# An Introduction to English Prosody

Elizabeth Couper-Kuhlen

# An Introduction to English Prosody

Edward Arnold

© Max Niemeyer Verlag Tübingen 1986

First published in West Germany by Max Niemeyer Verlag Tübingen

First published in Great Britain 1986 by
Edward Arnold (Publishers) Ltd, 41 Bedford Square, London WC1B 3DQ

Edward Arnold (Australia) Pty Ltd, 80 Waverley Road, Caulfield East,
Victoria 3145, Australia

Edward Arnold, 3 East Read Street, Baltimore, Maryland 21202, USA

**British Library Cataloguing in Publication Data**

Couper-Kuhlen, Elizabeth
An introduction to English prosody
1. English language — Intonation
I. An Introduction to English Prosody
421'.6      PE1139.5

ISBN 0-7131-6460-3 (Pbk)
     0-7131-6489-1

Text set in 9/11, 8/10, 8/9 pt Times Compugraphic
by Williams Graphics, Abergele, Clwyd, Great Britain.
Printed in West Germany by Allgäuer Zeitungsverlag GmbH, Kempten.
Bound in Great Britain.

# Contents

# Preface

It was in attempting to teach a course on English intonation at the University of Frankfurt that I became aware of the need for a book of this sort and it was in teaching subsequent courses at the University of Zürich and the University of Konstanz that I 'tried out' much of this material on my unsuspecting students. All in all, they have been a constant source of stimulation and encouragement for me and I feel it only fitting to dedicate this book to them.

The level at which I have aimed is introductory, in the sense that no prior knowledge of *prosodic* phonology is required. I do, however, assume familiarity with general linguistic and phonetic/phonological terms and notions. Where this is lacking, the reader is referred to current handbooks and dictionaries of linguistics and phonetics.

The book falls into two main parts, one dealing with prosodic form (Chs. I–V) and the other with prosodic function (Chs. VI–XI). In both parts illustrative material is taken from a corpus of spoken English data – primarily of the British variety and representative of varying degrees of spontaneity and formality – which I have recorded over the years. Excerpts from the corpus including most of the examples used in the text are on the accompanying cassette.

My original intention was to write an additional chapter on social and regional variation, comparing British and American intonation, and one on contrastive English–German intonation. But for reasons of time and space, I have had to abandon this project. My collection of references on these topics, however, has been added to the Bibliography.

The manuscript was completed in January 1984. More recent publications on prosody have not been taken into consideration.

During the latter stage of my work, I have benefited from the help of many friends and colleagues. My thanks go to Peter Williams and Hans Klingsohr for helping with the cassette, and above all to Richard Matthews, Bob Ladd, Dafydd Gibbon, Bill Barry and Wolf-Dietrich Bald, who read part or all of the manuscript and made invaluable suggestions for improvement. I hope the final result will do justice to the time and effort they have invested.

*Konstanz*                                                                 *E. Couper-Kuhlen*

# Symbols

| Symbol | Description |
|---|---|
| ‖ | tone-unit boundary |
| │ | onset |
| ↑ | pitch level higher than preceding syllable |
| ↑↑ | pitch level higher than preceding ↑ syllable or onset |
| → | pitch level same as preceding syllable |
| ↓ | pitch level lower than declination |
| ╲ | steep falling slope |
| ╱ | steep rising slope |
| ╲ᵢ | gradual falling slope |
| ╱ᵢ | gradual rising slope |
| ╰ | flattened fall |
| ╭ | flattened rise |
| ⌐ | fall to bottom of voice-range |
| ⌐ | rise to top of voice-range |
| ` | falling nucleus |
| ´ | rising nucleus |
| ᵛ | level or rising nucleus |
| ᵛ | level or falling nucleus |
| ˇ | falling–rising nucleus |
| ˆ | rising–falling nucleus |
| `+´ | falling + rising nucleus |
| ´+` | rising + falling nucleus |
| n | narrow nuclear pitch movement |
| w | wide nuclear pitch movement |
| h | higher than normal onset |
| l | lower than normal onset |
| [ ] | subordinate tone-unit |

Chapter I
# Prosody and prosodic features

## 1. Defining prosody

### 1.1 On the history of *prosody*

Terminological confusion is rampant in many fields of scientific inquiry but it is perhaps unmatched in the field of prosody. The term *prosody* itself can be traced back to the Greeks, who used the word προσῳδία to refer to features of speech which were not indicated in orthography, specifically to the tone or melodic accent which characterized full words in ancient Greek. Later, orthographic symbols which reflected the tonal accents were introduced and they too became known as prosodies. Syllables which bore an acute prosody in ancient Greek were spoken on a high tone, syllables with a grave prosody were said on a low tone, and those with a circumflex were given first a high, then a low tone.[1] *Prosody* was thus associated from the very beginning with the melodic features of spoken language.[2]

By the second century A.D., however, the term *prosody* had undergone an extension in meaning and was being used to refer generally to features which were not expressed in the segmental succession of vowel and consonant. Among these was vowel length. Eventually the tonal accents of Classical Greek disappeared and were replaced by dynamic accents, or stress. When this happened, *prosody* too narrowed in meaning and came to denote primarily stress distinctions. Thus it was via the link of vowel length and stress that, towards the 15th century, the term acquired the meaning 'versification', one of its primary denotations today.

So strong was the hold of 'metrical' prosody (deriving as it did from the study of the classical languages) that for a long time 'melodic' prosody was overlooked. Some scholars even claimed that the English language had no melody at all. For instance, Lord Monboddo, a learned Scottish judge, wrote in a six-volume treatise on *The origin and progress of language* (1773–92): "the music of our language ... (is) nothing better than the music of a drum, in which we perceive no difference except that of louder or softer". This claim, however, was soon countered by Joshua Steele, one of the first champions of 'melodic' prosody, in *An essay towards establishing the melody and measure of speech* (1775), later entitled *Prosodia rationalis*. Steele devised his own notation to transcribe the intonation (as well as the

---

[1] Later only the high and compound (high + low) tones were marked; all others were assumed to be low (Allen 1968:115).

[2] Cf. the Latin equivalent *accentus* (*ad* + *cano*) 'song accompanying words'.

stressing and pauses) used by David Garrick, a well-known Shakespearean actor of the time, and thus more than amply proved his case.

With this exception and a few others of its kind, 'melodic' prosody remained virtually forgotten until the late 1940's, when Firth revived the term to describe the approach he advocated towards linguistic analysis. While most linguists concerned with the auditory analysis of speech had their attention focused exclusively on single sounds or segments – this was referred to as *phonemic analysis* at the time – Firth argued that more emphasis should be placed on features which extend over a stretch of utterance. This he proposed to call *prosodic analysis*. The notion was embedded in a more far-reaching theory of *prosodic phonology* (Robins 1964:125ff., Lyons 1962) and was intended to cover more than merely 'force', length or quantity, and tone, features which other linguists (e.g. Jakobson/Halle 1956) later subsumed under *prosody*. It was Firth's merit, however, to have re-introduced the term, thereby paving the way to a new awareness of its original denotation.

Yet the notion of 'metrical' prosody has not vanished and in fact has recently been revived among generative linguists. Originally applied by Halle/Keyser (1966) to the distribution of stress in poetry, this use of the term *prosody* has now generalized to the distribution of stress in words and phrases, which according to recent hypotheses is metrically conditioned (Liberman/Prince 1977, Selkirk 1980, 1984).

## 1.2   Prosody vs. suprasegmentals

It has been customary among linguists working in the American structuralist tradition to use the term *suprasegmental* rather than *prosody*. These, however, are not wholly synonymous terms. Use of one rather than the other carries with it special connotations and often serves to indicate where one's linguistic loyalties lie.

Within the structuralist tradition, the speech continuum is thought to be segmentable into minimal units, the distinctive sounds of a language, which enter into a series of paradigmatic and syntagmatic relations with one another and form the primary sound system of a language. Not all sound phenomena or phonological facts can be accounted for at the level of single segments, however. Thus, some 'secondary' processes must be treated at a level above the segments, appropriately called the *suprasegmental* level. In the English language these processes would include not only stress, rhythm and intonation but also such phenomena as vowel length, sound reduction, elision, coarticulation, assimilation and dissimilation. In other languages, processes such as vowel harmony would also be included (Hyman 1975:186f.). In each case, more than just a single segment must be taken into consideration in order to explain the empirical facts. In this sense *suprasegmental* describes "features whose domain extends over more than one segment" (Lehiste 1970:1). Use of the term often implies not only adherence to this particular view of language but also the relegation of some sound phenomena to a secondary level.

In the British tradition, spoken language is typically approached from the so-called "context of situation", i.e. the communicative situation in which speech is embedded. The performance or perception of a speech event, depending on whether we look at it from the perspective of the speaker or the hearer, involves primarily vocal or auditory effects and visual effects (barring tele-communication). Study of the visual aspects of communication is more properly speaking the domain of kinesics. It is primarily the vocal or auditory aspects which concern the linguist. Auditorily, an utterance can be said to contain both segmental and non-segmental components. Setting aside the single sounds or segments of speech, what is left, the so-called "residue of utterance", is the domain of prosody in the British sense.

Naturally an utterance may contain vocal or auditory features which are not of a linguistic nature, and these must be carefully distinguished from prosody proper. For instance, we are usually aware of an individual's voice quality, and we may hear a sneeze or a cough along with the utterance. The former is a permanent, idiosyncratic feature which is physiologically determined. And the latter, sneezes and coughs, are for the most part involuntary physiological reflexes. To the extent that such features are not systematic, nor used conventionally or intentionally for the purpose of communication, they are referred to as the *non-linguistic* auditory aspects of speech.

In addition, a speaker may temporarily modify the voice in such a way that a whisper, creak, falsetto, etc. or a giggle, laugh, sob, etc. are produced. The former result from muscular adjustment in the vocal folds and the vocal tract above the glottis; the latter, from breath pulses out of phase with the syllable (Crystal 1969: 133).[3] Together, these are termed *paralinguistic* auditory effects and are excluded from the domain proper of prosody. Paralinguistic effects are only sporadically present in the speech signal, whereas prosodic effects are for the most part continuously present in speech: it is not normal to make utterances without them. We always use stress, rhythm, and intonation when we speak, although we may not always whisper, giggle or sob.

In sum, prosody may be defined negatively as those auditory components of an utterance which remain, once segmental as well as non-linguistic and paralinguistic vocal effects have been removed. Alternatively, prosody may be defined more positively as "sets of mutually defining phonological features which have an essentially variable relationship to the words selected" (Crystal 1969:5). That is, whereas an English word or phrase can be identified in terms of its segmental make-up, it is not individualized by its loudness, duration or pitch. A given word in English will not change its denotative meaning if it is articulated in one context, say, louder, longer or higher than in another.[4]

According to this definition then, what is traditionally called stress does not fall wholly within the domain of prosody. To a certain extent stress is used in English to distinguish one word from another. For instance, the noun *contrast* (with major stress on the first syllable) differs from the verb *contrast* (with major stress on the

---

[3] Whisper, creak, falsetto, etc. have been termed *voice qualifiers*, in contrast to laugh, cry, giggle, sigh, etc., termed *voice qualifications*. Only voice qualifications are mutually exclusive in speech (Crystal 1969:138).

[4] The situation is different in so-called tone languages, where words *are* identified by means of tones or melodic patterns (Ch. VI §5.1).

second syllable) primarily in terms of its lexical stress pattern. This type of stress does not belong to the domain of prosody. On the other hand, the same word in the context of an utterance may constitute a rhythmic beat and/or have pitch modulation, i.e. it may be 'stressed' or accented respectively (Ch.II), without changing its identity – and this is very much part of English prosody.

Defined in similar fashion, the term *prosody* subsumes at least the following auditory aspects of speech: loudness (a component of 'stress'), duration (a component of 'rhythm' and 'tempo'), pitch (a component of 'intonation') and pause.[5] Diagrammatically, these relationships could be sketched as follows:

Fig. I/1     Auditory components of speech in communication

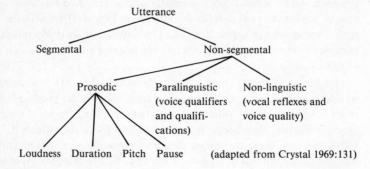

(adapted from Crystal 1969:131)

To summarize, the term *prosody* in the British sense is a category of auditory perception in a 'top-down' analysis of language, as it were. Prosodic features are on a par with paralinguistic and non-linguistic features; they encompass potentially more far-reaching aspects of speech than suprasegmentals do, although they generally do not apply to phenomena whose basic domain is smaller than the syllable. The term *suprasegmental*, on the other hand, stems from a 'bottom-up' approach to language and carries the connotation of being 'non-inherent', 'overlaid' or 'secondary' (Lehiste 1970:2; Bloomfield 1933:90). Its scope extends beyond that of *prosody* in that it can be applied to processes above the segment but below the syllable. However, the term is rarely applied to processes which have whole stretches of utterance as their domain.

---

[5] A certain case can be made for including *tension* as well in the domain of prosody. A word may be said with greater or lesser muscular tightness without affecting its identity; moreover, tension is continuous with speech and interacts closely with loudness and duration, other prosodic parameters. However, tension results largely from supraglottal muscular adjustments (rather than vocal cord mechanisms) and is therefore generally not considered to be a full-fledged prosodic feature (Crystal 1969:129, 165).

## 2.   Characteristics of prosody

In this treatment of prosody we shall assume a three-dimensional model of speech with

(i) an *articulatory* (motor or productive) dimension, i.e. speech viewed from the perspective of the speaker,

(ii) an *auditory* (perceptual or receptive) dimension, i.e. speech viewed from the perspective of the hearer, and

(iii) an *acoustic* dimension, i.e. speech viewed as an acoustic signal transmitted from speaker to hearer.

These dimensions are not wholly independent one of another. Normal speakers simultaneously hear themselves speak, and according to one theory of speech perception, hearers process speech signals by internally modelling the articulatory gestures which speakers would have to use in order to produce them (Ch. II §1.5). Nor is there a one-to-one relation between aspects of these dimensions. Not everything that is present in the acoustic signal is necessarily perceived by the hearer; features of the acoustic signal cannot always be traced back unequivocally to single articulatory positions or movements (Hammarström 1966; Ch. II §1). For these reasons it is extremely important, methodologically, to keep the dimensions apart.

### 2.1   Acoustic composition

So far we have considered prosody primarily from an auditory point of view. In fact, until the 20th century, it was hardly possible to do otherwise. However, with the advent of the oscillograph, the spectrograph and other modern acoustic instruments – and the possibility of computer digitalization of their output – the situation has changed radically. It has now become possible to 'objectivize' the auditory data and, it is hoped, to learn more about the nature of speech.

Acoustically, speech, like all sound, can be analyzed into three component parts: frequency, amplitude and time.

*Frequency* is the term used to describe the vibration of air molecules caused by a vibrating object, in our case typically the vocal cords (or folds) which are set in motion by an egressive flow of air during phonation. Frequency is measured in cycles per second or Hertz. A *cycle* is one back-and-forth movement made by a vibrating body (e.g. a vibrating air molecule). Thus the wave in the following diagram can be thought of as tracing the path of an air molecule which takes .01 second to move first in one direction and then in the other before returning to its place of rest. The frequency of its vibration is consequently 100 Hz.

Fig. I/2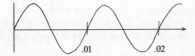

A speech sound, however, is much more complex. It consists of many different patterns of vibration at different frequencies. For instance, a speech sound might also contain this wave:

Fig. I/3

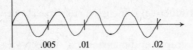

[It takes this wave .005 second to complete a cycle; in .01 second it repeats twice; thus its frequency is 200 Hz.]

And it might contain this wave:

Fig. I/4

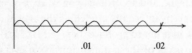

[Here the cycle repeats three times in .01 second; the frequency is thus 300 Hz.]

If these waves were combined, we would have a complex wave more like a speech sound:

Fig. I/5

The frequency of repetition of the complex pattern is referred to as the *fundamental frequency* (sometimes called $f_0$ or 'f zero') – in this case, 100 Hz. Fundamental frequency is in inverse proportion to fundamental period, or expressed as a formula, $f_0 = 1/t_0$. It is fundamental frequency which is largely responsible for our perception of pitch.[6] All other frequencies in a complex wave are typically whole-integer multiples of the fundamental frequency, thus $2 \times 100 \text{Hz} = 200 \text{Hz}$, $3 \times 100 \text{Hz} = 300 \text{Hz}$, etc. These are referred to as the second, third, etc. *harmonics*. All sounds produced by the vocal folds in the glottis have this basic composition.

A second acoustic component of sound is *amplitude*. To return to our model of a vibrating body, amplitude is the maximal displacement of a particle from its place of rest. For instance, compare the two waves below:

Fig. I/6

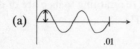 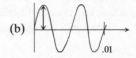

[6] However, acoustic and perceptual experiments have shown that there is not always a direct relationship between $f_0$ and pitch perception. For instance, regular increases in frequency, especially above 1000 Hz, will not necessarily be heard as regular intervals in pitch (Ladefoged 1962:77).

6

The back-and-forth movement in wave (b) is greater than in wave (a); thus it has a greater amplitude. [Notice that the two waves have the same frequency, however.] Amplitude is related to the *intensity* of a sound, which is usually measured in decibels (dB). It corresponds roughly to our auditory impression of loudness (cf., however, Ch. II §1).

The third component of sound viewed acoustically is *time*. Acoustic signals can be gauged along a time axis. An expanse of time is perceived auditorily as duration.

We have now progressed far enough to look at the relationship between the articulatory, acoustic and auditory dimensions of prosody:

Fig. I/7    Dimensions of prosody

| *Articulatory* | *Acoustic* | *Auditory* |
|---|---|---|
| Vibration of vocal folds ——————— | Fundamental frequency ($f_0$) ——————— | Pitch |
| Physical effort ——————— | Amplitude (intensity) ——————— | Loudness |
| Timing of articulatory movements ——————— | Time ——————— | Duration |

Figure I/7 should not be interpreted to mean that the various acoustic components of speech are wholly independent of other factors. On the contrary, they are subject to diverse outside influences. For one, *vowel quality* may interfere with fundamental frequency: vowels articulated high in the mouth have an intrinsically higher fundamental frequency than low vowels. Furthermore, vowel quality may affect intensity: high vowels tend to have less intrinsic intensity than low vowels. And vowel quality may influence duration: high vowels are generally shorter than low vowels. Second, the *point of articulation in consonants* may interact with duration: labial consonants, for instance, are intrinsically longer than alveolars and velars. Third, the surrounding sounds or the *phonetic environment* may influence the fundamental frequency of a segment: a vowel following a voiceless fricative, for instance, has a higher fundamental frequency on the average than a vowel following a voiced fricative. Phonetic environment may also influence the intrinsic duration of a sound: a vowel followed by a voiced consonant is regularly longer than the same vowel followed by a voiceless consonant in English. And just as the individual acoustic components are influenced by outside factors, so too they influence each other. Pitch, for instance, may affect intensity if fundamental frequency overlaps with formant frequency (cf. also Ch. II §1). As hearers we make automatic compensation for differences in fundamental frequency, amplitude and duration which are conditioned by factors such as these.

Notice that all three acoustic components function along two different axes. Every sound or segment has fundamental frequency and intensity of its own; furthermore, every sound extends in time. These are the so-called 'inherent' features, or *segmental* aspects of the sound continuum (i.e. related to the single sounds or segments). If, on the other hand, we consider the horizontal rather than the vertical axis, we find a succession of frequencies, a succession of intensity levels and a succession of time stretches. This explains how it is that we perceive the modulation of pitch over syllables, words, phrases, etc., the relative loudness of syllables, words, phrases, and/or the relative duration of syllables, words, phrases. These are the *prosodic* aspects of the sound continuum. Fig. I/8 presents a schematic view:

Fig. I/8   Acoustic composition of segmental and prosodic features

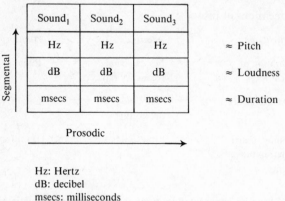

Hz: Hertz
dB: decibel
msecs: milliseconds
≈ : contribute to the perception of

It lies in the nature of prosodic features that they are of the same substance as segmental features. However, prosodic features derive from a *sequential* consideration of larger sections of the speech continuum:

> (S)uprasegmental features are established by a comparison of items in sequence, whereas segmental features are identifiable by inspection of the segment itself. (Lehiste 1976:225−6)

## 2.2   Relative vs. absolute norms

Much early investigation into intonation assumed that the pitch of the voice could be related to the musical scale. Joshua Steele, for instance, compared the pitches of his voice to notes on the bass viol. And Daniel Jones, using gramophone recordings, produced his well-known "intonation curves" (1909) by transcribing the pitch of spoken syllables onto a musical stave. There are, however, at least two objections to such a procedure. For one, the pitches of the musical scale have absolute frequency values;[7] yet the speaking voice does not use only these pitches or maintain precisely the intervals that have been established for music. Instead, it is capable of producing any number of semi-tones and quarter-tones − and frequently does so, although we are not then said to be "speak(ing) out of tune" (Schubiger 1958:4).

---

[7] Thus concert pitch 'A', for instance, is 440 Hz.

8

A second objection to using a musical scale is that no distinction can be made between systematic and idiosyncratic features of intonation. Speakers with different natural pitch ranges (men as opposed to women, children as opposed to adults) appear to be using different tunes on a musical scale, although the effect in linguistic terms may be quite similar.[8] In sum, it is not the absolute values of the pitches involved in speaking which are important, but the over-all pattern of pitch variation relative to surrounding pitches.[9]

Although arguments for prosodic relativity have come primarily from the area of intonation, the same points can be made concerning other prosodic features. Loudness, for instance, must be expressed in relative terms, since the same decibel level may be loud for one speaker but soft for another. Even tempo, it has been argued, should be viewed as a relative phenomenon. Although we often hear comments such as 'S/he speaks so fast/so slow', there are no absolute values with respect to rate of delivery.

To summarize, if certain syllables are heard as loud, they are not necessarily louder than some absolute decibel level, but are louder than other syllables that surround them or louder than the norm for a given speaker. Likewise, a speaker's rate of delivery may speed up or slow down — but primarily with respect to his/her normal tempo. And pitch variations may be perceived as low, medium or high but with respect to an individual's vocal range or the pitch level of surrounding syllables. Thus prosodic features are alike to the extent that they presuppose a *speaker-dependent norm* according to which variations can be measured.

On the other hand, however, a number of speaker-*independent* norms are also necessary at least in the analysis of intonation. As Crystal (1975b:77) has pointed out, we apparently do use norms or standards in auditory perception. For one, we can form a notion of 'natural speaking level' and are able to determine (regardless of individual voice range) when someone is speaking near the top or the bottom of his/her voice. Second, although it has often been claimed that the possibilities of human pitch variation are quasi-infinite, actually the number of pitches which the ear is capable of distinguishing from a given reference level is quite limited. This too can be seen as an argument against too strong a claim of prosodic relativity. And finally we must assume at least a minimum of standardizing ability on the part of analysts in the description of intonation; otherwise the analyst's task would be impossible. The conclusion is that certain absolute levels in intonation analysis simply cannot be avoided: indeed they form the framework within which more relative standards apply.

---

[8] As Pike points out, "the 'high' tonemes of a bass voice may be lower in absolute pitch than the 'low' tonemes of a soprano" (1945:20). [A *toneme* is a contrastive tone or pitch level.]
[9] Cf. Abercrombie: "... it is the position of the points in the pattern *relative to each other* that counts, not their frequency in terms of number of vibrations per second" (1967:107).

## 2.3 Syllable as domain

A third characteristic of prosodic features, in addition to their acoustic substance and their (limited) relativity, is their dependence on the syllable. Naturally, prosodic features may also extend over longer stretches of utterance, but the smallest possible domain over which they extend is the syllable. It is not the pitch of a sound, but the pitch of a syllable that we are concerned with; not the loudness or duration of sounds, but the loudness and duration of syllables. In this important respect prosodic features as defined here differ from those which Firth and his followers posit.

## 3. The syllable

Central to the study of English prosody is thus the notion of the syllable. Yet the syllable, an intuitive commonplace, is difficult to define in a water-tight manner.

### 3.1 The syllable vs. other linguistic units

Stating what the syllable is *not* is easier than stating what it is. In the first place, for instance, the syllable cannot be equated with an *orthographic unit*. The word-divisions which figure in most English dictionaries are guidelines for the written, not the spoken language. Most languages have conventions for the orthographic division of words. In English, for instance, it is considered undesirable to have only one letter on a new line. Furthermore, a double consonant starting a new line is considered improper.[10] Thus the word *slippery*, say, would be divided *slip-pery* or *slipp-ery* in writing; alternatives such as *slipper-y* or *sli-ppery* would be avoided for the reasons stated above. These are conventions which relate to the written language; the syllable, however, is a unit of the spoken language.

Second, the syllable cannot be equated with a *phoneme*. Although some syllables may consist of only one phoneme (/ə/, for instance, in *about*) it should be immediately obvious that not all single phonemes constitute syllables; indeed some by their very nature are incapable of doing so.

Third, the syllable cannot be equated with the presence of a vowel, or even a *vocoid*.[11] If a phonological vowel is defined as the nucleus of a syllable, it is obviously circular to define the syllable as consisting minimally of a vowel. And if the presence of a vocoid is made the defining feature of the syllable, then there is no way to account for the second syllable we perceive in words such as *garden* /gɑːd-n/ and *little* /lɪt-l/; in each case the sound forming the last syllable is a contoid, made with

---

[10] Orthographic conventions for word-division may vary from language to language. Thus in German -*st*- may not be divided, and a new line may not begin with a vowel (*Bega-bung*, not *\*Begab-ung*). These rules do not hold for English word-division.

[11] The term *vocoid* is used to refer to the phonetic notion of a sound which is articulated with no closure or narrowing of the vocal tract capable of producing friction. The term *vowel* is usually reserved in linguistics for the phonological notion of a sound which functions as the nucleus of a syllable.

closure in the vocal tract. Likewise, with the vowel-as-syllable nucleus definition, there is no explanation for intuitive monosyllabics such as *pst* or *fft*.

And finally, the syllable cannot be identified with a *morpheme*, the smallest meaningful unit of a language. The word *beautiful*, for example, contains two basic meaningful units: *beauti-ful*, but it has three syllables: /ˈbjuː-tɪ-fʊl/. Some morphemes do not constitute syllables at all, e.g. the plural marker *-s* in *hats*. In fact, morphemes may be non-syllabic, syllabic (e.g. *-ful*) or polysyllabic (e.g. *beauti-*). Any overlap with the syllable itself is mere coincidence.

In sum, the syllable cannot be defined with reference to any existing linguistic unit or category; it requires instead a definition in its own terms.


## 3.2   Defining the syllable

Native speakers can, in the majority of cases, agree on the number of syllables a given word in their language has. For instance, English speakers will agree that the word *reality* has four syllables (although they may not agree on where the syllable boundaries come). However, this is a feat which can be expected only of native speakers or near-native speakers of a language. Thus, a Japanese speaker with little exposure to English will claim to hear four syllables in the English word *sticks* /s-tɪ-k-s/, although English ears perceive only one. [The Japanese language has only open syllables and no initial consonant clusters.] The English word *biscuit* becomes *bisuketto* in Japanese; the English word *dribble* becomes the Japanese verb *doriburusuru*[12] (Firth 1948; 1973:63). This is of course a first indication that what we hear as a syllable may not have any objective reality as such but instead be conditioned by the structure of the language in question.

### 3.2.1  Physical definitions

Nevertheless, phoneticians have constantly sought a physical, indeed even a physiological basis for the syllable. Stetson ([2]1951), for instance, advanced the theory that the syllable is created by quick contractions of the intercostal muscles between the ribs, which, functioning in a manner similar to bellows, push the air in the inflated chest out in little puffs. These puffs or pulses, he claimed, are responsible for our perception of syllables. Known as the *chest-pulse theory* of the syllable, Stetson's results were intuitively pleasing, though later challenged by other acoustic researchers working with more sophisticated laboratory equipment (Ladefoged/Draper/Whitteridge 1958). Using a technique known as electromyography, which involves the registration of minute electrical discharges associated with muscular activity, they were able to show that in connected speech at least, segments perceived as syllables are not all necessarily accompanied by a burst of muscular activity. [Stetson's subjects had merely repeated a single word *pup-pup-pup*.] At times a single increase in muscular tension spans two or more syllables (e.g. as in *pity* or *around*); and at times

---

[12] In Japanese, *suru* 'to make' serves to change nouns into verbs.

there are two bursts of activity over a span of only one syllable (*sport, stay*). Thus Stetson's theory is generally discounted today.

Another theory advanced to explain the syllable in physical terms is based on the concept of *sonority*. The term itself was used as early as 1902 by Henry Sweet and has been associated with 'fullness' of voice, a notion related to the general audibility of a sound (Heffner 1950:74). Acoustically, sounds can be shown to have varying degrees of inherent sonority or acoustic energy. High on the scale are the vowels, especially [ɑ], as well as the lateral [l] and the nasals [m] and [n]. According to this theory, a syllable is formed by a *peak of sonority*. By way of illustration, if different levels of sonority are represented with numbers such that [p, t, k] = 4; [ç, tʃ] = 3.5; [b, d, g] = 3; [m, n] = 2.5; [f, s, x, h] = 2; [i, u] = 1.5; [ɑ] = 1 (cf. Bloomfield 1933:120f. and Selkirk 1982:380), the word *unspoken* could be represented as follows:

Fig. I/9      Sonority and the syllable

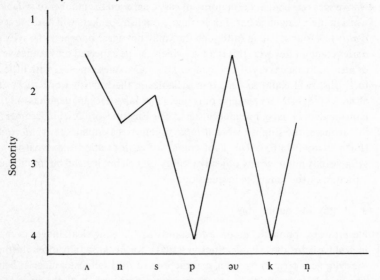

The three peaks of sonority created by /ʌ/, /əʊ/ and /ŋ/ correspond to the three syllables we perceive.

The peak-of-sonority theory accounts quite nicely for syllables formed by sonorants such as /n/ and /l/, e.g. /gɑ:d-n/, /lɪt-l/. However, it does not offer per se any guidelines for determining exactly where in the 'valleys' the syllable boundary comes. What are the first two syllables of *unspoken*? /ʌ-nspəʊk/, /ʌn-spəʊk/, /ʌns-pəʊk/ or /ʌnsp-əʊk/?

One way of accounting for the placement of some syllable boundaries is to appeal to the notion of juncture. *Juncture* can be defined as the way segments are joined together at boundaries. To take a well-known example, *I scream* is said to differ from *ice-cream* in that in the former /aɪs/ is given open juncture, in the latter close juncture. In this example, juncture is actually none other than difference in degree of co-articulation, a term used to describe the overlapping of articulatory movements

12

in speech. In *ice-cream* /s/ is coarticulated with the preceding diphthong, i.e. its voicelessness shortens the duration of /aɪ/, whereas /s/ in *I scream* is co-articulated with /kr/ and /aɪ/ retains full length.[13] In short, if there is no syllable boundary, then sounds stand in phonetic contiguity and assimilations of this sort may result. Given examples like these, it seems quite reasonable to think of the syllable as a peak of sonority optionally preceded or followed by less sonorous sounds which are 'bound' to it via coarticulation.

There are, however, two major objections to this view of the syllable. First of all, there are cases in which variation in the number of perceived syllables does not correspond to variation in the number of peaks of sonority. For example, most English speakers distinguish (a) *hidden aims* /hɪdn̩eɪmz/ from (b) *hid names* /hɪdneɪmz/ by using a syllabic /n/ in the former, thereby increasing the number of syllables to three. And yet both (a) and (b) have the same number of peaks of sonority:

Fig. I/10

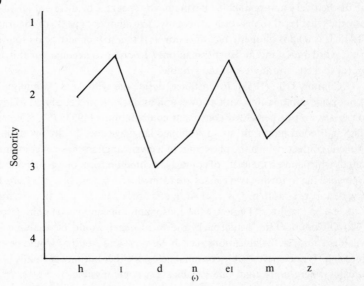

It may be countered that this distinction is not always maintained in informal spoken English. But the point is that it can be made, and yet is inexplicable in terms of sonority peaks.[14]

Another objection to a theory of the syllable based on sonority is that, even together with the notion of coarticulation, it does not always provide an explanation for syllable boundary placement. Despite clear examples such as *I scream* vs. *ice-cream*

---

[13] Similarly, in *peace talks* the first /s/ is coarticulated with /iː/, thereby shortening it, and the /t/ of *talks* is fully aspirated. But in *pea-stalks* the first /s/ is coarticulated with /t/ causing it to lose its aspiration, and /iː/ has full length (Jones 1918, 1976:327f., Jones 1931).

[14] Similar distinctions which the theory of sonority cannot account for are: *lightning* (two syllables) vs. *lightening* (three syllables); *codling* (two syllables) vs. *coddling* (three syllables).

(where syllable and word boundary coincide), not all syllable boundaries are clearly marked in terms of articulation — nor do we always clearly perceive them. Thus, in a word like *slippery*, we may agree that there are three syllables (corresponding to the peaks of sonority ɪ-ə-ɪ), but how do we determine, for instance, to which syllable /p/ and /r/ belong? /slɪ-pə-rɪ/, /slɪp-ər-ɪ/, /slɪp-ə-rɪ/ or /slɪ-pər-ɪ/? In this case the placement of the syllable boundary cannot be determined auditorily, nor is it reflected in the articulation of the word.

The conclusion must be that the theory of sonority is not wholly satisfactory as a basis for defining the syllable either. Since no other, more satisfactory explanations have been forthcoming, most linguists believe that it is impossible to account for the syllable and syllabication in physical terms alone.

### 3.2.2 Phonological definitions

Another reason why physical definitions of the syllable are unsatisfactory is that they are by their very nature unable to explain why speakers of different languages perceive the syllables of some words differently. The number of peaks of sonority a given word has is a hard phonetic fact. Yet how is it that a Japanese hears four syllables in the word *sticks* and an Englishman one? In order to account for this, we must appeal to a structural view of the syllable.

O'Connor/Trim (1953), for instance, define the syllable as ''a minimal pattern of phoneme combination with a vowel unit as nucleus, preceded and followed by a consonant unit or permitted consonant combination'' (1953; 1973:259).[15] 'Vowel unit' and 'consonant unit' are determined language-specifically by tabulating the phonetic contexts which the phonemes of a given language have in common. Those sounds which have a majority of contexts in common form one distributional class. In English the following two classes are formed: (1) /p, t, k, b, d, g, tʃ, dʒ, f, ɵ, s, ʃ, h, v, ð, z, ʒ, r, l, m, n, ŋ, j, w/; (2) /i:, ɪ, e, æ, ɑ:, ɒ, ɔ:, ʊ, u:, ʌ, ɜ:, ə, eɪ, əʊ, aɪ, aʊ, ɔɪ, ɪə, eə, ɔə, ʊə, jʊ/.[16] These are the consonant units and vowel units respectively.

In O'Connor/Trim's approach, the word *anger* would be analyzed into two syllables /æŋ-gə/. Syllabications such as /æ-ŋgə/ and /æŋg-ə/ would be excluded, since /ŋg/ is not a permissible consonant cluster either initially or finally in English. In cases where more than one syllabication is permissible — e.g. *aster* /æs-tə/, /æ-stə/ or /æst-ə/ — it is relative probability which is to serve as a criterion, according to O'Connor/Trim. For instance, there are 277 possible phoneme combinations in a final VC sequence and 421 combinations for initial CV, i.e. the division VC-CV can be said to have a 'relative probability' of 277 + 421 = 698. This is much higher than the number of possible phoneme combinations in V (12) + initial CC (26) = 38, or in final CC (59) + V (12) = 71. Thus the preferred syllabication would be VC-CV: /æs-tə/.

---

[15] A vowel unit, rather than a consonant unit, is chosen as nucleus because it does not occur as often side by side with other members of its bloc and because it can stand alone (1953; 1973:252).

[16] O'Connor/Trim's symbols have been translated here into those in current use today (English Pronouncing Dictionary, 14th edition).

This view of the syllable is based on *phonotactics*,[17] the study of the combinatory possibilities of phonemes in a given language. It presents a convincing account of syllables as functional entities whose structure is language-dependent. However, it does not address the question of whether the syllable is in any way a universal phenomenon.

It is with respect to this point that the work of Pulgram (1970) is noteworthy. For Pulgram too the syllable is a "linguistic unit composed of phonemes that are arranged according to certain phonotactic criteria" (1970:22). However, here more explicitly than before, the syllable is viewed in much the same way as the word. That is, it is expected to demonstrate the same restrictions with regard to phoneme combination at its beginning (*onset*) and at its end (*coda*) as does a word in the same language at its beginning or end. Consider, for instance, *slippery* again. A syllabication */slɪ-p.../ would not be permissible, since lax vowels such as /ɪ/ generally do not occur at the end of words in English.[18] Furthermore, */slɪp-ər-ɪ/ would not be acceptable in British English, since there are no standard words that end in /r/. The only remaining alternative which reflects the phonotactic possibilities of words in English is /slɪp-ə-rɪ/.[19]

Not only is Pulgram's heuristic for syllabication an improvement over the O'Connor/Trim 'relative probability' count; it is also more ambitious in its claims. Thus Pulgram states:

> ... one cannot but suspect that the phonotactic rules, though realized differently in different idioms, are capable of being stated in a general universal manner that finds specific realization and application in the various tongues. (1970:45)

To the extent that the syllable is operational in all known languages, it is a universal phenomenon, even though the specific rules for syllable structure in each language obviously vary in accordance with the respective phonotactic constraints. Pulgram posits the existence of three basic principles of syllabication, formulated in such a way that they are applicable to all languages, although their implementation differs depending on the language in question:

(i) *Maximal open syllabicity.* Every syllable is open provisionally.

This principle reflects an over-all universal tendency towards open syllables. No (known) language has only closed syllables (Malmberg 1963).

(ii) *Minimal coda and maximal onset.* If rule (i) produces a deviant onset or coda, then as many consonants as are necessary – but no more – are transferred from that onset to the preceding coda or, in the case of a deviant coda, from the following onset to that coda in order to meet minimal phonotactic requirements.

This rule provides a unique syllabication for words like *extra* /ekstrə/ [which

---

[17] Cf. also Haugen (1956).

[18] The fact that the sound at the end of words such as *pretty, city* is sometimes transcribed with the symbol /ɪ/ is a convention and need not affect our argumentation.

[19] According to Haugen (1956:219) there is a traditional rule of English syllable division that a single intervocalic consonant goes with a preceding 'short' (simple) vowel, but not with a preceding 'long' (complex) vowel [e.g. /pæt-ə/ but /faɪ-lɪŋ/]. Application of this rule would also result in the correct syllabication here.

15

O'Connor/Trim were unable to do (1953; 1973:257)]: /ek-strə/. The syllabications */eks-trə/ and */ekst-rə/ would be excluded because the codas of the first syllable contain more material than absolutely necessary to fulfil the phonotactic requirements of English. The general rule in cases where several syllabications are phonotactically permissible is to keep codas short and, where necessary, make onsets long.

(iii) *Irregular coda.* If several possible syllabications result in phonotactic irregularity and none is wholly permissible, an irregular coda is to be preferred over an irregular onset.

A good example of this situation can be found in German, where 'I go by bicycle' in some dialects is syncopated from /iç ra:dələ/ to /iç ra:dlə/. If /ra:dlə/ is syllabicized as (a) /ra:-dlə/, a phonotactic constraint is violated, since no words in German begin with /dl-/. But if it is syllabicized as (b) /ra:d-lə/, another constraint is violated, since German devoices all obstruent consonants in final position. Following Pulgram's rules, alternative (b) would be preferable to (a), since languages are more likely to tolerate irregularity at the ends of words and syllables than at the beginning.[20]

### 3.2.3 Physical vs. phonological unit

In summary, syllables can be viewed both physically and phonologically. A wholly satisfactory physical explanation for the syllable, however, has not yet been advanced. Phonologically, the syllable is a well-attested fact, although not all the problems of analysis have been solved as yet. One major difficulty is that physical and phonological boundaries do not always correspond. A case in point here is the word *bedroom*. Speakers sometimes distinguish 'room in which one sleeps', syllabicized /be-dru:m/ as evidenced by coarticulation of /dr/ and possible affrication to /dʒr/, from 'space for a bed', syllabicized /bed-ru:m/ (Hyman 1975:190). Phonologically, however, only the latter syllabication is permissible. We must thus conclude that the phonological syllable does not always overlap fully with the phonetic syllable. In cases like this, Pulgram would maintain that only the unit determined phonologically is a syllable. For example, although the phonological syllabication of *rooster* is /ru:-stə/, he admits that a speaker might also articulate /ru:st-ə/ or /ru:s-tə/ (using allophonic boundary signals or inserting a glottal stop or a silence at the appropriate spot). However, this kind of phonetic division should not be called real syllabication, according to Pulgram:

> Syllabation ... remains a phonological-phonotactic process, even though the stream of speech can be phonetically cut into all sorts of pieces, some of which, if they contain one vowel and are pronounceable, may sound like 'syllables'. (1970:57)

Yet if we disassociate the phonological unit wholly from phonetic division, we may find ourselves dealing with abstractions which lack intuitive value. As far as is possible, the syllable even as a phonological entity should be phonetically motivated.

---

[20] Example from Vennemann (1972). According to Vennemann, speakers of 'refined Standard' use (a), whereas 'northern Standard' speakers use (b) but devoice the final consonant /ra:t-lə/. Tolerance for onset irregularity thus seems greater in Standard German pronunciation.

Furthermore, there is increasing evidence that we must be prepared to put up with some indeterminacy in dealing with the syllable. Native speakers of American English, for instance, cannot seem to agree even on the number of syllables in words such as *pearl, squirrel, jewel, towel* (final-r and glide-liquid sequences). And there are many more cases in which the placement of syllable boundaries is indeterminate. This is in particular true of single consonants preceding unstressed vowels: *attic* /ætɪk/, *apple* /æpl̩/, *any* /enɪ/ (Bell/Hooper 1978:17). A phonotactic approach can 'resolve' the problem but the phonological 'solution' does not necessarily reflect speaker intuition. In these cases many speakers would intuitively assign the consonant to both syllables (known as 'ambisyllabicity').

Furthermore, there may be no such thing as a fixed syllabication of words in context. Evidence is accumulating, for instance, that syllabication varies according to tempo and/or style. Thus Bailey (1978; 1980) has discovered a tendency for stressed syllables in rapid speech to attract consonants and become heavier, while unstressed syllables tend to lose consonants and become more reduced:

Lento: as-paragus, Wis-consin
Allegro: a-sparagus, Wi-sconsin

Here the unstressed vowels in the allegro versions would undoubtedly reduce to schwa /ə/, which is permissible at the end of words (and syllables); thus no phonotactic violation is involved.

But in casual speech even the phonotactic rules of a language may be violated: e.g. *potato* /pteɪtə/, *tonight* /tnaɪt/, *fatality* /ftælɪtɪ/ (Bell/Hooper 1978:18). This makes syllable variability and indeed indeterminacy seem all the more plausible.

### 3.2.4 Is the syllable necessary?

A number of linguists have argued that the problems involved with syllables are so thorny that we would be better off in linguistic analysis without them. For instance, according to Kohler:

> ... it can be demonstrated that the syllable is either an UNNECESSARY concept, because the division of the speech chain into such units is known for other reasons, or an IMPOSSIBLE one, as any division would be arbitrary, or even a HARMFUL one, because it clashes with grammatical formatives. (1966:207)

Likewise, Chomsky/Halle's *The Sound Pattern of English* (1968), a generative account of English phonology, makes no provision for a syllabic level of organization.[21]

On the other hand, however, the notion of syllable has played an important role in the development of writing systems, some of the oldest of which are syllabaries (e.g. Semitic). Furthermore, the syllable has always been an important component of language play and language art. For instance, secret languages such as Pig Latin appeal to a notion of syllable. And one of the most widely observed metrical traditions

---

[21] More recent metrical theories, however, appeal crucially to the notion of syllable (e.g. Liberman/Prince 1977, Selkirk 1982, 1984, etc.).

in English literature requires lines in verse to have an equal number of syllables. Finally, and perhaps most convincingly, it has been shown that spoonerisms and slips of the tongue cannot be accounted for without recourse to the notion of syllable (Fromkin 1971; 1973). How else are we to explain the fact that it is not sounds in random positions in the word which are interchanged, but invariably sounds at similar positions in the syllable? Thus:

elephant  /e-fə-lənt/
pancakes  /kæn-peɪks/  (Fromkin 1971: 39f.)

In sum, there are historical, psychological and cultural reasons for believing in the syllable. Despite its indefinite, at times indeterminate nature, it is a basic building block in the view of prosody taken here.


## References

Full references will be found in the Bibliography. * Asterisks mark particularly useful sources recommended for further reading.

Abercrombie 1965
Alkon 1959
Allen, W.S. 1968
Allen, W.S. 1973
Anderson 1969
Bailey 1978
Bailey 1980
Bell/Hooper/Bybee 1978
*Crystal 1969 (§§3, 4)
*Crystal 1975b
Denes 1959
Fallows 1981
Firth 1948
Fromkin 1971
Fromkin 1973
Fudge 1969
Gibbon 1976 (Ch. 2)
Gimson [3]1980 (§5.4)
Hadding-Koch/Studdert-Kennedy 1964
Hála 1961
Halle/Kaiser 1966
Hammarström 1966
Hammarström 1976
Haugen 1949
*Haugen 1956
Hill 1961
Hooper 1972
*Hyman 1975 (§§6−6.1.1.1)
Jakobson/Halle [2]1971
Jones 1909
Jones [9]1976

Jones 1931
Kohler 1966
*Ladefoged 1962 (Chs. 1, 2, 6)
Ladefoged 1975
Ladefoged/Draper/Whitteridge 1958
Lea 1977
Lehiste 1970
Lehiste/Peterson 1961
Liberman, A.M. 1957
Liberman/Cooper/Harris/MacNeilage 1963
Liberman/Prince 1977
Lyons 1962
Malmberg 1955
Malmberg 1963
Meyer-Eppler 1957
O'Connor/Trim 1953
Pike 1945
*Pulgram 1970
Robins 1972
Rosetti [2]1963
Rosetti 1961
Selkirk 1980
Selkirk 1982
Selkirk 1984
Steele 1775
Stetson 1945
Stetson 1951
Stevens/Volkman/Newman 1937
Stevens/Volkman 1940
Tillman 1964
Vennemann 1972

Chapter II
# Stress and accent


## 1. The phenomenon stress

What many phoneticians and linguists have called *stress*, and what most laymen readily understand under this term, refers to nothing more than the fact that in a succession of spoken syllables or words some will be perceived as more salient or prominent than others.[1] What this perceived prominence is due to, however, is a highly complex question which has caused a considerable amount of discussion in past years. As one linguist has put it: "... stress appears to be a chameleon whose nature changes according to the experiment set up to detect its true color" (Frank 1974:60).

### 1.1 Definitions of stress

*Stress* has been given a variety of scholarly definitions involving such disparate notions as emphasis, weight, intensity, sound pressure, etc. (Crystal 1969:113). For some it is considered to be an aspect of speaker activity, e.g. "the degree of force with which a sound or syllable is uttered" (Jones [9]1976:245). In this case it is related to the physiological phenomenon of greater articulatory effort. Others, however, view stress as an auditory sensation of the hearer, e.g. "degree of loudness" (Trager/ Smith 1957:36), loudness being a perceptual dimension. And at least one scholar has combined articulatory and auditory dimensions by defining stress as the activity of "speaking one of (the) syllables (in a word) louder than the other or others" (Bloomfield 1933:90).

But these definitions are not merely different ways of saying the same thing. Loudness and greater articulatory effort cannot be equated in any simple or straightforward fashion, as Fig. II/1 illustrates:

Fig. II/1    Articulatory and acoustic dimensions of LOUDNESS

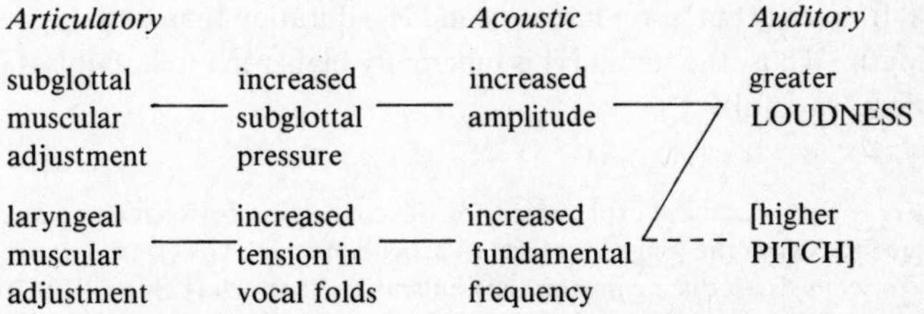

| Articulatory | | Acoustic | Auditory |
|---|---|---|---|
| subglottal muscular adjustment | increased subglottal pressure | increased amplitude | greater LOUDNESS |
| laryngeal muscular adjustment | increased tension in vocal folds | increased fundamental frequency | [higher PITCH] |

---

[1] Prominent *words* in phrases or clauses are sometimes signalled in written texts by underlining, italics or capitalization; prominent *syllables* within words are usually not marked.

The auditory sensation of loudness has two different acoustic correlates: an increase in the amplitude of the sound wave [more energy reaching the ear per unit of time] and/or an increase in the rate of vibration of the vocal folds [more pulses reaching the ear per unit of time] (Lehiste 1970:144). The latter is due to the "integrating time-constant" of our ear (Lehiste 1976:236). Furthermore, one of the acoustic correlates of loudness, increased fundamental frequency, can have two different physiological sources: pulmonic muscular activity and/or laryngeal muscular activity. Yet only the former is involved in greater articulatory effort. The relation between loudness and articulatory effort − and, more generally, between perception and articulation − is thus a highly complex one which defies simple equation.

But even if the two could be equated, it would still be insufficient to define stress in these terms only. In English at least, duration and pitch are also involved in perception of prominence. For instance, in the word *inSULT* (v.), the second syllable is not only louder than the first, but also perceptibly longer than the first. And if the word is pronounced in citation form, the first syllable has a level pitch, whereas the second has a perceptible pitch glide. Consequently, when we perceive the second syllable of *inSULT* as more prominent than the first, this may be because it is louder, or longer, or because it has a glide, or because of some combination of these features.

## 1.2   Acoustic correlates of stress

Scientists have understandably had little success in locating a unique acoustic correlate of stress. As we might surmise, there are at least three *primary* acoustic cues which may be expected in the vowel or syllable nucleus of a stressed syllable: higher intensity, greater duration, and higher fundamental frequency (cf., however, §1.4.3). Furthermore, there are a number of (optional) *secondary* cues to stress, primarily of a segmental nature. For instance, in English a glottal stop, an aspirated plosive, or a non-central vowel − if present − are usually signs of stress (although they are not obligatory). By the same token, a syllabic sonorant or a weak central vowel such as [ɨ] or [ə] may signal absence of stress.

However, none of the secondary or, for that matter, primary criteria can serve unequivocally as markers of stress because of certain *interfering factors*. These include:

(a) *Vowel identity.* Every vowel has inherent intensity, duration and frequency. For instance, vowels articulated high in the mouth have ceteris paribus higher fundamental frequency but lower intensity and less duration than vowels produced low in the mouth.[2] Thus, the sound [i] is inherently higher in pitch, but less loud and less long than, say, [ɑ].[3]

---

[2] There is a physiological explanation for the connection between high vowels and greater frequency: when the tongue is raised to articulate a high vowel, the laryngeal muscles are also stretched, producing greater tension and higher pitch (Lehiste 1970:70f.).

[3] These differences, which are physiologically determined, may pass unnoticed in speech: they are compensated for in perception processing. However, they obviously interfere with an exact acoustic determination of stress.

(b) *Consonantal context.* The intensity, duration and fundamental frequency of vowels is also conditioned by surrounding consonants. For instance, preceding voiceless consonants cause a sudden rise in fundamental frequency in the following vowel; following voiceless consonants tend to reduce the length of the preceding vowel.

(c) *Position in the phrase or sentence.* Intensity and fundamental frequency tend to decrease over a phrase or sentence; vowels at the end of phrases and clauses tend to be lengthened.

(d) *Rate of speech.* In rapid speech unstressed vowels are more reduced in length than stressed vowels, and fundamental frequency tends to be higher (Lea 1977:114).

It is in part due to such interfering factors that stress cannot be identified acoustically with perfect accuracy.[4]


## 1.3    Physiology of stress

Abstracting from the inherent features of individual sounds, the greater *intensity* in connected speech, it is thought, is produced pulmonically by the use of greater muscular force or energy. During expiration, muscular contraction decreases the volume of the chest cavity, which automatically produces an increase of pressure in the air below the glottis. Expiratory muscular activity occurs in bursts (the so-called chest pulses which Stetson believed were responsible for the syllable; Ch. I §3.2.1). Consequently, there tend to be *peaks in subglottal pressure* at given intervals during an utterance. Experiments by Ladefoged et al (1958) suggested that these peaks in subglottal pressure correlate with major stresses in connected speech. However, more recent research has corroborated this finding only for emphatically stressed syllables (Ohala 1977).

The greater *duration* associated with stressed syllables is thought to be related to the greater and more forceful movements of the articulators which have been documented with the help of cine X-ray techniques. However, here too the effect appears only in emphatically stressed syllables.

The articulatory origin of *pitch variation* in speech has been a subject of controversy in recent years. While most phoneticians assume that muscular adjustments in the vocal cords are primarily responsible for changes in fundamental frequency, Lieberman (1967) advanced the challenging theory that it is uniquely changes in subglottal pressure which correspond to changes in fundamental frequency, except for the rising pitch of questions, where vocal cord activity increases as well (Ch. IV §3.1). However, Lieberman's theory has been disproved by subsequent experiments which show that laryngeal muscular activity actually increases significantly during stressed syllables (Ohala 1977).

It appears then that the physiology of emphatic stress is understood far better than that of normal, non-emphatic stress. Whereas greater force and energy affecting the

---

[4] According to Lea (1977), however, it is possible to detect approximately 89% of the stresses in connected speech by using algorithms which weight acoustic cues differentially (1977:115).

pulmonic, laryngeal and vocal-tract muscles have been found with the former, the only articulatory feature consistently present in the latter appears to be increased laryngeal activity, which ceteris paribus may result in greater loudness or in higher pitch.

## 1.4 Stress as an auditory phenomenon

If on articulatory and acoustic levels at least two and sometimes three primary components of stress can be identified, the question which arises is how these factors interact to produce the auditory impression of stress. What part – and how necessary a part – does each component play? Can the presence of one component compensate for the absence of another in a so-called trading relation?

### 1.4.1 The part of intensity

Gimson once remarked that if a nonsense word with English sounds such as /iːvɒlɪmæ/ is uttered on a monotone or in a whisper with approximate equal syllable length, native speakers usually hear the second syllable as prominent (1956, 1973:98). That is, if pitch and length are held constant, intensity – here the greater inherent sonority of the vowel /ɒ/ as opposed to that of the other vowels – appears to determine stress perception.

Fry (1958, 1960) investigated this hypothesis experimentally by synthesizing noun-verb pairs of the sort *SUBject–subJECT* and systematically varying one acoustic component at a time. Listeners' noun vs. verb judgments indicate to what extent the variable under consideration is responsible for stress recognition. Increasing the intensity of the first vowel with respect to the second vowel in the word *subject*, for instance, resulted in listeners increasingly perceiving stress on the first syllable, i.e. hearing the noun rather than the verb. Although some scholars have maintained that intensity plays no part at all in perception of stress (e.g. Bolinger 1958b:149), a more balanced view of the matter is that it is at least sufficient to cue a stress judgment, although it may not be necessary.

### 1.4.2 The part of duration

As pointed out earlier, the difference in stress between the two syllables of *inSULT* is based in part on a difference of perceived syllable length, the second syllable being longer than the first. This rhythmic pattern might be expressed in musical notation /♩♩./. However, there is no equivalent difference in length between the two syllables of the corresponding noun *INsult*. The rhythmic pattern here is not /♩.♪/ but /♩♩/. Thus, it appears that a syllable perceived as prominent need not necessarily be longer than an adjacent syllable. What seems to be more important is the distinctive rhythmic pattern.

Furthermore, it is not simply the relative length of a vowel with respect to surrounding vowels which cues our perception of prominence (Fry 1958a:128). For example, although the vowel of the first, stressed syllable in the word *morbid* is what is traditionally called a 'long' vowel and may indeed in this case be longer than the so-called 'short' vowel /ɪ/, we do not determine stress simply by comparing the length of the two adjacent vowels in absolute terms. If we did, we would probably hear the first syllable of the word *morbidity* /mɔ:bɪdɪtɪ/ as being stressed, since its vowel /ɔ:/ is typically somewhat longer than the adjacent /ɪ/ vowels. Instead our perception of stress is based on a judgment of relative length with respect to vowel quality. That is, we compare the length of /ɔ:/ in *morbidity* to the length of /ɔ:/ in *morbid* — or, more abstractly, we judge the length of a particular instance of a vowel with respect to a norm for that particular vowel. The norms for given vowels are independent of each other and may vary significantly. In absolute terms an /ɪ/ may be shorter than or equal in length to an /ɔ:/; however, if the former is relatively long with respect to its norm and the latter relatively short with respect to its norm, then the syllable with /ɪ/ will be heard as having greater prominence than that with /ɔ:/ (Fry 1958a).

The part that length norms for given vowel qualities play in perception of prominence is not taken into consideration in Fry's (1958a) stress experiments. Thus, his results can only be considered valid to the extent that the norms for the vowels involved are comparable. However this may be, by systematically increasing the duration of the first vowel with respect to the second vowel in the word *subject*, Fry was able to show that listeners' judgments increasingly changed from *subJECT* (verb) to *SUBject* (noun). But most importantly, compared to the same test with increasing intensity, increased duration in the first vowel influenced more listeners to hear the noun than did increased intensity. Fry interprets these results to mean that, of the two factors, duration is more important than intensity in the perception of syllable prominence.[5]

### 1.4.3 The part of pitch

We noted earlier that in the citation form of the verb *inSULT*, the pitch patterns on the two syllables are quite distinct. This can be expressed diagrammatically as ⎺\. But notice that the noun *INsult* is not produced with an inverse pitch pattern. Its melody in citation is not \⎺, i.e. a glide followed by a static tone, but instead a high static tone on *IN-* followed by a low static tone on *-sult* ⎺_. Thus rather than correlating stress with pitch glide, it would be more appropriate, here too, to speak of distinctive pitch patterns.

What the stressed syllables in both noun and verb do have in common is sudden pitch height. Indeed there is a certain amount of experimental evidence showing a link between pitch step-ups and perceived stress (cf. Crystal 1969:119 for references). The results of Fry's (1958a) experiments support this hypothesis to a great extent. By synthesizing a step-up in pitch from one syllable to the next in the word *subject* Fry was able to show that more listeners hear the verb (*subJECT*) than the noun,

---

[5] In reality stress judgments are probably rarely made on the basis of duration alone. One noteworthy case, however, is the intoning of prayers in church. Here the relative prominence of syllables is realized by lengthening alone, since pitch and loudness are usually held constant (Gimson 1956, 1973:99).

whereas with a step-down in pitch, more listeners hear the noun (*SUBject*) than the verb. [Interestingly enough, the size of the step-up or step-down was irrelevant.] Furthermore, by simulating stress patterns such as (a) \ __ and (b) __ \ and imposing them on the word *subject*, Fry was able to show that for (a) there is a majority of noun judgments (*SUBject*) even when the duration of the second vowel with respect to the first is increased maximally, whereas for (b) there is a majority of verb judgments (*subJECT*) even when the duration of the first vowel with respect to the second is increased. The conclusion he draws is that pitch variations are not only important; they may indeed outweigh duration altogether.

It would be mistaken, however, to assume that only pitch height is responsible for stress recognition. Simple experimentation will show that a sudden step-down in pitch also triggers stress recognition. For instance, pronouncing the nonsense word /iːvɒlɪmæ/ on the pitch pattern ‾ ‾ _ ‾ will usually lead native speakers of English to perceive the third syllable as stressed. In a sentence such as "Did you say 'INsult'?", the pitch pattern will be ‾ ‾ — ˌ_ ‾. Here the prominence on the first syllable of *INsult* corresponds to extra low pitch with respect to surrounding syllables (Gimson 1956, 1973:99).[6] This type of observation, coupled with experimental evidence, convinced Bolinger that it is *pitch obtrusion*, "a rapid and relatively wide departure from a smooth or undulating contour" (1958b:112) – either up or down – which is responsible for perception of prominence. Thus his introduction of the term *pitch accent* to reflect the fact that pitch change is an essential component of what others call stress (§2.2).

### 1.4.4 Trading effects and neutralization

From both Bolinger's and Fry's experiments on stress, a clear hierarchy emerges among the acoustic cues to stress in English: (in order of importance) fundamental frequency, duration, intensity.[7] Some linguists, however, assume that – regardless of relative position in the hierarchy – there is a *trading relation* between these factors such that one or two may compensate for lack of differentiation in the other (Lieberman 1960:451). For instance, the fact that we hear stresses in whispered speech, where fundamental frequency is absent, would imply that some compensatory mechanism is at work here. Furthermore, the fact that some syllables which have pitch but no pitch obtrusion are perceived as prominent (e.g. in pre-nuclear position; Ch. V §1.2) may require an explanation in terms of trading effects.

On the other hand, there is evidence that stress distinctions are *neutralized* if fundamental frequency is excluded as a distinguishing factor. This phenomenon has

---

[6] Some English nursery rhymes are performed with extra pitch height on unstressed syllables; the stressed syllables are thus low with respect to their neighbors (Gimson 1956, 1973:100). Cf.:

*Round and round the garden / Walks a teddy bear ...*
Likewise in rising 'glissando' intonation (Ch. V §2.4), stressed syllables are accompanied by a step-down in pitch.

[7] Needless to say, this hierarchy might look different for other languages.

been amply attested, for instance, in post-nuclear position. Thus listeners are reportedly unable to distinguish consistently between the verb *imPORT* (a) and the noun *IMport* (b) in:

(a)  He said (Mr) *Wood* imports wood
(b)  He said *wood* imports would     (Scott, cit. in Gimson 1956, 1973:99)

nor can they distinguish (Br.E.) *LOOK-out* ('man on watch') from *look-OUT* ('fault/risk') in:

That's your *own* look-out     (Sharp 1958:135)

nor an adjective + noun construction (e.g. *a green HOUSE*) from a compound construction (e.g. *a GREENhouse*) in:

I know very *well* it's a green house
I know very *well* it's a greenhouse     (Faure et al 1980:76f.)

In cases where pitch distinctions are minimized, duration and intensity differences may be present but are rarely perceived as such and do not relate in any consistent fashion to the perception of prominence in post-nuclear position (Huss 1978). In one series of experiments Huss determined that listeners were actually making post-nuclear stress judgments in accordance with the prevailing rhythmic pattern. For instance, in realizations of *Did you say the GERmans import sinks?* (where *import* is used as a verb) vs. *Did you say the GERmans' import sinks?* (where *import* functions as a noun), subjects were unable to determine which version they had heard when the two sentences were excised from their respective contexts. However, the stress judgments were not wholly random. Significantly more listeners claimed to hear the noun *import* than the verb, presumably because the noun fits better in the rhythmic pattern of alternating stressed and unstressed syllables (*the 'Germans' 'import 'sinks* vs. *the 'Germans im'port 'sinks*) (1978:98). This type of evidence lends strong support to a rhythmic view of stress (§2.5).

## 1.5   A theory of stress perception

The assumption behind much of the research on stress has been that the ear acts as a filter on the acoustic signal, transforming phonetic input into perceptual 'bits', which are then transmitted to the brain for interpretation. This is known as the *transducer* model of speech perception (McNeill/Repp 1973:1325). The (misguided) philosophy behind this model has been described in the following terms:

> ... we have taken for granted that most of the information which listeners used to perceive prosodic meaning was there in the acoustic signal; all the investigator had to do was to find out where that information was located and how it was signalled. If listeners could identify prosodic functions in speech, then so could an intelligent acoustic analysis. (Grundstrom 1979:43)[8]

---

[8] Cf. also Cooper (1972), who points out that the speech signal was long assumed to be an acoustic *cipher*, implying a one-to-one correspondence between minimal units of the original and final message, whereas it is actually a *code*, in which the original message is restructured and usually shortened.

Yet, although we can set up laboratory experiments to assess the role of individual acoustic components in stress determination and although we can devise algorithms to locate stress automatically, there is growing doubt that we are thereby learning more about how human beings perceive stress. Long before psychoacoustic evidence was available, at least one phonetician intuitively suspected that stress is a construct of our minds: according to Daniel Jones, a hearer familiar with the language does not perceive stress objectively. Instead, "the sounds he hears call up to his mind (through the context) the manner of making them, and by means of immediate 'inner speech' he knows where the stress is" (1918, [9]1976:245).

Today this view of stress perception has found confirmation in psychoacoustic studies. The evidence suggests that perception of speech involves at once less and more than the simple transferral of acoustic signals to the brain. The reasons for this are several. For one, the auditory system processes phonetic material at a much slower rate than that at which speech can be generated. This means that a great deal of phonetic information must simply be ignored. Second, other kinds of information can be transmitted to the auditory center of the brain and theoretically be used to interpret auditory material. One psychologist has thus concluded that "... by virtue of the structure which the listener imposes upon the incoming acoustic signal, he need perform only a cursory examination of that signal. We perceive according to the probabilities we have used to generate expectancies" (Sanders 1977:156).

In sum, listeners do not use all the phonetic information available to them in perceiving speech, and in fact they use more than just this restricted phonetic input. What other types of information are necessary and precisely how this process works is not fully understood. Some scientists believe the answer lies in a *motor theory of speech perception*. According to this theory, speech perception is a mediated or 'active' process, whereby "articulatory movements and their sensory effects mediate between the acoustic stimulus and the event we call perception" (Liberman 1957:122). The contention is that we perceive speech sounds by reference to the articulatory movements which we ourselves would have to make in order to produce the same sounds. In its more modest version this view does not claim that we actually mimic the incoming speech sounds and respond to the sensory feedback of our articulatory movements. Instead, "we must assume that the process is somehow short-circuited — that is, that the reference to articulatory movements and their sensory consequences must somehow occur in the brain without getting out into the periphery" (Liberman 1957:122).[9]

With respect to perception of stress, a motor theory would help explain how, in spite of the indeterminate nature of the acoustic cues, we are able to make the stress distinctions we do: speakers presumably 'know' which physiological mechanisms are at play, since quite different organs are involved. Listeners compare their 'inner' knowledge as speakers to the input from the acoustic signal in making stress judgments (Lehiste 1970:145).

---

[9] In a more explicit model known as *analysis-by-synthesis*, it is hypothesized that the perception of speech involves "the internal synthesis of patterns according to certain rules, and a matching of these internally generated patterns against the pattern under analysis" (Stevens/Halle 1967:88).

## 2. Linguistic views of stress

Linguists have been faced with two separate problems in dealing with the phenomenon of stress: (i) determining what degree of stress differentiation is necessary and establishing appropriate taxonomic categories, and (ii) accounting for the location of stresses in the utterance. It is to the first of these that we turn our attention now.

### 2.1 Stress phonemes and contours

For structuralists such as Trager/Smith (1957), stress was thought to have phonemic character, differing degrees of stress representing independent phonemic entities. These *stress phonemes* were assumed to function wholly independently of pitch, which itself was analysed in terms of 'pitch phonemes' (Ch. IV §2.1). In English four degrees of stress and thus four stress phonemes were postulated: primary ( ´ ), secondary ( ^ ), tertiary ( ` ) and weak stress ( ˘ ) (1957:36f.). All significant stress contrasts, so the claim, can be expressed with these four categories. For instance, the fact that the noun *rebel* differs from the verb *rebel* can be expressed by the assignment of strong (primary) stress followed by weak stress to the former: *rébĕl*, and weak stress followed by strong (primary) stress to the latter: *rĕbél*. Moreover, the fact that the verb *animate* differs from the adjective *animate* can be expressed by attributing tertiary stress to the last syllable of the former: *ánĭmàte* (v.) and weak stress to the last syllable of the latter: *ánĭmăte* (adj.). Finally, the difference between two original primary stresses when combined in a compound can be accounted for by postulating a secondary stress phoneme. For instance, we have *élĕvàtŏr* and *ópĕràtŏr* individually, but as compounds we can distinguish between *élĕvàtŏr ôpĕràtŏr*, 'someone who runs the elevator', and *êlĕvàtŏr ópĕràtŏr*, 'the operator as opposed to the elevator repairman'. Secondary stress is said to be perceptually slightly stronger than tertiary, but slightly weaker than primary stress.

Generative grammarians have inherited the structuralists' strict separation of stress and pitch but no longer assume that one or the other has phonemic status. According to Chomsky/Halle (1968), for instance, *stress contours* are predictable from the application of a small number of basic stress rules to the labelled formatives (roughly, syntactically categorized morphemes) of the surface structure. At the word level three phonologically conditioned rules apply (Main Stress Rule, Alternating Stress Rule, Stress Adjustment Rule) yielding lexical items which have maximally one syllable with primary stress (indicated by a small numeral 1 placed above the vowel).[10] Thus we might have *astonish, maintain, eat, domain, America* or *hurricane*. Above the word level two further rules apply:

---

[10] The *Main Stress Rule* assigns primary stress to (a) the penultimate syllable of verbs and adjectives if the following cluster is weak (i.e. contains a lax vowel followed by no more than one consonant), and (b) to the last syllable elsewhere. The *Alternating Stress Rule* places primary stress on the antepenultimate vowel and reduces other primary stresses to secondary stresses in words of three syllables or more. The *Stress Adjustment Rule* reduces secondary stresses to tertiary stresses within the word.

(i) *Compound Stress Rule.* This rule assigns primary stress to the *leftmost* primary stressed vowel in lexical categories (N,A,V), automatically reducing all other stresses by one.

Ex.
$$\left[ [\text{bl}\overset{1}{\text{a}}\text{ck}]\ [\text{bo}\overset{1}{\text{a}}\text{rd}] \right] \qquad \left[ \text{bl}\overset{2}{\text{a}}\text{ckbo}\overset{1}{\text{a}}\text{rd} \right]$$

(ii) *Nuclear Stress Rule.* This rule assigns primary stress to the *rightmost* primary stressed vowel in phrases (NP, VP, PP) or sentences, automatically reducing all other stresses by one.

Ex.
$$\left[ [\text{bl}\overset{1}{\text{a}}\text{ck}]\ [\text{bo}\overset{1}{\text{a}}\text{rd}] \right] \qquad \left[ \text{bl}\overset{2}{\text{a}}\text{ck bo}\overset{1}{\text{a}}\text{rd} \right]$$

In more complex structures these rules apply cyclically, i.e. first to the innermost string of formatives, then − once these brackets have been erased − to the next larger string of formatives, and so forth until the whole string has been completed. Since with each cyclical application primary stress is assigned anew and all other stresses are automatically weakened by one degree, complex sentences may ultimately have a large number of different degrees of stress. Furthermore, depending on the environment in which a structure appears, one and the same compound or phrase may have different stress contours (in terms of the degrees involved): for instance, Chomsky/Halle have reckoned that *sad plight* would have the stress contour /21/ in isolation, in *consider his sad plight* the stress contour /31/, and in *my friend can't help being shocked by anyone who would fail to consider his sad plight* the stress contour /81/ (1968:23). The number of degrees of stress is potentially unlimited in this approach, although readjustment rules to cancel distinctions beyond a certain degree of refinement have been proposed (Chomsky/Halle/Lukoff 1956).[11]

What characterizes this view of stress in particular, however, is the conviction that "the shape and the degree of differentiation of a stress contour are largely determined by obligatory rules" (Chomsky/Halle 1968:25):

> Once the speaker has selected a sentence with a particular syntactic structure and certain lexical items (...), the choice of stress contour is not a matter subject to further independent decision. That is, he need not make a choice among various 'stress phonemes' ... With marginal exceptions, the choice of these is as completely determined as, for example, the degree of aspiration. (1968:25−6)

In sum, the factors which determine stress contours, according to this view, are phonological structure (at word level) and syntactic structure (above word level).

---

[11] Bierwisch (1968) suggests instead that the operation of the CSR and the NSR must be blocked at a certain stage depending on the length of a constituent or the number of accents in it.

## 2.2   Pitch accents

The theory of the separation of stress and pitch, which underlies structuralist and generative approaches, has not gone unchallenged. In particular, Bolinger's *pitch accents* – and accompanying experimental evidence that pitch obtrusion is central to the perception of stress (§1.4.3) – have constituted a major challenge.

Bolinger (1958b) proposes to use the term *accent* for prominence in the utterance. In his view, a syllable is heard as accented only when it has *pitch* prominence. The prominence may be due to pitch movement (i) down from, (ii) up to (or from), or (iii) down to the accented syllable.[12] For example, in:

```
(i)    Hz 120 |             be ea
          110 |
          100 | wouldn't it      sier to wait
```

listeners were unanimous in hearing *easier* as accented; likewise in

```
(ii)   Hz 120 |                      wait
          110 |
          100 | wouldn't it be easier to
```

listeners heard *wait* as accented, and in:

```
(iii)  Hz 120 |             be
          110 |
          100 | wouldn't it    easier to wait
```

listeners heard *easier* as accented (1958b:129). Bolinger calls these configurations different types of *pitch accent* and refers to them as A, B and C respectively. Diagrammatically, the three types can be represented as follows (with arrows signalling skips; solid lines, essential parts; and dotted lines, optional parts of the contours):

Fig. II/2   Bolinger's pitch accents

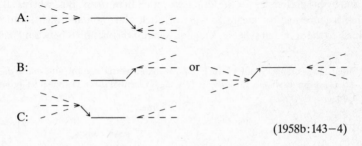

(1958b:143–4)

---

[12] Bolinger's categories thus in essence 'phonemicize' type of pitch obtrusion (high vs. low) and position of this obtrusion (before vs. after the accented syllable). These features are reminiscent of Isačenko/Schädlich's (1970) pre-ictic vs. post-ictic falls and rises.

Note that central to Bolinger's approach is the conviction that (lexical) stress and pitch work together to define accent. Thus pitch modulation alone will not always provide the proper cue. Compare, for instance:

(a) it's the man who      (b) it's the man
          broke it              who broke it

If accent depended on pitch alone, we should hear either *who* or *broke* in (a), and either *man* or *who* in (b) as accented. Instead, however, only *broke* in (a) and *man* in (b) have accents. This, Bolinger claims, is because when we learn the lexicon of our language, we learn that some syllables shun pitch accents.[13] Consequently, when these "unaccentables" do appear with pitch prominence, our foreknowledge prevents us from hearing them as accented. Thus it is the interaction of our knowledge of lexical stress patterns, *stress* being understood as potential for pitch accent, together with (primarily) pitch obtrusion, which accounts for perception of accent.[14]

According to Bolinger, the pitch accents are responsible for all-or-none contrasts. That is, the substitution of one pitch accent for the other produces an entirely different meaning, not merely more or less of the same or a similar meaning. It is the all-or-none contrast which characterizes pitch accent; gradient contrasts, on the other hand, belong to the domain of 'intonation'. [Cf., however, the definition of intonation adopted here, Ch. IV.]


## 2.3   Kinetic and static tones

For Kingdon (1958a, 1958b) the stress phenomenon − Bolinger's accents − may be viewed from two different perspectives. *Word stress* is "the relative degree of force used in pronouncing the different syllables of a word of more than one syllable". *Sentence stress* is "the relative degree of force given to the different words in a sentence" (1958a:1). The domain of word stress is the syllable: the domain of sentence stress, the word. All polysyllabic words have word stress, but in the utterance both polysyllabic and monosyllabic words may have sentence stress if they are spoken with greater emphasis relative to the words surrounding them.

Similar to Bolinger, Kingdon incorporates pitch into his account of stress, as witnessed by his preference for the term *tone* rather than *stress*. But, whereas Bolinger is more concerned to categorize types of pitch obtrusion and their location with respect to the accented syllable, Kingdon's major distinction is between *kinetic* and

---

[13] Some unaccentable syllables belong to polysyllabic words, e.g. *di-, -ti-, -ble* in *digestible*; others are monosyllabic words themselves, e.g. existential *there*. Despite pitch prominence, as in:

  di                        there
     ble                        trouble
   gesti                 wasn't any

we still do not hear these 'flanking unaccentables' as accented.

[14] For Bolinger intensity is "negligible both as a determinative and as a qualitative factor in stress" (1958b:149). However, duration can be seen as an ancillary feature: it is "to a large extent a co-variable with accent" (1958b:138).

*static* tones. The former are syllables which are prominent by virtue of a pitch movement: falling (`insult`) or rising (´insult), falling–rising (ˇinsult) or rising–falling (ˆinsult).[15] The latter are syllables which are prominent by virtue of their being pitched on a steady level tone either relatively high in the voice range or relatively low in the voice range. High level tones (') occur on fully stressed syllables and only before kinetic tones. For example: 'photo`graphic. Low level tones (ˌ) occur on syllables which are partially stressed (but contain non-reduced vowels) and may come either before or after kinetic tones. For example: ˌvi`bration, `attiˌtude.

As Kingdon remarks, partially stressed syllables need not be marked at all; however, doing so makes it possible to distinguish syllables without vowel reduction from those with vowel reduction. For instance, of the pair *postman – mailman*, only *postman* has a reduced vowel /pəʊstmən/ [vs. /meɪlmæn/]. This difference can be expressed as follows: `postman, `mailˌman. Since partial stress is linked to a full vowel and weak stress (or no stress) to a reduced vowel, it is a general rule that whenever a reduced vowel occurs [/ə/ and sometimes /ɪ, ʊ, ɪə, ʊə/], the syllable is unstressed. Other vowels and diphthongs are non-reduced; therefore the syllables they occur in are either partially or fully stressed.

## 2.4 Stresses and accents

Whereas for Bolinger the only type of perceptual prominence conceivable is accent or pitch prominence, Crystal (1969) argues that both stress and accent may be realized in the utterance. The difference between stress and accent does not depend (*pace* Kingdon) on whether the domain of prominence is a syllable or a word, but on whether loudness plays the major role in perception of prominence – in which case we speak of *stress* – or whether pitch plays the major perceptual role – in which case we speak of *accent* (1969:120). For Crystal, it is theoretically conceivable that a syllable could be perceived as prominent although it has no pitch obtrusion at all. This might occur, for instance, in whispered speech or in monotone utterances. Or it might occur in parts of a normal utterance which have no pitch prominence, for instance, in the body of a tone-unit unmarked for pitch-range or in the tail (Ch. V §§1.2.2, 1.4). In such cases, Crystal hypothesizes, perception of syllable prominence is due primarily to loudness (as well as length and secondary cues). On the other hand, judgments of syllable prominence in which pitch plays a predominant role are found typically in the nucleus or in the onset and other parts of the tone-unit body marked for pitch-range (Ch. V §§1.1, 1.2.1).

Note that within this terminological framework what has often been investigated under the name of *stress* is actually *accent*, since pitch prominence is involved. According to this model, stress is not restricted to words of more than one syllable;

---

[15] Kingdon rightly notes that a word spoken in isolation is normally treated as an utterance and given pitch movement. Therefore he represents the stress patterns of polysyllabic words in terms of kinetic and static tones as well. For the sake of simplicity, however, he uses a *falling* tone mark /´/ for the kinetic syllable of all lexemes in isolation. Ex.: `private.

furthermore, polysyllabic words may be wholly unstressed. What has traditionally been called *sentence stress* now falls under *accent* in pitch-prominent parts of the utterance and under *stress* in non-pitch prominent parts of the utterance. *Lexical stress*, on the other hand, becomes an abstract concept; it is the potential pattern of syllable prominence in polysyllabic words, compounds and groups of words. It figures in lexical entries such as:

(i) ˈan-ti-ˈdis-es-ˈtab-lish-men-ˈ*tar*-i-a-nis-m
(ii) ˈ*black*-board-e-ˈra-ser
(iii) and ˈ*so* on

[where ˈ indicates potential loudness prominence and italics potential pitch prominence].

Defined in this manner, lexical stress patterning belongs to the lexicon and not to the domain of prosodic analysis as we are using the term here. Prosodic features were described earlier as those having "an essentially variable relationship to the words selected" (Ch. I §1.2). The relationship of the word to its lexical stress pattern is, however, non-variable for the most part; changing the stress or accent from one syllable to another will often alter the meaning of the word: ˈ*desert* vs. de*ˈsert*, ˈ*record* vs. re*ˈcord*, etc. [A small percentage of words in English do have variable stress patterns (§3.2; Ch. III §4.2), but this subset is too small to justify giving lexical stress the status of a prosodic feature.] For these reasons lexical stress will not receive further consideration here.

As for types of prosodic stress and accent, Crystal argues that syllables may have differing degrees of prominence due to loudness: i.e. they may be *strongly stressed* (ˮ), *stressed* (ˈ) or *unstressed*. And they may have differing degrees of prominence due to pitch: i.e. *primary accent* (if they incorporate a glide or similar nuclear pitch movement, Ch. V §1.1), *secondary* or *tertiary accent* (if they represent significant steps up or down from the slowly descending reference line; Ch. V §1.2.2). Furthermore, syllables may have combinations of stress and accent, or both pitch and loudness prominence in varying degrees. The two systems, however, are claimed to be ultimately independent one of the other (Crystal 1969:158).

But this purported independence is undermined by the fact that in Crystal's model secondary and tertiary accent (and in effect primary accent) are themselves defined with respect to stress. For instance, secondary accent can only be attributed to a *stressed* syllable marked for pitch, and tertiary accent can only apply to *unstressed* syllables marked for pitch. Only primary accent can theoretically be defined in its own terms – say, with a pitch glide as its identifying feature. But even here problems would conceivably arise in the treatment of glissando and of nuclei with pitch jumps rather than pitch glides (Ch. V §§1.1.2, 2.4). In the latter case the presence of stress is a sine qua non for primary accent as well.

Moreover, Crystal's stress-accent dichotomy – although it is intended to bring some clarity into the confused relation between loudness and pitch – actually obscures an important distinction, namely that between nuclear and non-nuclear prominence (Ch. V §1.1). Since both his accented and stressed syllables may be either nuclear or non-nuclear, the nucleus cannot be identified with accent – nor even with primary accent, for that matter: although all primary-accented syllables are presumably nuclei, not all nuclei are primary-accented (level nuclei being a case in point). Therefore, distinguishing stress and accent as loudness vs. pitch prominence is not as useful as it might appear.

## 2.5  Rhythmic stress beats

An alternative to the view of stress-as-loudness or stress-as-accent is stress-as-rhythm (Ladd 1978:36). This view is just beginning to emerge in work on English prosody, although linguists have long known that stress and rhythm are closely linked (cf. Jassem 1952; Jassem/Gibbon 1980). According to Allen (1972a, 1972b), in addition to the lexico-grammatical role of stress in English, it also serves "... as a unifying marker around which the rhythm (of speech) is organized" (1972b:192). That is, the sequential production of stressed syllables is organized in such a way as to produce rhythmic patterns (Ch. III).

The view of stress-as-rhythm claims that we perceive syllables as stressed when they coincide with a rhythmic beat. Thus, for Abercrombie (1976), a salient syllable is "the syllable on which the beat of stress-timing falls" (1976:52) (Ch. III §2.1). Viewing stress this way has a number of advantages. For one, it provides a convincing explanation for the distinction between pairs such as (i) *líght housekeeper* vs. (ii) *líghthouse keéper*. Trager/Smith (1957) could only account for the difference between (i) and (ii) by positing an independent phoneme, "internal juncture", separating *light* from *house* in (i) and *house* from *keeper* in (ii). However, if stress is viewed rhythmically, then given the basic rhythmic principle of isochrony, according to which beats come at approximately equal intervals in time (Ch. III §2.2), the difference between the members of this pair can be described wholly in terms of stress: in (i) the interval between the stresses on *light* and *house* is lengthened to maintain the proper spacing in time between the two stress beats, whereas in (ii) the same interval requires no significant lengthening since the stress beats on *light-* and *keep-* are separated by *-house*. This explanation accords with instrumental measurements of recordings of these phrases which show that *light* plus the following 'disjuncture' is longer in duration in (i) than in (ii) (Ladd 1978:62).[16]

A second advantage of viewing stress in rhythmic terms is that it provides a principled account of the phenomenon of *stress shift*, which in other approaches must be treated as an exception. By way of illustration consider the word *un'known* in the following contexts:

(a)  a 'quite un'known ef'fect
(b)  a 'largely 'unknown 'land

Whereas in (a) *unknown* maintains lexical stress on the second syllable, in (b) it shifts its stress from the second to the first syllable. If we view stresses as rhythmic beats,

---

[16] Liberman (1975) proposes a similar explanation for *'John struck 'out my 'friend* vs. *'John 'struck out my 'friend* (1975:293).

then we can account for this shift by appealing to a basic rhythmic principle of English, i.e. that stressed and unstressed syllables alternate regularly in speech (Ch. III §4.1). The stressing of *unknown* and other words like it can thus be shown to depend systematically on the rhythmic pattern of the context in which they occur (§4.2).

A third advantage of a rhythmic theory of stress is that it can incorporate the phenomenon of *silent stress*. Abercrombie (1971) first introduced this term to refer to "a pause where a beat, according to the timing already established, might be expected to come, a pause which fills a gap which otherwise would be filled by a stressed syllable" (1971:148). For example: *boys₊stop here* vs. *boys stop here*, *making the green₊one red* vs. *making the green one red*.[17] Such 'phonological' pauses, Abercrombie argues, are not discontinuities in the utterance but are perceived as part of the utterance. Thus they cannot be ignored, or treated as hesitations, since this would make the rhythm appear amiss, or misrepresent the rhythmic phrasing. Needless to say, a view of stress as loudness or as pitch obtrusion renders the concept of silent stress meaningless. However, if stresses are rhythmic beats, then there is nothing contradictory about the claim that some are realized as pauses.

A number of recent generative approaches have sought to link stress and rhythm in the phonological component of the grammar. For instance, according to one model, Liberman/Prince's (1977) *metrical theory of stress*, the perceived stressing of an utterance results from the combination of constituent-structure − on which relative prominence in terms of strong /s/ and weak /w/ syllables is defined − and metrical "grid" assignment.[18] The latter fits the structure in question to a rhythmic hierarchy with different "metrical levels". For example, the phrase [ [ [*law degree*] *requirement* ] *changes*] would have the following relative prominence pattern based on constituent structure:

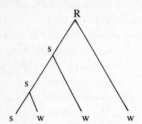

law degree requirement changes                                              (R = root)

The corresponding metrical grid would look as follows:[19]

Level 3    x
Level 2    x       x       x           x
Level 1    x    x  x   x   x       x       x  x
           law degree requirement changes        (1977:324)

---

[17] Whereas these silent stresses are more or less obligatory, many are optional and of a more stylistic/rhetorical nature: e.g. *the time is nine and a half minutes₊to nine, BBC Television₊ from Scotland* (Abercrombie 1971:151).

[18] Above word level, /s, w/ reflects compound stressing, /w, s/ phrasal stressing.

[19] We adopt the convention of using *x*'s to represent 'beats' (instead of numerals, as in Liberman/Prince). See Ch. III §4 for more on the construction of metrical grids.

34

This grid reflects the fact that *law* is metrically the strongest syllable in the phrase, that *de-, re-, -ment, -es* are metrically weak and *-gree, -quire, chang-* are of intermediate metrical strength. In other words it reflects to a certain extent degrees of stress. Moreover, it indicates that the phrase *law degree requirement changes* is metrically well-formed, in that for every two adjacent beats on an upper level there is an intervening beat on the next lower level. In other words the stressed and unstressed syllables alternate regularly. The advantage of metrical grids is that they offer a principled explanation for when and how stress changes (e.g. deletion, addition, shift) in rhythmically less well-formed structures occur (Ch. III §4). Metrical theories of this sort have grown directly out of the view of stress as rhythmic beat.

To recapitulate, we have looked at five different linguistic approaches to prominence, ranging from a theory which would restrict the phenomenon to pitch obtrusion alone, to one which would distinguish two independent types of prominence based on loudness and pitch respectively, and finally to one which would equate prominence with rhythmic beat. Probably none of these theories is wholly right. Granted for a moment that we do recognize different degrees of prominence in non-pitch prominent parts of speech, the theory of prominence as pitch obtrusion must be found lacking: it accounts for most but not all instances of prominence. Likewise, the theory of the independence of loudness and pitch is lacking, in that its categories cannot be defined independently one of another. At the moment it is the rhythmic approach to prominence which appears most promising and it is this view which we shall adopt here. The rhythmic beats in the utterance will be referred to as *stresses*; those rhythmic beats which are additionally prominent through some unspecified combination of loudness, pitch and length will be called *accents*.

## 3. Principles of stress distribution

We turn now to the question of what principles determine the location of stresses, understood as rhythmic beats, in the utterance.

### 3.1 Word category

One of the oldest and most venerable theories of stress distribution in the utterance is that described by Jones (1918) in the following terms:

> As a general rule it may be said that the relative stress of the words in a sequence depends on their relative importance. The more important a word is, the stronger is its stress. (1918, [9]1976: 262)

It was Pike (1945), however, who first associated "importance" with word categories. He identified *content* words as those which carry the major semantic weight of the sentence and are typically "nouns, main verbs (...), adjectives, demonstrative and interrogative pronouns, interjections, indefinite pronouns, adverbs of time, place, and manner". *Function* words, on the other hand, are those which have little semantic content of their own and serve primarily to mark grammatical relationships in the sentence; they are typically "auxiliary verbs, prepositions, reflexive and personal pronouns, adverbs of degree, and connectives". The former, Pike claimed, were normally stressed, the latter unstressed (1945:118).

Pike's categorization corresponds surprisingly well to that of Kingdon (1958b), whose discussion of the stress potential of word categories is, however, much more detailed. The following chart summarizes and illustrates his major points (illustrative words are set in italics):

*Word categories typically stressed*

| | |
|---|---|
| Nouns[20] | The 'noise of the 'train in the 'tunnel was 'deafening |
| Pronouns | |
|     Demonstrative | 'That's what I 'told you |
|     Possessive | I 'didn't 'know 'his was 'there |
|     Indefinite (as subject) | 'Somebody must have 'lost it |
|     Interrogative | 'Who's 'coming |
| Determiners | |
|     Demonstrative | 'That 'coat's very 'nice |
|     Negative | There's 'no 'doubt about 'that |
|     Quantifying | There are a 'few 'small ones |
|     Interrogative | 'Which 'route did they 'come by |
| Adjectives | This 'narrow 'valley was the 'scene of a 'famous 'battle |
| Main verbs | 'Don't for'get your 'homework |
| Auxiliaries | |
|     Negative[21] | He 'doesn't 'like them |
| Adverbs | |
|     Manner | I can 'do 'that 'easily |
|     Place | 'Tell him to 'come 'in |
|     Time | I shall 'see him to'night |
|     Frequency | It's 'usually 'hotter than 'this |
| Interjections | 'Oh |

*Word categories typically unstressed*

| | |
|---|---|
| Pronouns | |
|     Personal[22] | They 'didn't 'give me one |
|     Reflexive | I've 'just 'cut myself |
|     Reciprocal | I 'heard them 'speaking to each other |
|     Indefinite (as object) | I've 'seen someone a'bout it |
|     Relative | 'This is the 'girl who 'typed the 'letter |

---

[20] However, not nouns of 'wide denotation' (e.g. *thing, person, place*): *'That's a 'nice thing.*

[21] Also the following positive auxiliaries in statements:

| | |
|---|---|
| *should* ( = inference) | We 'should be 'there 'soon |
| *will* ( = insistence) | He 'will 'talk while I'm 'writing |
| *would* ( = disposition) | You 'would do a 'thing like 'that |
| *may* ( = possibility) | They 'may 'wait for us |
| *must* ( = inference) | They 'must come 'every 'day |
| *do* ( = polarity contrast) | She 'does look a little 'sick |

[22] However, *you* in imperatives is typically stressed: *'You 'make the 'tea.*

| Determiners | |
|---|---|
| Possessive | I 'saw *your* 'daughter and *her* 'husband 'yesterday |
| Relative | Is 'that the 'man *whose* 'daughter 'plays the 'cello |
| Articles | 'Is *the* 'book on *the* 'table *a* 'good one |
| Partitives [23] | 'Has she 'brought *any* 'sugar |

| Auxiliaries | |
|---|---|
| Affirmative (statements) [24] | She'*s* 'waiting for you |

| Adverbs | |
|---|---|
| Degree | It's *about* a 'mile from 'here |
| Relative | 'That's the 'reason *why* I 'don't 'like him |

| Prepositions | 'What are they 'staring *at* |
|---|---|

| Conjunctions | |
|---|---|
| Co-ordinating | *Both* 'he and 'I are 'ready |
| Subordinating | I pro'pose *that* we should 'wait for him |

(Kingdon 1958b:160–207)

Note that this categorization is valid only for so-called 'normal' stressing; it does not apply when contrastive meaning is present. In fact, function words *are* typically stressed or accented when used contrastively: *It's 'my book* (*not yours*) or *She 'is waiting for you* (*she hasn't left*). For the moment, however, we shall ignore contrastivity (cf. §4.3).

## 3.2   Rhythm and tempo

Yet the word-category principle alone cannot account for the location of all rhythmic stress beats in English speech utterances. It should come as no surprise that rhythmic principles, themselves related to considerations of tempo, interact with word-category membership to determine stress location in the utterance.

As noted earlier, it is a basic principle of English speech rhythm that stressed and unstressed syllables alternate rather regularly (§2.5; Ch. III §4.1). Consequently if an utterance contains a succession of, say, three monosyllabic words from stressable word categories, e.g. *'big 'black 'bugs*, the intermediate stress may be dropped in order to achieve a more regular alternation, e.g. *'big black 'bugs*. Similarly, if an utterance contains a succession of, say, monosyllabic words belonging to non-stressable word categories, e.g. *they will have been there be'fore*, then stresses may be added to ensure a more even rhythm: *'they will have 'been there be'fore*. Finally if two major stresses are adjacent to one another in a phrase or utterance, e.g. *thir'teen 'men*, under certain conditions one may be moved forward: *'thirteen 'men* (cf. stress shift, §2.5; Ch. III §4.2) in order to more nearly approximate an alternating rhythm.

The rhythmic principle of alternation is, however, intimately tied up with

---

[23] But *some* meaning 'a certain' and *any* meaning 'no matter which' are stressed: *'Some 'idiot has 'broken 'this*, *'Any 'newspaper'll 'do*.

[24] In affirmative questions, auxiliaries may either be stressed or unstressed: *Am I to 'wait for you*, or *'Am I to 'wait for you*.

considerations of speech tempo. Thus, several stresses *can* be articulated in immediate succession if the syllables bearing them are lengthened appropriately, or if a pseudo-pause is inserted: *'big— 'black— 'bugs, thir'teen — 'men*. Likewise, additional stress beats need not be added in a sequence of unstressed syllables if the rate of delivery is appropriately fast. As a rule, the faster the rate of delivery, the further apart in terms of number of intervening syllables the stresses may be. Conversely, the slower the rate of delivery, the closer together the stresses come.

Almost any short passage of spoken English will illustrate these rhythmic principles at work in the determination of stress beats in the utterance. Here and in the following we shall refer to a small corpus of BBC radio recordings (excerpts of which will be found on the accompanying cassette) for illustrative purposes. [To the extent possible, only RP and/or modified RP speakers will be considered.] Consider, for instance, the following utterances:

(a) of 'course these women 'care about the 'fate of what's in their 'womb (A1/BD$_4$)*
(b) 'thirteen hundred 'odd members of the 'Transport and General Workers 'Union (E3/DJ$_3$)

In (a), had all possible stresses been used, the utterance would have been: *of 'course 'these 'women 'care about the 'fate of 'what's in their 'womb*. However, in order to articulate so many stresses in immediate or close succession it would be necessary to adopt an appreciably slower rate of delivery than that which the speaker is using. Similarly, in (b) it is the fact that the speaker is articulating at such a fast rate which accounts for the missing stresses on *'hundred, 'members, 'General*, and *'Workers*.

Now consider:

(c) and 'this of 'course uh was 'caused ·'by· there 'being 'no 'paint on the 'timber (D)
(d) and its 'rights 'must 'be re'spected (F)

In these cases the speakers are articulating at a slow, deliberate pace and stresses on *by, being* (c), and *must, be* (d) have been added.

Finally, in

(e) 'disapprove 'powerfully (E1/SW$_1$)
(f) 'trade union 'movement (F)

the lexical stresses on *disap'prove* and *trade 'union* have been shifted forward to avoid a concentration of stresses in immediate or close succession (cf. also Ch. III §4.2).

It is interesting to note that there are restrictions on stress addition and deletion, as Giegerich (1978) has shown. For instance, stresses cannot be added just anywhere in the utterance. If we have a string of unstressed syllables such as *he has been in the pub* we cannot say (with normal, non-contrastive meaning) *\*he 'has been in the 'pub* but instead we must say *'he has 'been in the 'pub*. Likewise if an extra stress is to be added in *'interest in the 'idea* it cannot be added on the determiner but must be added on the preposition: *'interest 'in the i'dea*, not *\*'interest in 'the i'dea*. Based on evidence of this sort, Giegerich establishes an ordering convention for stress addition such that:

---

* Notation to be read as 'Excerpt A1, speaker BD's fourth turn'.

That is, demonstratives are more likely to receive stresses than are *wh*-words, these in turn are more likely to receive additional stresses than are modals, and so forth respectively for pronouns, auxiliaries, prepositions and conjunctions. The above categories are in turn more likely to have extra stressing than all others (i.e. articles, relative adverbs and determiners, possessive determiners, etc.). This hierarchy is of course a tentative one and may require revision once more data is examined. However, it illustrates nicely how intricately interwoven the word-category and rhythmic principles are.

## 3.3   Expressive determinants

Yet there is still a residue of rhythmic stress beats which cannot be explained even when word-category, rhythm and tempo are taken into account. Consider, for instance,

(a)  that 'nobody 'really wants to 'solve (A2/EP)
(b)  'makes me feel 'very em'barrassed (A3/EP)

The speaker in (a) could very well have said *that 'nobody really 'wants to 'solve*, and in (b) *'makes me 'feel very em 'barrassed*. The stressing in these alternatives is equally as acceptable as the speaker's actual stressing. In cases such as these the speaker is exercising a free choice as to which one of several permissible stress patterns to use. Although strict cognitive meaning per se is not affected, the choice of one pattern as opposed to another reflects a particular attitudinal disposition towards some aspect of the message (e.g. stress on *very* rather than *feel* in (b) may emphasize that the speaker feels strongly about the degree of embarrassment).

## 4.   Principles of accent placement

Whereas stress distribution in the sense used here appears fairly uncontroversial, accent placement in contrast has been the subject of heated debate over the past two decades. Few areas of intonation have been more widely discussed but remain so poorly understood. Most discussion has centered around the question of whether the principles of accent placement are strictly syntactic or whether they are determined by semantic, pragmatic, discourse, or other considerations. And the question has been treated as if it had an either-or answer.

At the center of the controversy is the Chomsky/Halle (1968) hypothesis that stress contours are wholly determined by syntactic structure, once lexical items and their word stress have been determined (§2.1). Recall that the Nuclear Stress Rule (NSR), ordered after the Compound Stress Rule (CSR), assigns primary stress to the rightmost primary stressed vowel of major constituents, proceeding in a cyclical fashion. Accent in this model is thus equivalent to primary stress on the last cycle of the NSR. For example:

[ [Mary] [ [teaches] [engineering] ] ]
S       VP   teaches            VP  S

| 1 | 1 | 1 | (word stress) |
|   | 2 | 1 | 1st cycle: NSR |
| 2 | 3 | 1 | 2nd cycle: NSR  (Bresnan 1971:258) |

Since it is *engineering* which receives primary stress on the last cycle, it is consequently accented: *Mary teaches engiNEERing*. Note that according to this model it is always the rightmost item capable of taking (lexical) stress which receives the accent in 'normal' stress contours. Contours with so-called 'emphatic or contrastive stress' must be handled separately (§4.3).

But Chomsky/Halle's theory of accent placement has been attacked on a number of grounds. For one, Bresnan (1971) shows that the application of the NSR to surface structure would make it impossible to distinguish:

(i)  George has plâns to leave ('George has plans which he intends to leave')
(ii) George has plans to leàve ('George is planning to leave')
(examples originally from Newman 1946)

Applied to surface structure the NSR would provide both of these with /231/ contours. Based on this and other evidence, Bresnan argues that the NSR should apply earlier in the derivational process, i.e. after all the syntactic transformations *in each transformational domain*. This means that sentences with embedded clauses — for instance, those above — would have the NSR apply to the most deeply embedded sentence (S) at the end of the first transformational cycle and then again to the next higher S on a subsequent transformational cycle. Consequently the derivation of a sentence similar to (i) would look as follows:

[Helen left [directions [for George to follow directions] ] ]
S          NP        S                               S NP S

| 1 | 1 | 1 | 1 | 1 | 1 | (word stress) |
|   |   |   | 2 | 2 | 1 | 1st cycle: NSR |
|   |   |   |   |   | ø | 2nd cycle: Syntax |
| 2 | 2 | 1 | 3 | 3 |   | 3rd cycle: NSR |

(Bresnan 1971: 260)

Since the direct object of the embedded sentence *directions* is deleted on the second transformational cycle, the NSR, when it applies again, assigns primary stress not to *follow*, because its stress has already been reduced, but to *directions* in the matrix sentence, thus yielding: *Helen left diRECtions for George to follow*. Bresnan's proposal represents a rather radical departure from the orthodox generative view that stress assignment is part of a phonological cycle which merely interprets surface structure. Instead her contention is that stress — and with it intonation — depends systematically on underlying structure. The basic assumption that it is syntax which determines accent placement, however, remains unchallenged.

Yet precisely this assumption has been called into question by linguists such as Berman/Szamosi (1972), Bolinger (1972b), Schmerling (1976) and others. The NSR − or in fact any rule based wholly on syntactic structure, they argue − would be unable to account for sentences with identical underlying (and/or surface) structure but different accentual patterns. For instance:

(i) John amused MARy (agentive subject)
    John aMUSed Mary (abstract subject)    (Berman/Szamosi 1972:315f.)

(ii) I have a POINT to make
     I have a point to EMphasize    (Bolinger 1972b:633)

(iii) JOHNson died
      Truman DIED    (Schmerling 1976:42f.)

What emerges from this at times polemic discussion is primarily the (negative) conclusion that position of accent cannot be explained on the basis of syntax alone. More positively, however, it is still unclear whether the non-syntactic criteria for accent placement are semantic, pragmatic or discourse-related − and moreover whether they are to serve in addition to or in place of syntax. At least three other principles of accent placement have been proposed: *focus, default, contrast/emphasis*. We shall review each of these in the following.

## 4.1 Focus

The term *focus* in conjunction with accent has been used in two different but related ways − one, introduced by Chomsky, in which it is opposed to presupposition; the other, introduced by Bolinger, in which it is linked to information.

### 4.1.1 Focus and presupposition

A question such as *Does John write poetry in his STUDY?*, Chomsky (1971) points out, may have as a natural response *No, John writes poetry in the GARDEN.*[25] What both question and answer have in common is the fact that John writes poetry somewhere; this is *presupposed* by the sentences in question. What is *focused* is where, i.e. in the study or in the garden. The focus of a sentence is consequently that part of the sentence which when replaced by a variable $x$ yields the presupposition of the sentence. For example:

Sentence:         *Is it JOHN who writes poetry?*
Presupposition:   x writes poetry
Focus:            John

Since in cases such as these the focus also contains the intonation center or accent of the sentence, a principle of accent placement based on focus might state that the accent falls on the word focused in the sentence.

---

[25] Chomsky subscribes here to the widely held view that although accent affects only one, lexically determined syllable in the word, its significance attaches to the whole word (cf. also Brazil/Coulthard/Johns 1980:41).

This, however, would be only partially true. In a sentence such as *Was he warned to look out for an ex-convict with a red SHIRT?*, although the accent falls on *shirt* the focus could conceivably vary [italics marking focus and capitals, the accent-bearing word]:

| FOCUS | NATURAL RESPONSE |
|---|---|
| (a) shirt | No, he was warned to look out for an ex-convict with a red *TIE* |
| (b) a red shirt | No, he was warned to look out for an ex-convict with *a CARNATION* |
| (c) with a red shirt | No, he was warned to look out for an ex-convict *wearing DUNGAREES* |
| (d) an ex-convict with a red shirt | No, he was warned to look out for *an AUTOMOBILE salesman* |
| (e) to look out for an ex-convict with a red shirt | No, he was warned to *expect a visit from the FBI* |
| (f) warned to look out for an ex-convict with a red shirt | No, he was simply *told to be more CAUTIOUS* |
| (g) was he warned to look out for an ex-convict with a red shirt | No, *nothing was said to ANYONE* |

(Chomsky 1971:200ff., Jackendoff 1972:232ff.)

In other words, although the focus may coincide wholly with the accented word as in (a), it may also extend beyond the accented word, as in (b) – (g). As a result, a rule for accent placement which appeals to focus must also specify *which* word or syllable within the domain of focus is to receive primary stress. Jackendoff's proposal is the following:

> If a phrase P is chosen as the focus of a sentence S, the highest stress in S will be on the syllable of P that is assigned highest stress by the regular stress rules. (1972:237)

This does not specify what the "regular stress rules" are – perhaps with good reason, since there is as yet no real consensus on the matter. It is worth noting, however, that Jackendoff's treatment, while not explicitly excluding syntactic determination of accent within the domain of focus, nonetheless introduces non-syntactic criteria in the definition of focus. Thus he describes focus as denoting "the information in the sentence that is assumed by the speaker not to be shared by him and the hearer", and presupposition as denoting "the information in the sentence that is assumed by the speaker to be shared by him and the hearer" (1972:230). Such a conception of focus comes closer to the definition which non-generativists such as Bolinger, Chafe and Halliday have given it.

### 4.1.2 Information focus

One of the first linguists to associate accent placement and information was Hultzén; in his opinion, whether a word "has relatively stronger stress in the larger intonational pattern is a matter of information, not of structure" (1956:199). Hultzén argued from a strict information theoretical point of view that an element which is highly probable in a given context carries less information than one which is not probable. Bolinger (1972b) called elements with low probability "points of information focus" and argued that it is these which are accented in sentences. Thus in the example cited above – *I have a POINT to make* vs. *I have a point to EMphasize* – *make* has less semantic weight because it is predictable in the phrase *point to ...*, whereas *emphasize* is less predictable in the phrase and consequently has more semantic weight. However, Bolinger is careful to point out that it is not simply lexical predictability but ultimately "relative semantic weight" which determines accent placement. That is, it is the context, including the context of situation, which helps determine where the point of information focus lies.[26]

Schmerling (1976), however, criticizes the criterion of predictability as advocated by Bolinger. She reports having heard the news of the death of two former U.S. Presidents on different occasions as follows:

(i)   JOHNson died
(ii)  Truman DIED

The difference in accent placement, she argues, is a result of the contexts these utterances occurred in. Thus, Johnson was in relatively good health at the time of his sudden fatal heart attack, whereas Truman's health was known to be poor; in fact he was hospitalized in critical condition at the time of his death. Yet if Bolinger's criterion of predictability is applied, the accent should fall on *Truman* in (ii) since his death was highly predictable, and on *died* in (i) since Johnson's death was so unpredictable. This obviously will not do. Instead, according to Schmerling, we must distinguish "news" sentences such as (i) above from "topic-comment sentences" such as (ii).[27] In the former, the verb receives lower stress than subject or object if there is one.[28] In the latter, both topic and comment are stressed, a supplementary 'rightmost' rule accounting for heavier stress (i.e. accent) on the last stress in a succession of stresses.[29]

In a sense Schmerling's distinction harks back to older theories of information and information structure (e.g. Halliday 1967b, Daneš 1967, Firbas 1972), according to which sentences are structured in terms of given and new information (Ch. VII). In these theories it is typically the tonic or nuclear accent of a tone-group which signals

---

[26] This assumption is also central to much of Gunter's work on accent (1966; 1974).

[27] The latter are described by Schmerling as being sentences " 'about' the subject of the sentence rather than an entire event or state of affairs" (1976:93).

[28] Bresnan (1972) likewise acknowledges the necessity of a rule which she calls 'topical stress' to assign primary stress to the subject of sentences such as *The SUN is shining*.

[29] This is indeed one of the oldest accounts of accent placement: "When no expressive accents disturb a sequence of heavy stresses, the last heavy stress in an intonational unit takes the nuclear heavy stress" (Newman 1946: 176).

information focus, and "what is focal is 'new' information ... in the sense that the speaker presents it as not being recoverable from the preceding discourse" (Halliday 1967b:204) (see also Ch. VII). However, whereas information structure will account for accent placement in (ii) above, it does not furnish a satisfactory explanation for early accenting in all-new sentences such as (i). Halliday's rules stipulate that in unmarked, neutral cases the tonic falls on the last stressed item under focus (1967b:207). Yet if the focus extends over the whole sentence in (i) this would produce *Johnson DIED* rather than *JOHNson died*.[30] Schmerling is thus to be credited with producing data which not only an NSR-type rule but also an information-focus rule cannot account for.[31] In conclusion, it appears that if the principle of information focus is to be a valid one for accent placement, then some additional account must be given of which element or elements in all-new sentences receive(s) the accent (Ch. VII §2.1.2.1).[32]

### 4.1.3 Focus in discourse

But the principle of information focus requires modification on other grounds. In traditional accounts, whether an element is given or new can be decided by examining the co-text, or previous discourse, to determine whether it is 'recoverable' or not. However, there are no clear-cut guidelines as to how far back in discourse an element may lie and still be recoverable (Chafe 1976). It is thus to a certain extent at the speaker's discretion to determine whether an item should be treated as given or new. Brazil/Coulthard/Johns (1980), for instance, cite the example of a teacher who accents the same word (similarly) in a succession of four utterances; s/he obviously judges the information to be subjectively 'new' for the pupils each time, although after first mention it is no longer technically so (1980:17).

Both Bolinger (1972b) and Gunter (1966) have likewise emphasized that information focus is negotiable: the speaker him/herself may decide whether to treat a piece of information as new or not. The following example demonstrates a striking application of this principle:

A: John can paint SPLENDID pictures
B: John CAN paint splendid pictures sometimes    (Gunter 1966:96)

Here B appears to be agreeing with A's opinion of John's painting ability, although a new meaning component in the word *sometimes* has been added. By not accenting this word, B treats it as if it were shared knowledge.

Once the information focus principle is viewed as exploitable according to speaker

---

[30] According to Halliday (1967b) a sentence such as *JOHNson died* would have 'marked' focus, in which case the domain of focus would be limited to the constituent itself. Yet (i) is surely not contrastive in the sense outlined in §4.3.

[31] Other criticisms of the information-focus theory of accent placement will be discussed in Ch. VII.

[32] Indeed, according to Fuchs (1976), we should actually consider multiple accenting to be the norm for all-new utterances, e.g. *JOHNson DIED*. In a second step we can then ask why one (or more) of the accents may be suppressed, as in *JOHNson died* (cf. also Ch. VII §2.1.2.1).

intention, then accent placement comes to depend on the motives behind speaker choice. Recent research offers evidence that a speaker's accent placement may be influenced by discourse-regulatory or organizational principles. Thus a speaker may accent what is objectively given material in order to hold or regain the floor. Or a speaker may use accent placement to introduce new topics or set off digressions from the topic at hand (Lehman 1977; Abdul-Ghani 1978; Yule 1980a; also Chs. VII & XI).

Brazil/Coulthard/Johns (1980) also emphasize that accenting, or "prominence" in their terms, may have less to do with objectively informing matter than with "more general *social* meanings of convergence/divergence, or solidarity/separateness":

> ... quite a lot of what speakers say is not in any real sense informing and is usually marked as not informing by not being made prominent. But there are times when such items are made not simply prominent but even tonic. (1980:51)

In these cases accent has a social meaning which may vary from "'we are in some unspecified sense at one with each other'" to "the speaker is (...) reserving his position in some general way or perhaps staking a proprietory claim to the view expressed in the ensuing discourse, or simply emphasizing the likely lack of agreement on a point" (1980: 51f.). Such an interactional theory of accent, however, must still answer the question of how speakers know which words (among the objectively non-informing words) to attach these social or discourse meanings to.


## 4.2   Default

The converse of a principle of accenting whereby the accent is placed on a particular item under certain conditions is a principle of de-accenting which states that the accent is 'removed' from a particular element when these conditions are not met. In certain trivial respects, of course, the principles of accenting and de-accenting are complementary. If, for instance, we take one accenting rule to be that the accent falls somewhere within the information focus formed by 'new' material, the corresponding de-accenting rule will state that the accent may not be placed on 'given' material in the utterance. [By 'given' we mean here material that is recoverable from the discourse or conventionally shared (Ch. VII).] Thus we can account for the following either by an accenting or a de-accenting rule:

(a) I've left my spectacles at home.
   Why don't you buy a SECond pair of glasses?

(b) D'you drink Bourbon?
   I'm afraid I don't LIKE whisky.

(c) John's got a sore knee.
   It looks like he'll have to REST his leg.      (adapted from Allerton 1978:141)

The de-accenting rule explains why the accent does not fall on *glasses*, *whisky* or *leg* in the sentences above: they are in each case co-referential 'substitutes' for aforementioned items. [Note that the semantic relation need not be one of equivalence; synonymy, hyponymy and part-whole relations also permit co-reference (Allerton

1978).] And the accenting rule explains why the accent does fall on *second, like, rest*: they belong to the focus of information.

According to Ladd (1978), however, there is a non-trivial sense in which accenting is not the converse of de-accenting; this he dubs *default accent*. Consider, for instance, the following hypothetical dialogue:

A: Has John read *Slaughterhouse-Five*?
B: No, John doesn't READ books.    (1978:115)

Now since *Slaughterhouse-Five* is a book, the word *books* in B's answer is co-referential and therefore shuns the accent. However, the accent does not then fall on *read* due to an accenting principle associated with information focus, but instead appears to fall on this item by default. [Note that the speaker is not interpreting *read* contrastively, i.e. the implication is not 'John doesn't read books, he writes them instead'.] The item accented is simply that one immediately to the left of the given item,[33] or, as in the following, to the right: *We've got lots of books, but we haven't got any bookCASES* (Ladd 1978:130). The default principle of accent placement thus states that the accent is moved to some item immediately to the left or to the right in order to avoid accenting a given item.

Two points can be made concerning default accent. First, observe that the item which is accented by default need not belong to an inherently 'stressable' category:

(i)　A: John's gone to North Dakota to study the mating habits of the native linguist.
　　　B: But there aren't any linguists IN North Dakota!    (Cutler/Isard 1980:252)

(ii)　He keeps insisting that we countersign it, but there's nothing TO countersign.
(Bolinger 1961a: 88)

(iii)　This is necessary because of the use of contrastive stress twice in the same sentence ....
Note that (the items) can BE contrastive only by virtue of the "normal" reading.
(Stockwell 1972:88)

This means that in some cases a different rhythmic structure must accompany default accent. Compare:

there 'aren't any 'linguists in $^{()}$North Da'kota
there 'aren't any $^{()}$linguists 'in North Da'kota

The consequences this might have for a stress/accent hierarchy (Jassem/Gibbon 1980) remain to be investigated.

Second, the default rule of accent placement as it stands now can hardly be maintained in such an ill-defined form. The insight as such is a valuable one; linguists must now explore and positively specify the conditions under which it occurs.[34]

---

[33] Why *read* in B's answer does not count as 'given' may have something to do with its different phonetic form /ri:d/ vs. /red/ or with its different temporal reference: *has read* vs. *does read*.

[34] Gussenhoven 1983a takes an important step in this direction by distinguishing 'counter-assertive' sentences such as *The house ISn't on fire* from 'counterpresuppositional' sentences such as *The house isn't ON fire*. [Default accent is presumably a feature of the latter.] In counterpresuppositional sentences, he maintains, the nucleus goes to the penultimate element of the VP or to the rightmost preposition or *to* particle, if present (1983a:411). [Cf. also Fuchs 1984.]

## 4.3 Contrast and/or emphasis

Much of the discussion concerning accent placement has ensued based on one important premise, namely that rules for accent placement which appeal to focus or information focus are valid only in so-called 'normal' cases. Chomsky, for instance, explicitly excludes "expressive or contrastive" processes which may for "obscure" reasons shift the intonation center (1971:199). It is unclear whether this is intended to imply that there are two different types of accent assignment principle in addition to focus and default, or whether these are alternative designations for one and the same general principle. For reasons which will become obvious shortly, we shall assume the latter.

The contrastive principle of accent placement has two interpretations, one formal and one notional. From a formal point of view, it has been assumed that every sentence has a 'normal' stress contour or accent pattern.[35] According to some models, this normal pattern is determined by syntactic structure; according to others, by (unmarked) information focus. Common to most models, however, is the assumption that only inherently stressable word categories are involved and that in a series of stressed items it is the final one which receives the accent. Accordingly, any accent pattern in which a non-stressable word is accented or in which some stressed item other than the final one receives the accent is called *contrastive*. In this sense then the term means 'deviation from the normal pattern'.

The term *contrastive*, however, also has a notional sense based on the meaning of *contrast*. This has been described by Bolinger as '*A* rather than *B*' (1961a:87) and by Pike in the following terms:

> When the context (words, idiom, gesture, material situation, or cultural history) implies that two or more items are potentially available for selective attention, the actual selection of the one contrasts it sharply with the other; the affirmation of the one implies a denial of the other .... (1945:45)

Implicitly many linguists have tended to assume that there is a one-to-one correspondence between contrastive (i.e. deviant) accent placement and semantic contrast. However, upon closer examination it becomes obvious that a semantic contrast may be present although the accent falls in a 'normal' position − e.g. *the book is JOHN'S* ('not Susie's'), *I gave it to my MOTHer* ('not my father'), etc. Furthermore, accent placement may deviate from the norm without there being any semantic contrast, e.g. *did you REALLy climb the Eiffel Tower?*, *John is VERy pleased with his new bicycle*, etc. It is of course for this reason that some linguists speak of "contrastive or expressive/emphatic" accent placement. It is important to remember, however, that semantic notions such as contrast and emphasis have a much broader scope than the terms *contrastive* or *emphatic accent placement*. In the following we shall restrict ourselves to these notions only to the extent that they affect accent placement. [See

---

[35] Cf., for instance, Stockwell: "there is (...) a 'neutral' or 'normal' or 'colorless' intonation contour for any sentence, serving as a baseline against which all other possible contours are contrastable, and thereby meaningful" (1972:87f.).

Ch. VII §2.2.2.2 for a discussion of contrast and emphasis with respect to pitch configuration.]

A number of linguists have recently cast doubt on the validity of a normal-contrastive dichotomy. Schmerling (1976), for instance, points out that there are some sentences for which there is no normal accent pattern at all but only a contrastive one: *even a TWO-year-old could do that, John was killed by himSELF* (1976:49). Furthermore, even sentences which do have normal accent placement make special assumptions. For instance, *my mother is COMing* requires either a context in which 'mother' is thematized or a citation context such as 'How would you pronounce this sentence?'. In an out-of-the-blue context, which makes no special assumptions, the appropriate contour would be *my MOTHer is coming*. Therefore it appears that there is no such thing as normal accent placement if we mean by *normal* that it involves no special assumptions and that it contrasts with accent placement where semantic contrast is involved. And if normal accent is meaningless, contrastive accent is too – or so the argument goes.

But although the normal-contrastive dichotomy is unsatisfactory in its extreme form, some linguists have pointed out that the notions do appear to correspond to differing domains of focus (Fuchs 1976, Ladd 1978). For instance, with what is typically called contrastive accent placement, e.g. *JOHN ate the cookies* or *he gave it to ME*, the domain of focus is restricted to one word: *John* ('not Tom') and *me* ('not you'), respectively. However, with so-called normal accent placement, e.g. *John ate the COOKies, he GAVE it to me*, the domain of focus is potentially very broad. In fact, it can encompass the whole sentence if the context is 'What happened?'. [Of course, in the same sentences the domain of focus could also be narrow: *cookies* ('not cakes'), *gave* ('not sold'). This corresponds to the phenomenon of semantic contrast with normal accent placement.] Thus the suggestion has been made that we should actually view the normal-contrastive dichotomy as a continuum of broad to narrow focus, with 'normal' and 'contrastive' referring to the more extreme ends (Ladd 1978).[36] The advantage of such a proposal is that it makes it possible to put sentences with contrastive accent placement and sentences which are semantically contrastive but have normal accent placement all under one roof. The effect is to shift the burden of accent placement wholly to focus (and default) principles, although contrastivity is still implicit in the notion of narrow focus.

---

[36] As Ladd (1978) points out, even with 'contrastive' accent placement, i.e. narrow focus, there may still be a variety of focal interpretations, e.g. *Even a nineteenth century professor of CLASsics wouldn't have allowed himself to be so pedantic*. Depending on the context in which this sentence is embedded, it could have *classics, professor of classics* or *a nineteenth century professor of classics* as focus (Ladd 1978:120).

# References

Abdul-Ghani 1978
*Abercrombie 1971
Abercrombie 1976
*Allen, G. D. 1972a (pp. 72–75)
*Allen, G. D. 1972b (pp. 190–194)
Allerton 1978
Andrew 1980
Armstrong/Ward [2]1931
Berman/Szamosi 1972
Bierwisch 1968
Bing 1983
Bloomfield 1933 (§7.3–7.7)
Bolinger 1958a
*Bolinger 1958b
*Bolinger 1961
*Bolinger 1972b
Brazil/Coulthard/Johns 1980
Bresnan 1971
Bresnan 1972
Brown/Currie/Kenworthy 1980 (Ch. 5)
Catford 1977
Chafe 1976
Chomsky 1971
Chomsky 1972
Chomsky/Halle 1968 (Ch. 2 §§1, 2)
Clark/Clark 1977 (Ch. 5)
Coleman 1914
Cooper 1972
Couper-Kuhlen 1984
Crystal 1969 (§4.10)
Crystal 1975a
Currie 1981
Cutler 1980
Cutler/Isard 1980
Daneš 1967
Enkvist 1979
Faure/Hirst/Chafcouloff 1980
Firbas 1972
Frank 1974
Fromkin 1977
*Fry 1958a
Fry 1960
Fuchs 1976
Fuchs 1980
Fuchs 1984
Gazdar 1980

Giegerich 1978
Gimson 1956
*Grundstrom 1979
*Gunter 1966
Gunter 1974
Gussenhoven 1983a
Gussenhoven 1983b
Halle/Stevens 1964
Halliday 1967b
Householder 1957
Hultzén 1956
Huss 1978
Hyman 1977
Isačenko/Schädlich 1970
Jackendoff 1972 (Ch. 6)
*Jassem/Gibbon 1980
Jones [9]1976 (Ch. 29)
Kingdon 1958a
Kingdon 1958b
*Ladd 1978 (Ch. 1 §§4, 5; Ch. 2)
Ladd 1979
Ladd 1983c
Ladefoged 1967 (Ch. 1)
Ladefoged/Draper/Whitteridge 1958
Lakoff 1971
Lakoff 1972
Lane 1965
*Lea 1977
Lehiste 1970 (Ch. 4)
Lehman 1977
Liberman, A. M. 1957
Liberman/Cooper/Harris/MacNeilage 1963
Liberman, M. Y. 1975
Liberman/Prince 1977
Lieberman 1960
Lieberman 1967 (Ch. 7)
Lipka 1977
McNeill/Repp 1973
*Mol/Uhlenbeck 1956
Newman 1946
Ohala 1977
Pike 1945
Sanders 1977
Schmerling 1974a
Schmerling 1974b

Schubiger 1963

Selkirk 1984

Sharp 1960

Stevens/Halle 1967

Stockwell 1972

Studdert-Kennedy/Liberman et al 1970

Taglicht 1982

Trager/Smith 1957

Vanderslice/Ladefoged 1972

Yule 1980a

Chapter III
# Rhythm

## 1. The nature of rhythm

There has been much debate among linguists − as well as among literary critics and psychologists − on the nature of rhythm. According to one critic, the term "is frequently used for any kind of repetition or periodicity in the physical world, also for any kind of correspondence in aesthetic experience, and, generally, for practically anything connected with verse experience as long as it is not clearly defined" (de Groot [2]1968: 541). In fact, it is to be feared that we are hardly much closer to understanding rhythm today than half a century ago.

Basically the controversy can be reduced to two competing views of what rhythm is: a temporal, or a non-temporal phenomenon. Those who support the former point of view define rhythm as the recurrence of an event at regular intervals in time; those who prefer the latter see rhythm as a pattern of events related to one another in terms of salience.

### 1.1 The temporal view

Central to the temporal view of rhythm are the concepts of periodicity and isochrony. By *periodicity* we mean the recurrence of an event at regular periods or intervals. By *isochrony* we mean the equal duration of these intervals in time. According to a temporal understanding of rhythm, a sudden burst of machine-gun fire or the regular dripping of a water faucet are rhythmic phenomena, since both involve the recurrence of the same or a similar event at equal intervals in time.

Proponents of this view emphasize that rhythm in its most natural form is to be found in the movements of the body − e.g., the beat of the heart, respiration, or walking. Here normally two different motions alternate: a heavy movement, or *thesis* [Gr. 'setting down'] and a light movement, or *arsis* [Gr. 'raising'] (Steele 1779:20). It is the regular alternation of these two movements which characterizes the natural rhythm of human motor activity.

However, at least as far as voluntary motor activities go, human beings do not generally *produce* wholly isochronous movements. The variability is said to be between 3−11% of the length of the time interval involved (Allen 1975:79). Nor, it might be added, do human beings *perceive* isochronous intervals wholly objectively. A sequence of identical clicks similarly spaced in time, for instance, is typically perceived as groupings of two to six stimuli,[1] one of which in each group is perceptually

---

[1] The groups tend to have more stimuli in them the faster the clicks follow one another.

stronger than the others. In other words, it is a natural human tendency to impose structure on perceptual stimuli. One of the better known examples of this is the fact that we hear the regular swinging of the pendulum of a clock as tick-*tock*, not tick-tick. It is evidence of this sort which has carried the most weight with those who support the non-temporal view of rhythm.

## 1.2   The non-temporal view

Proponents of the non-temporal approach to rhythm would undoubtedly deny that the sound of water dripping or a machine gun firing is inherently rhythmic. Instead, they argue, rhythm is something created in the mind of the listener when s/he perceives a series of sensory impressions as a whole rather than as a succession of unrelated events. According to this view, in order to form a rhythmic unit, the sensory impressions must be related to one another in terms of salience: some must be more prominent than others. And the sensory impressions must be spaced close enough so as to be perceived as a group [according to one investigator, no more than 3.0 seconds apart] but not so close as to be perceived as overlapping [i.e., more than 0.1 second apart] (Allen 1975:75). Within certain temporal limits then, a sequence of stimuli may have a structure imposed upon it in terms of salience.

Naturally the rhythmic pattern imposed on a series of impressions is determined in part by their objective characteristics. For instance, the typical rhythmic patterns of runs and pauses used by typists in writing familiar words are determined in part by the relative location of the keys on the keyboard with respect to the possibilities of manual movement. Similarly the rhythms of speech are determined in part by the physical mechanism of pronouncing certain sequences of sounds.

The main difference between this view of rhythm and the temporal view sketched above is that repetition or recurrence is not thought to be a necessary component of rhythm as a non-temporal phenomenon. The claim is that if repetition occurs at all, it only serves to draw one's attention to the pattern. The movements of a dancer, for instance, are perceived as rhythmic if they are structured in terms of salience; whether the pattern recurs or not is secondary.

This approach clearly views rhythm as a perceptual phenomenon. Yet psychological studies on perception have also shown that, given a succession of intervals of differing duration, we tend to over-estimate the length of the short intervals and underestimate the length of the long ones. That is, we tend to hear time intervals as more equal than they really are. This would appear to support the temporal view of rhythm, if a more modest claim is made – say, that we merely *perceive* the intervals between beats as isochronous. In sum, at the moment there appears to be psychological evidence both for and against the 'timers' and the 'accenters', as advocates of the temporal and non-temporal views of rhythm have been called respectively.

Some researchers (e.g. Brown 1911, Adams 1979) have suggested, however, that one point of view need not necessarily preclude the other: "A rhythm is temporal in so far as there is any regular return of similar features. But at the same time such a rhythm will also be accentual since there must always be points of emphasis whose return can be marked" (Brown 1911:344). That is, to a certain extent both views see rhythm as dependent upon the impression of regularity:

> Some hold that this impression arises from the regular recurrence, in time, of certain features of the rhythmic series; others claim that the regularity resides in the structure of the elements composing the series. (Brown 1911:336)

To this extent the competing views of rhythm are, at a superficial level at least, reconcilable.

## 2.  Speech rhythm

If rhythm – whether isochronous or not – is found in all human body movements, it is naturally also to be expected in the motor activity of speaking. And so it is that we find both temporal and non-temporal views of speech rhythm.

### 2.1  Syllable-timing vs. stress-timing

According to a temporal view of speech rhythm, which is the one most linguists adopt, a similar event recurs at regular intervals in time. What constitutes this event, however, is not the same in all languages. Pike (1945) distinguished two major types of speech rhythm: (i) syllable-timed rhythm, in which the *syllables* come at equal intervals in time, and (ii) stress-timed rhythm, in which the *stressed* syllables occur at regular intervals. Languages belonging to the former category are said to include French, Spanish and Italian, those belonging to the latter, English and Russian.[2] Whereas French rhythm has been compared to that of a machine gun, English rhythm is likened to that of Morse code.[3]

### 2.2  Isochrony

While Pike's classification is generally accepted as valid, the concomitant principle of isochrony in speech has not gone unchallenged. Classe (1939), for instance, measured the time intervals between stresses instrumentally in a number of prepared sentences read aloud and concluded that more or less perfect isochronism can only be found under the right conditions: (a) the number of syllables (in each rhythmic group) must be approximately equal, (b) the phonetic structure of the syllables must not be too different, and (c) the grammatical structures involved must be similar (1939:85). If any of these conditions is not met, then isochrony may be obliterated, although it "remains an underlying tendency" (1939:90).

---

[2] Delattre (1964) argues that German assumes a position midway between French and English with respect to rhythm and other phonological features.

[3] If the timing of syllables in French is indeed like the firing of a machine-gun, then according to a strictly non-temporal view French would not be rhythmic at all. However, provided a broader definition of rhythm is adopted [i.e. if we recognize rhythms of alternation *and* succession (Allen 1975:77)], then all languages have inherent rhythm.

Still more damaging evidence against the principle of isochrony in speech is offered by Shen/Peterson (1964), who measured the time lapses between stresses in passages of English read by three different speakers. Their results showed that there was almost no overlap in time measurements, either between speakers or for a given speaker. Critics have objected, however, that no distinction was made in their study between time intervals with terminal juncture and those without (Ch. IV §2.1). Obviously, at the end of a clause or sentence a longer pause will be made and isochrony may suffer as a consequence. Moreover, no allowance was made for silent stress beats, although these reportedly serve to "keep the isochronous stress-pulse going" (Abercrombie 1971:148). Thus it is possible that, had Shen/Peterson established the intervals to be compared somewhat differently, a greater degree of isochrony would have been found.

On the other hand, O'Connor (1965) showed that even when a speaker is trying to produce isochrony [e.g. in 'doggerel' verse], the real durations of feet (§3.1) vary between 488 and 566 milliseconds. That is, even isochrony which is consciously aimed for by the speaker and perceived as such by the hearer is only 'isochrony ± 39 msecs'. This result, however, is consonant with physiological and psychoacoustic evidence, according to which human variability averages from 3–11% in the production of regular rhythms (Allen 1975:82). Furthermore, the threshold for just noticeable differences of duration in speech is reported to be at least 30–100 milliseconds, if not more (Lehiste 1977:258). Consequently, even though the intervals in a sentence (or tone-group) are not absolutely isochronous, they may be perceived as such.[4] Finally, as Lehiste (1977) points out, there is even some evidence that speakers unconsciously aim at isochrony in production, to the extent that adjustments are made in the length of sounds depending on the sequence in which they occur.[5] [Cf. also Hoequist 1983a.]

We can conclude then that the principle of isochrony in speech – despite the counter-evidence – is far from dead. In fact, in the light of recent physiological and psychological studies, it is enjoying a revival. However, it must be admitted that even perceived isochrony is not likely to be encountered everywhere to the same degree. Verse may sound more isochronous than prose, for instance. And certain styles of spoken language are likely to be more isochronous than others (Séguinot 1979). Furthermore, production interference as a result of fatigue, memory failure, poor speaker planning, etc. may influence the degree of achieved isochrony. It is for this reason that Crystal (1969) proposes a prosodic scale ranging from *rhythmic* to *arhythmic*, along which values are assigned depending on the degree to which isochrony is realized.

---

[4] Rees (1975) proposes that the tone group rather than the sentence or some larger unit be considered as the domain in which isochrony can be expected. [Cf. also Donovan/Darwin 1979.]

[5] For instance, consonants are shorter in clusters than when they are alone. In other words, "the duration of a word as a whole is changed less than it would have been if new segments had been added without adjustment in the duration of the segments already present" (Lehiste 1977:260).

## 2.3   Rhythmicality

On a broader, less strictly temporal view, speech can be said to demonstrate various types of rhythm, rhythm based on duration being just one. If rhythm is a salient/non-salient grouping, then patterns can conceivably arise in which other auditory dimensions of prominence play a role. For instance, contrasting degrees of loudness may create an impression of rhythm – or rather of *rhythmicality*, to distinguish strictly non-temporal from temporal patterns. Crystal (1969) provides a scale *staccato-legato* for this, characterized by "heavily prominent arsis and very light thesis" (1969:164).[6] Or rhythmical patterns might arise through contrasting degrees of pitch height. One type of rhythmical pitch pattern is provided for by Crystal's scale *spiky-glissando*, the former referring to "sharp and rapid jumps between syllables", the latter to "smooth and usually fairly slow glides" (1969:164) (Ch. V §2.4).

In sum, provision for features relying not only on contrasts of duration but on contrasts of loudness and pitch as well reflects the fact that there are differing types of rhythmicality, and differing degrees within each type.


## 3.   English speech rhythm

### 3.1   The foot

If all speech is naturally rhythmic, then, many scholars feel, there may be a basic rhythmic similarity between prose and verse. It is thus not surprising that some of the terminology originally used to describe rhythm in verse has been adopted to describe rhythm in speech. Abercrombie, for instance, uses the term *foot*, which he defines, for prose and for verse, as "the space in time from the incidence of one stress-pulse up to, but not including, the next stress-pulse" (1964a, 1973:11).[7] To illustrate with a well-known example, the first line of the nursery rhyme

'This is the 'house that 'Jack 'built

has four stresses, as marked, and consequently four feet. Using vertical bars to indicate foot boundaries, we could represent this as follows:

|This is the |house that |Jack |built

If the first syllable of a line or utterance is not stressed, we have an upbeat. For instance:

A |tisket a |tasket
A |green and yellow |basket

Upbeats, however, do not constitute feet on their own.

---

[6] As the terminology indicates, duration is a concomitant factor. Some other set of terms referring solely to an alternation of loud/soft might have been more appropriate.

[7] Use of the term *foot* in rhythmic analysis is thought to stem from the alternate raising and lowering movements of the human foot in walking (Allen 1973:122).

A foot may also consist of a silent beat (Ch. II §2.5), and any unstressed syllables following it, as at the end of the first line of the limerick:

There |was an old |man in a |tree |ˎ
Who was |horribly |bored by a |bee |ˎ    (Abercrombie 1964a, 1973:11)

Rhythmic phenomena of this sort occur not only in verse but also in speech. Thus, the utterance *A funny thing happened to me, on my way here this evening* can be analyzed rhythmically into six feet, one of which contains a silent stress:

A |funny thing |happened to |me |ˎ on my |way here this |evening
(Abercrombie 1964a, 1973:9)

## 3.2 The consequences of stress-timing

If we accept for a moment the principle of isochrony and the fact that English is a stress-timed language, then we would expect the stress-pulses as marked in our examples above to be separated by intervals of time which are perceived as approximately equal. The fact that it is the stresses and not the syllables which are isochronous has a number of important consequences for English rhythm.

### 3.2.1 Syllable length

First, if rhythmic feet are approximately equal in length, it follows that the length of a given syllable in a foot will depend in part on how many other syllables are in the same foot with it. Returning to our example from above, consider:

|This is the |house that |Jack |built

Since each foot is approximately the same length, the syllables *Jack* and *built*, which stand alone in their respective feet, will be longer than *this*, *is* and *the* or *house* and *that*, which share their intervals respectively. This could be represented perhaps more appropriately as:

|This is the|house that| J a c k | b u i l t |

In other words the syllables in a foot must either be stretched out (if they are few) or squeezed together (if they are many) in order to maintain the rhythm of the phrase. This adjusting of syllable length occurs independently of vowel length. Thus in

|four |large |black |dogs
/ɔ:/  /ɑ:/  /æ/  /ɒ/

the third foot is judged as long as the first, second and fourth, although its syllable contains a so-called 'short' or 'lax' vowel (Abercrombie 1964b:217).

### 3.2.2 Relative syllable length in the foot

Yet the length of a syllable is not wholly determined by the number of syllables with which it must share a time interval. In feet with two syllables, for instance, the time interval may be divided in different ways between the syllables in it. This can be seen by comparing two versions of the phonemic sequence /ˈteɪk ˈgreɪtə ˈlʌndən/. The same succession of phonemes with identical syllable division and stress can become one of two utterances:

(a) |take |Grey to |London
(b) |take |greater |London

The difference between these two is due solely to the different rhythmic patterns in the second foot. In order to demonstrate this, let us assume that a foot with two syllables is in three-quarter time. The patterns can then be represented as:

(a) ♩♪    (b) ♩. ♪.

That is, the first syllable of the second foot in (a) is perceived as approximately twice as long as the second syllable, whereas in (b) the two syllables in the second foot are perceptually of more equal length.[8] Notice that the foot with ♩♪ rhythm contains a word boundary. It is generally the case that two-syllable feet with a long–short rhythmic pattern contain word boundaries in English. However, it is not necessarily the case that all feet with word boundaries have a long–short rhythm, as we shall see shortly.

The patterns in (a) and (b) above are not the only two rhythmical possibilities for disyllabic feet in English. According to Abercrombie (1964b), there is a third possibility, namely ♪♩ . This type of short–long rhythm can be heard (at least in one variety of RP English) in disyllabic feet with words such as *shilling, never, atom, cuckoo*. These words have in common the fact that their first syllable contains a 'lax' vowel and a single consonant (C).[9] A word whose first syllable has any other phonetic make-up – e.g. a 'tense' vowel or diphthong + C, or a vowel + CC(C) – reportedly has an equal–equal rhythm in disyllabic feet.

To summarize, the following rhythmic patterns exist for disyllabic feet:

(a) ♩ ♩           Grey to, mine are, -board a
(b) ♩. ♩.         greater, minor, border
(c) ♪ ♩           shilling, never, atom, cuckoo

Type (a) is characterized by the existence of a word boundary within the foot; type (b), by the presence of a diphthong or a tense vowel and a single consonant, or any vowel and a consonant cluster in the first syllable; and type (c), by the presence of a lax vowel and a single consonant in the first syllable. The difference between type (a) and the other two is immediately noticeable for speakers of English and has a clearly distinctive function. The difference between (b) and (c), on the other hand, is for many native speakers less obvious and has no distinctive function in English.[10]

---

[8] Other minimal pairs which demonstrate this contrastive rhythmic patterning are: *mine are official* vs. *minor official, aboard a liner* vs. *a border liner* (Gimson 1980:260f.).

[9] Notice that the short–long rhythm may be present even in words with lexical stress on the first syllable.

[10] According to Abercrombie, relative syllable lengths in the disyllabic foot, in particular (b) and (c), may vary from dialect to dialect.

A final point should be made with respect to disyllabic feet containing word boundaries. Feet such as *Tell him* or *Stop it* are not said with a long–short rhythm (a) but rather with an equal–equal (b) or short–long rhythm (c). Thus, not all feet with word boundaries necessarily use pattern (a). Pronouns in imperatives or interrogatives (*Stop it, Is she?*); *there* in interrogatives (*Is there?*); and *of* in certain expressions (*piece of* ) are examples of monosyllabic words whose length is determined by the phonetic nature of the preceding syllable, thus calling for pattern (b) or (c) in disyllabic feet. For this reason, they are called *enclitics* (Abercrombie 1964b:220).

It goes without saying that in examining disyllabic feet we have done no more than touch the surface of relative syllable length in English feet. The number of conceivable rhythmic patterns multiplies rapidly when feet of three, four and more syllables are considered. What rhythmic differences are to be found here remains to be investigated (cf., however, Sumera 1980).

### 3.2.3 Weak-forms

A third consequence of the stress-timed nature of English rhythm is the phenomenon of so-called *weak-forms*. Since it is typically content words (rather than grammatical words) which are given prominence in the utterance, it follows that grammatical words will tend to be unstressed. Rhythmically, as unstressed syllables, the grammatical words cluster around a stressed word or syllable within a foot or rhythmic group. The consequence is that grammatical words are most likely to undergo 'squeezing' in order to fit into the constant time interval between two stressed syllables or words. This is such a common occurrence in English speech that many grammatical words are said to have two forms: a *full* form (full phonemic realization) used on occasions when the word is stressed or accented, and one or several *weak* forms (with vowel weakening, consonant elision, etc.) used on occasions when the word is unstressed and must be fitted into a pre-determined rhythmic pattern. For example, consider the following grammatical words in stressed/accented positions:

| | |
|---|---|
| Yes, we 'have | /hæv/ |
| Yes, it 'was | /wɒz/ |
| That's what it was 'for | /fɔ:/ |
| He's 'the man | /ði:/ |

Now observe what happens when the same words occur in unstressed positions:

'What have you (·) done with the 'meat that was for our 'dinner
  /əv/        /ðə/   /ðət/ /wəz/ /fər/

In each case the grammatical word has had its vowel reduced to /ə/ (and the initial /h/ of *have* has been elided).

To what extent a grammatical word will be weakened or reduced depends of course on the rhythmic interval into which it must be fitted and on the rate of delivery. But the occurrence of weak-forms is wide-spread in all forms of spoken English, regardless of the degree of formality of the situation. The fact that weak-forms exist follows logically from the nature of English rhythm and stress and the way the two systems interact.[11]

---

[11] See Gimson (1980:262f.) for a more complete list of English weak-forms.

## 3.3   Rhythmic grouping

It should be pointed out that an approach to English rhythm based on the foot, although widely popularized by the work of Abercrombie and Halliday, is by no means the only approach.[12] Some scholars (e.g. Jones, Gimson, etc.) have preferred to speak of the *rhythmic group* as the basic unit of English rhythm. A rhythmic group is usually defined as a group of syllables which belong together grammatically and contain one major stress. Based on this definition, a rhythmic group does not necessarily overlap with a foot. Consider, for instance, /ˈdəʊnt ˈweɪtəz ˈlɒŋ fərɪt/. This phonemic sequence, which has at least two different rhythmic realizations, would be divided as follows into feet:

(ai)   |Don't |wait as |long for it
         or
(aii)   |Don't |waiters |long for it

However, in terms of rhythmic groups, i.e. taking grammatical boundaries into consideration, the division would be either

(bi)   |Don't |wait |as long for it
         or
(bii)   |Don't |waiters |long for it

The contrast between (ai) and (aii) divided into feet depends upon the relative length of the two syllables in the second foot. The same contrast between (bi) and (bii) divided into rhythmic groups, however, is due to the placement of the boundary, which in turn depends on the grammatical construction involved. To account for the rhythmic difference between (bi) and (bii), a distinction is made between so-called *leading* syllables, those which precede a stressed syllable in a rhythmic group, and *trailing* syllables, those which follow a stressed syllable in a rhythmic group. [The syllable /əz/ would be leading in (bi) and trailing in (bii).] It is then stated as a general principle of English rhythm that trailing syllables are longer than leading syllables. However, this is approximately equivalent to stating that the rhythmic pattern of the second foot in (ai) is ♪♪, whereas in (aii) it is ♩♩. The rhythmic group and the foot are thus different but, for all practical purposes, equivalent units of English rhythm.[13]

---

[12] See Jassem 1952 and Jassem/Hill/Witten 1984, for example, for a different approach to the treatment of unaccented syllables in rhythmic units.
[13] Séguinot (1979), however, finds greater isochrony if rhythmic groups rather than feet are measured.

# 4.  Rules of English speech rhythm

## 4.1  The principle of rhythmic alternation

In addition to being conditioned by the principles of isochrony and stress-timing, English rhythm is characterized by the principle of *rhythmic alternation*. This principle underlies not only verse but also — and more fundamentally — natural spech:

> Verse rhythm is based on the same alternation between stronger and weaker syllables as that found in natural everyday speech. Even in the most prosaic speech, which is in no way dictated by artistic feeling, this alternation is not completely irregular: everywhere we observe a natural tendency towards making a weak syllable follow a strong and inversely.
>
> (Jespersen 1900, 1970:254)

Whether the tendency for strong and weak syllables to alternate with one another is ultimately physiologically or psychologically conditioned, there is reason to believe that rhythmic alternation is a universal principle governing the rhythms of natural language (cf. also Selkirk 1984).

The sceptic may object here that speakers surely do not choose their words according to lexical stress pattern. How is it then that regular alternations of stressed and unstressed syllables result? The answer is that once the lexemes of an utterance have been selected, a set of rules (among them, rhythm rules) applies to determine their phonological realization in context. A rhythmically well-formed structure in terms of the alternation principle requires no adjustment by the rhythm rules. However, a structure which is 'ill-formed' in terms of the alternation principle is modified by the rhythm rules so that it conforms more closely to the ideal pattern. The rhythm rules operate to add stresses, delete stresses, and/or to move stresses (Ch. II §3.2), as we shall demonstrate below.

## 4.2  Rhythmic hierarchies

To state that these rhythm rules apply to the linear concatenation of words, however, would not be wholly accurate. As recent research has shown, in order to account for the patterns encountered in speech, we must assume that utterances are hierarchical structures with different levels of rhythmic organization.

For example, the rhythm rules do not apply blindly at the 'surface' level of concatenated lexical items to ensure that every stressed syllable is followed by one and only one unstressed syllable. This can be demonstrated with a (hypothetical) utterance such as *it was organized on the model of a gallon of worms*. A sequence of four unstressed syllables follows the lexical stress on *or-*, and a sequence of three follows the lexical stress on *mod-*. Yet the rhythm rules do not require beats to be added to break up these sequences of unstressed syllables: *\*it was 'orga'nized on the 'model 'of a 'gallon of 'worms*. On the other hand, the rhythm rules *do* require that not only just *worms* be stressed (or accented here) but also *or-* or *mod-*. To account for why these beats must be added and where, it is necessary to appeal to a rhythmic hierarchy.

Rhythmic hierarchies are best demonstrated by a so-called metrical grid.[14] If we mark all syllables at the lowest rhythmic level of an utterance with $x$, all phonologically strong syllables at level /2/ with another $x$, and one main stress within each word by another $x$ at level /3/, then the lexical stresses in this utterance can be represented as follows:

```
3        x            x      x      x
2        x   x        x      x      x
1    x x x x x    x  x    x x x x x x x    x
     it was organized on the model of a gallon of worms
```

The presence of phrasal stress (assigned by the NSR or a similar rule) or compound stress (assigned by the CSR or a similar rule) can be represented by another $x$ at level /4/. In this example the phrasal stress rules would assign a stress beat to *worms*:

```
4                                           x
3        x            x      x              x
2        x   x        x      x              x
1    x x x x x    x  x    x x x x x x x     x
     it was organized on the model of a gallon of worms
```

We can now see why this utterance would be rhythmically ill-formed if realized as indicated on the topmost level; there is only one beat at level /4/ corresponding to a sequence of four beats at level /3/.

To become rhythmically well-formed, this utterance requires an additional beat at level /4/. Since beats at level /4/ may only be added to the top of columns which have reached level /3/, and since they are added in an alternating fashion, this means that either *or-* or *mod-* would qualify, depending on whether we move from left to right or from right to left. But, syllables such as, say, *-ized* or *of*, would not qualify for an additional beat. The rhythmic hierarchy thus accounts for why and where beats must be added (or, in other contexts, deleted) to create rhythmically well-formed utterances.

Rhythmic hierarchies are likewise needed to account fully for the phenomenon of *stress shift*, or the movement of stresses. Here, it will be recalled, a lexical stress may be moved forward to a preceding syllable in the environment of a following stress (Ch. II §§2.5, 3.2): *thir'teen* → *'thirteen 'men*. However, it is not necessary for two stresses to be immediately adjacent at a lower level of the rhythmic hierarchy in order for a stress shift to occur. There may even be a number of intervening unstressed syllables. But if two stresses are immediately adjacent on an upper level, with no intervening beats at the level below, this is known as a stress *clash* and a stress shift may occur. Consider, for instance:

```
(i)     4       | x     x |          x        x
        3    x  | x     x |          x   x    x
        2    x  x     x           →  x   x    x
        1    x  x  x  x  x           x  x  x  x  x
             trade-union movement    trade-union movement
```

---

[14] We adopt Selkirk's (1984) conventions for grid construction.

(ii)

```
    4        x        x              x              x
    3   x    x        x              x   x          x
                              →
    2   x   x       x   x          x   x          x   x
    1   x   x  x    x   x x         x   x   x      x   x x
         self-righteous attitude       self-righteous attitude
```

In both (i) and (ii) unstressed syllables intervene on level /1/ between the stressed syllables *u-* and *move-*, and *right-* and *at-* on level /2/; however, at level /4/ *u-* and *move-* are immediately adjacent, as are *right-* and *at-*, with no beats intervening at level /3/.[15] This clash is one prerequisite for the application of a rhythm rule to move stress.

The other prerequisite is that the syllable to which the stress is to be moved must itself have a beat at least on level /2/, i.e. it must be a phonologically strong syllable. This prerequisite is fulfilled in (i) and (ii) above, and thus the stresses on *u-* and *right-* are shifted leftwards to *trade-* and *self-*.[16] But *pre'vailing 'winds* does not become *\*'prevailing 'winds*, nor does *in'sipid 'coffee* become *\*'insipid 'coffee*, because the syllables *pre-* and *in-* are themselves not strong.[17]

The development of a theory of rhythm which will account for the complex phenomenon of stress shift (or, more generally, beat deletion and addition) in English is one of the major aims of current research in prosody.

## References

Abercrombie 1964a
\*Abercrombie 1964b
Abercrombie 1971
\*Adams 1979
\*Allen, G. D. 1975
Allen, W. S. 1973
Brown 1911
Catford 1977 (pp. 84–91)
Classe 1939
Crystal 1969 (§4.11)
Crystal 1975d
Delattre 1964
Donovan/Darwin 1979
Faure/Hirst/Chafcouloff 1980
Gimson ³1980 (§§10.03, 10.04)
de Groot ²1968
Hoequist 1983a
Hoequist 1983b

Hoequist 1983c
Jassem/Hill/Witten 1984
Jespersen 1900
\*Lehiste 1977
Liberman/Prince 1977 (§§0, 1, 3)
O'Connor 1965
Pike 1945 (§3.6)
Rees 1975
Séguinot 1979
Selkirk 1980
Selkirk 1984
Shen/Peterson 1964
Sonnenschein 1925
Steele ²1779
Sumera 1980
Uldall 1971
Uldall 1972
Uldall 1978

---

[15] We assume here that *trade-union* and *self-righteous* have lexical stress on *u-* and *right-* respectively.

[16] According to Liberman/Prince (1977), stress never shifts to the right in English. Thus we do not have *'sports 'contest → \*'sports con'test* or *'verb 'paradigm → \*'verb para'digm*.

[17] In Kingdon's terms, the words *prevailing* and *insipid* do not have high or low level stresses (Ch. II §2.3).

62

# Chapter IV

# Intonation

The term *intonation* has a variety of denotations ranging in scope from the very broad to the very narrow. For some linguists the term covers not only pitch, but also stress and pause phenomena on a suprasegmental level (e.g. Wode 1966). For others, *intonation* is restricted to the (non-lexical) manifestations of melody in speech (Ch. VI §3). And for a strict follower of Bolinger, *intonation* is reserved exclusively for gradient contrasts due to pitch, e.g. steep vs. gradual pitch movement, type of melodic approach to the accented syllable, relative height of pitch peaks (Ch. II §2.2). Here and in the following we shall adopt the second of these definitions, i.e. *intonation* as speech melody.

## 1. Levels of analysis

From an auditory point of view intonation is related to the perception of pitch, perceived pitch in turn being related to the fundamental frequency of the vibration of air molecules set in motion during speech. It may be well to remind ourselves, however, that the relationship between acoustic $f_0$ and auditory perception of pitch is by no means simple or direct. For one, we do not perceive a change in pitch whenever there is a change in fundamental frequency. Nor do we perceive regular increments in frequency as regular intervals of pitch.[1] In fact, psycho-acoustic studies have shown that some quite sizeable changes in $f_0$ are not perceived at all, while other, minimal changes may produce clear differences in perceived pitch. In sum, "the extent of $F_0$ changes as such is no reliable measure for their perceptual relevance" ('t Hart/Cohen 1973:310).

As 't Hart/Collier (1975) have pointed out, there are three different levels at which intonation can be analyzed, each reflecting a different degree of abstraction. At a concrete, *acoustic* level intonation can be seen as a succession of fundamental frequency curves in time. Since, however, many of these acoustic phenomena are not perceived at all by the human ear or only selectively perceived, a second, *phonetic* level must be distinguished, at which intonation can be viewed as a succession of perceivable pitch 'events'. However, not even all the pitch events which are in principle capable of being distinguished by the human ear are necessarily relevant in understanding the utterances of a given language. That is, a third, more abstract *phonological* level of intonation analysis can be identified at which potentially distinct

---

[1] Below 1000 Hz our ear perceives pitch change when the fundamental frequency varies by as little as 2 to 3 Hz. Above that, a larger variation in frequency must be made before we detect a change (Ladefoged 1962:75).

pitch events are grouped together into 'meaningful' categories. Since we usually listen to speech in order to grasp meaning, many of these otherwise perceptible distinctions are simply not registered. A good example of this is an experiment by Hadding/ Studdert-Kennedy (1964) in which more than 50% of the American subjects heard the following $f_0$ sequences as final *falling* contours [presumably because they were identified as statements]:

Fig. IV/1

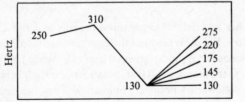

(1964, 1972:355)

The authors comment that "listeners were unable to follow the terminal glide with anything like the precision that might have been predicted from simple pure tone pitch discrimination" (1964, 1972:357). And in a set of experiments designed to test pitch variability within given contours, Gårding/Abramson came to the conclusion that "each contour has a considerable margin within which changes can be made without any effect on perception, as long as these changes do not disturb a certain pattern" (1965:75).

However, although most linguists will agree that the amount of actual variation in pitch far exceeds that which is systematically relevant in a given language, there is much less consensus on which aspects of the melodic 'line' – an undifferentiated, quasi continuously varying pitch continuum extending in time[2] – should be considered most significant. In the following we shall examine some of the phonological models of English intonation which linguists have proposed in recent years.

## 2. Phonological models

### 2.1 Levels

Influenced by American structuralist tradition and by his experience with Amerindian tone languages (Ch. VI §3), Pike (1945) viewed the intonation contour as 'segment- able' into a sequence of distinctive pitch levels, each level representing a *pitch phoneme*. Four levels are postulated in order to describe the significant intonation contrasts of English: /1/ extra high, /2/ high, /3/ mid, and /4/ low pitch.[3] These levels are obviously not constant from speaker to speaker, but they are assumed to

---

[2] Strictly speaking, fundamental frequency is only present when the vocal cords are vibrating, i.e. during the voiced parts of speech. The $f_0$ line is interrupted when voicing is cut off, as, for instance, in the articulation of voiceless consonants. However, interruption due to phonetic influence is rarely perceived as such in speech (Lea 1977:101).

[3] Presumably for mnemonic reasons, the numbering was later reversed so that /1/ would correspond to low pitch and /4/ to high pitch (Trager/Smith 1957:42).

be relatively constant for any given speaker. The pitch phonemes combine in various ways to produce *intonation morphs*, linguistic units which carry meaning. Thus if we imagine an utterance such as *He wanted to do it* with a melodic line approximately as follows:[4]

Fig. IV/2

Pike would describe this as a /2−4/ contour,

Fig. IV/3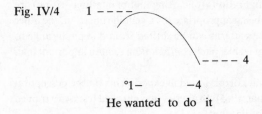

which might contrast with, say, a /1−4/ contour:

Fig. IV/4     1 − − − −

                          − − − − 4

              °1−           −4
           He wanted  to  do  it

Substituting level /1/ for level /2/ here is responsible for a change in meaning, which might be glossed as 'insistence', 'excitement' or 'conviction'. Thus it can be argued that /1/ and /2/ are pitch phonemes, which alone or in combination with other pitch phonemes form intonation morphs such as /2−4/ and /1−4/.

Note that the pitch levels are assigned independent of considerations of stress.[5] In Pike's model the only necessary connection between intonation and stress is that all pitch contours begin on a stressed syllable (marked with / °/). Otherwise, significant intonation contrasts are assumed to be describable in terms of the four pitch phonemes alone.

To these Trager/Smith (1957) later added three *terminal junctures*, types of pitch transition from phrase to phrase or from phrase to silence:

# a quick fall down to silence
‖ a terminal rise in pitch
| sustention of pitch     (1957:46)

Terminal junctures mark the boundaries between intonation contours.

---

[4] These curves represent an abstraction from the $f_0$ contours which would emerge in instrumental analysis, where voiceless segments interrupt the continuity of the line.

[5] Trager/Smith admit that stress may influence a pitch level slightly, but this produces only "allophones of a pitch phoneme" (1957:43; cf. also Bolinger 1958:122).

## 2.2　Configurations

The four-level approach to intonation, however, came under attack by Bolinger (1951), whose main criticism was levelled at the theoretical status of the pitch levels. If, as Pike and Trager/Smith claim, the pitch levels are wholly relative (except that /4/ is always higher than /3/, /3/ always higher than /2/, etc.), then in the absence of context, Bolinger argued, a single absolute pitch could correspond to any one of the four pitch phonemes. Furthermore, even if context were present, it would be impossible to distinguish, say, a /123/ contour from a /234/ contour. Bolinger concluded that "those who adopt the four-level analysis are not talking about PURELY relative tones, but about tones that may rove each in its own bailiwick but no farther" (1951:200).

If the pitch ranges are mutually exclusive, Bolinger continued, then there should be semantic contrasts from one level to another, but little or no significant contrast within the pitch range of one level. Yet Bolinger's own experiments showed that curves with different levels but similar configurations are sometimes synonymous, i.e. capable of being used interchangeably in the same context, whereas curves with approximately the same levels but different configurations (one rising and one falling–rising) are sometimes non-synonymous, one being appropriate for a genuine question, the other not. Bolinger concluded that since patterns can be shifted from one pitch range to another without becoming unrecognizable, pitch *configuration* is more important than pitch range or level.

Several years later, this view was corroborated in experiments on the perception of intonation by linguists (Lieberman 1965). In a series of controlled tests with trained linguists, Lieberman found, inter alia, that:

(i) Competent linguists independently transcribing 'non-emotional' and 'emotional' utterances differ as much as 60% of the time when the Trager/Smith system of pitch levels and terminal junctures is used.

(ii) The pitch levels do not correspond either to mutually exclusive ranges or to discrete relative ranges of $f_0$, even when the intonation of just one speaker is being transcribed by one linguist. What is transcribed as pitch level /1/ (low) may have the same $f_0$ or even greater $f_0$ than pitch level /2/ for one and the same speaker.

(iii) Linguists were only able to distinguish two degrees of stress (stress and non-stress) when transcribing fixed vowels modulated with the $f_0$ and amplitude of the original. However, when they heard the complete speech signal, they could distinguish four.[6]

(iv) Tonetic transcription (§2.3) of the original was more consistent with the $f_0$ and amplitude information than the Trager/Smith notation (Lieberman 1965; 1967:123ff.).

These findings cast serious doubt on the theory of pitch levels as conceived of by Pike, Trager/Smith, Wells and others. [Cf., however, Crompton 1980 and §2.5.]

---

[6] This suggests that secondary and tertiary stresses may be inferred from knowledge of the words themselves rather than gleaned from the acoustic signal.

## 2.3 Tones and tunes

The British school of intonation analysis can be traced from its beginning with Sweet (1892) through Palmer (1924) and Armstrong/Ward (²1931) to Kingdon (1958b), Schubiger (1958) and O'Connor/Arnold (²1973).[7] Two trends can be distinguished: *tone* or tonetic analysis and *tune* analysis. These are not mutually exclusive, however; indeed there have been a number of successful amalgamations. But for purposes of presentation we shall treat the two separately, beginning with Kingdon's tonetic system (1958b).

### 2.3.1 Tonetic analysis

In contrast to the American structuralist school but in accord with Bolinger, the British tradition fully acknowledges the interrelatedness of stress and pitch in intonation. It is the stressed syllables in an utterance which are treated as the frame upon which the melodic line is 'hung', so to speak. Only the pitch of the stressed syllables is considered relevant for the characterization of intonation patterns. The pitch of unstressed syllables is assumed to be predictable in the majority of cases, based on that of the surrounding stressed syllables.

Among the stressed syllables in an utterance a distinction is made between kinetic and static tones (Ch. II §2.3). The types of pitch movement typically encountered in kinetic tones include falls, rises, and combinations thereof, i.e. fall–rises, rise–falls, etc. Both kinetic and static tones may be placed relatively high or relatively low in the voice range. Thus there is a binary option for each, as summarized in the following chart:

Fig. IV/5 Tones and tonetic marks [based on Kingdon 1958b]

*Kinetic tones*

| | | | |
|---|---|---|---|
| Fall | High (ˋ)<br>Low (ˎ) | Fall–rise | High (ˇ)<br>Low (ˬ) |
| Rise | High (ˊ)<br>Low (ˏ) | Rise–fall | High (ˆ)<br>Low (‸) |

*Static tones*

| | |
|---|---|
| Level | High (ˈ)<br>Low (ˌ) |

Provision is also made for *emphatic* kinetic and static tones; these are transcribed with double tonetic marks.

---

[7] Cf. Scherer/Wollmann (²1977:228ff.) and Gibbon (1976a:101ff.) for historical surveys.

With respect to our example *He wanted to do it* Kingdon would single out the stress and pitch on *wanted* as the significant part of the trajectory:[8]

Fig. IV/6

and transcribe the intonation as *He `wanted to do it*. The (`) mark indicates that the following syllable is at once stressed and kinetic, with pitch movement starting relatively high in the voice range and descending to near-bottom. The surrounding syllables are not marked in any way because (a) they are unstressed, and (b) their behaviour is predictable: in a post-tonic position, they simply continue the movement of the kinetic tone, i.e. in the case of *-ed to do it*, they descend slowly in pitch.

Kingdon's tonetic notation tends to record less pitch variation than the Pike-Trager/Smith notation does. Whereas Pike advocated marking pitch level at the beginning and the end of every contour (of which there is one for every primary stress), Kingdon recognizes in general only one kinetic tone in an intonation group (§3), which in his view normally overlaps with the sentence or utterance.[9] Thus compare Pike's notation of

a) It's ten o'clock; I've got to go home
   3-  °2--3-°2-4  4-            °2-4     (1945:79)

with the equivalent in Kingdon's notation:

b) It's 'ten o"clock ‖ I've got to go `home ‖

The pitch movement recorded in (a) from *ten* to *o'* would not be marked in (b), since unstressed syllables are simply assumed to descend slowly in pitch. The pitch of the initial unstressed syllable *it's* in (a) would not be noted in (b), since normal pre-heads are assumed to be pitched slightly above the bottom of the voice range. If necessary, the fact that the pitch of the second pre-contour *I've* is lower than that of the first could be captured in (b) by use of the Low Pre-head mark ( _ ). [The latter, however, is usually reserved for added contrast before emphatic kinetic tones (Kingdon 1958b: 47ff.).]

In addition to recording in general less pitch variation, the tonetic approach – rather than demanding that the analyst identify a given pitch with respect to some arbitrary pitch level – relies on judgments relative to speaker voice-range.[10] Thus,

---

[8] We adopt Scherer's convention of a thicker printed line for the simultaneous notation of pitch and stress (Scherer/Wollmann [2]1977:229).

[9] Kingdon does allow for the occurrence of two or more intonation groups in a sentence; this happens in particular, he states, in conversation and in the reading aloud of written (narrative) texts (1958b:68).

[10] For instance, the High Rising Tone begins on a pitch 'slightly below the middle of the normal voice range, and rises to the top'; the Low Rising Tone begins 'at or near the bottom, and rises to about the middle, of the normal voice range'; the Falling Tone begins 'according to its tonetic context, anywhere from the top to near the bottom, and finishes on the bottom, of the normal voice range' (Kingdon 1958b:7ff.).

all in all, the tonetic approach places fewer (and perhaps more reasonable) demands on the analyst with respect to the phonetic details of intonation and stress. It may be for this reason that tonetic notation has been found more consistent with actual frequency curves (Lieberman 1965).

### 2.3.2 Tune analysis

A second trend in the British approach to intonation has been called tune analysis and is associated primarily with the names of Jones and Armstrong/Ward. Much as its name suggests, tune analysis reduces the intonational system of a language to a small set of holistic contours or tunes, with variations allowed for special circumstances. For example, according to Armstrong/Ward, English intonation has Tune I, which for unemphatic sentences can be illustrated as follows (dashes represent stressed syllables and dots, unstressed syllables):

Fig. IV/7

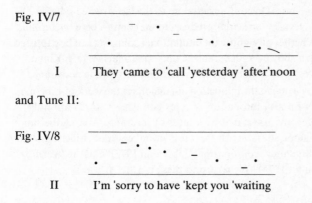

I    They 'came to 'call 'yesterday 'after'noon

and Tune II:

Fig. IV/8

II    I'm 'sorry to have 'kept you 'waiting

Whereas in Tune I the pitch of the voice *falls* to a low level at the end, in Tune II the voice *rises* on any unstressed syllables that follow the last stressed syllable. If there are none, then the rise occurs within the last stressed syllable:

Fig. IV/9

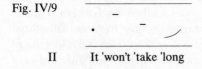

II    It 'won't 'take 'long

Although admittedly "there are other varieties and greater wealth of detail than are here recorded" ([2]1931:1), Armstrong/Ward claim that for all practical purposes, English intonation can be reduced to these two tunes, one with final falling, one with final rising pitch movement. Variations for emphatic sentences include increased stress as well as widened, or narrowed and lowered pitch range.

With respect to our example *He wanted to do it* (Fig. IV/2), Armstrong/Ward would classify the melodic line as Tune I. If the same utterance were realized, say, as follows:

Fig. IV/10         or

these too would be classified as Tune I. What is essential for Tune I is the falling movement of the (final) stressed syllable.

Given the expressly didactic aim of the tune approach, it is understandable that a certain amount of generalization is necessary. Armstrong/Ward only claim to describe "one type of intonation that is essentially English" ([2]1931:1). However, it should be obvious that although the tunes as illustrated here may indeed be authentic in R.P. (Armstrong/Ward's dialect), they are not necessarily appropriate for the description of non-R.P. varieties of British English, nor for American English and other varieties.[11]

However, even with respect to an R.P.-variety of British English, tune analysis makes a very strong claim about the amount of pitch variation which is significant. Since Tune I and II are identical in configuration up to the last stressed syllable, the amount of distinctive pitch variation actually reduces to the contrast between terminal fall and terminal rise. Whether all significant intonational contrasts can be captured by this single distinction is, however, debatable. Competing analyses (e.g. Kingdon, Halliday, Crystal) suggest that a much greater repertoire of tunes is necessary.

Recently, tunes have re-entered the intonation discussion via the work of Liberman (1975). Liberman views English intonation as a lexicon whose words are holistic contours, or tunes, which are associated with units of meaning. Among the tunes which have been investigated so far are the 'contradiction' contour (Liberman/Sag 1974), the 'surprise/redundancy' contour (Sag/Liberman 1975), and the 'warning/ calling' contour (Liberman 1975). We return to these in Ch. IX.

### 2.3.3 Tone–tune analysis

There have been other attempts to reduce the melodic complexity of speech to a didactically manageable size. O'Connor/Arnold, for instance, follow initially the tone approach in distinguishing six *nuclear tones* (as well as various pre-heads, heads and tails), but then point out that although all the parts of a "tune" (i.e. intonation group) could theoretically combine freely with each other, this is in point of fact rarely the case. Instead, some combinations are much more frequent than others. Moreover, some combinations can scarcely be said to differ from others in terms of meaning. O'Connor/Arnold thus establish ten *tone groups*,[12] or "grouping(s) of tunes all conveying the same attitude on the part of the speaker" ([2]1973:39). With these it is said to be possible to convey all the meaningful intonational distinctions in English. For each 'tone group' there is a specified obligatory nucleus and occasionally a specified obligatory head. Other parts of the tune are specified but are optional. Thus O'Connor/Arnold's approach represents a combination of the tone and tune

---

[11] In fact, the intonation of some varieties, in particular American English, is said to differ noticeably from R.P. intonation in the nature of the melodic line before the kinetic tone.

[12] Not to be confused with the basic unit of intonation, also sometimes called *tone group* (§3).

approaches, with the added advantage that tunes are grouped together as allophonic varieties of a fixed number of distinctive (phoneme-like) classes.

In similar fashion, Halliday (1970a) distinguishes five *primary* tones: /1/ falling, /2/ high rising, or falling–rising (pointed), /3/ low rising, /4/ falling–rising (rounded), and /5/ rising–falling – each of which in turn can be subdivided into a number of *secondary* tones, representing finer distinctions within the primary tones. The configuration of the whole contour [which Halliday divides into a pre-tonic and a tonic segment[13]], however, is 'fixed' in a manner reminiscent of tune analysis:

> As far as the primary tones are concerned, the pretonics are fully determined, and there is no separate choice involved; once a choice of tone has been made this not only specifies how the tonic is to be spoken but sets limits to the form of the pretonic as well.     (1970a:9)

Thus Halliday too prescribes the nature of the preceding melodic line for each nucleus or tonic type and so is able to reduce the amount of pitch variation in speech to a limited set of characteristic patterns, which are claimed to be responsible for the significant intonational contrasts of English.

## 2.4   Prosodic features

Despite its eminent suitability for didactic purposes, the tune approach to intonation imposes a rather rigid frame on the melodic line. Although the tune categories established may be adequate for the description of one variety, they are hard to transfer to the description of other varieties without loss of descriptive adequacy. Characteristic tunes often vary from dialect to dialect and transferring whole melodies from one to the other inevitably involves the distortion of reality to make it fit pre-established patterns. Considerations of this sort have led some linguists to adopt an approach to intonation based on *features*, which combine more or less freely with one another to create the intonational patterns of a given variety. Positing a set of general and somewhat abstract features, together with relatively free combinatorial potential, provides a flexible basis for the description of both distinctive and non-distinctive intonational patterns in language varieties.

The feature approach is embodied in the model developed by Crystal/Quirk (1964), originally in conjunction with the Survey of English Usage (cf. Quirk et al 1972), and subsequently elaborated upon by Crystal (1969). Intonation in the restricted sense of speech melody is viewed in this model as a manifestation of the interaction of several prosodic features, first and foremost *tone* (pitch direction) and *pitch-range* (pitch height and pitch width). Other prosodic features such as loudness, rhythmicality, pause, etc. may, however, also enter in – in which case we are speaking of intonation in its broadest sense, or prosody. The prosodic feature model, in slightly modified form, has been adopted here and will be presented in fuller detail in the following chapter.

---

[13] The *tonic segment* extends from the tonic syllable (kinetic tone or nucleus) up to the end of the tone group; the *pre-tonic* is an optional part of the tone group preceding the tonic segment (1970a:5).

## 2.5   The return to levels

Although the criticism levelled by Bolinger, Lieberman and others at the structuralist pitch-level approach to intonation made it appear that any further attempt to describe contours as a succession of levels was doomed, this has in effect not proved to be the case. Many of the phonological models being developed today [Bruce/Gårding 1978 for Swedish; Thorsen 1978 for Danish; Pierrehumbert 1980, Hirst 1983, Ladd 1983 for English] employ some sort of pitch level analysis – for instance, following in the tradition of Vanderslice/Ladefoged (1972), in the assignment of binary features such as [ + High] and [ + Low] to fixed points in the melodic line. How can they do so and yet avoid the pitfalls of the Pike-Trager/Smith system?

For one, current phonetic/phonological models do not assume the independence, but instead the interdependence of stress and pitch in establishing pitch accents. Intonation contours are thus not segmented exhaustively into discrete pitch levels irrespective of stress, but instead pre-established pitch accents are described in terms of two, more abstract levels: High and Low. The justification for doing so has been formulated by Bruce (1977) as follows:

> ... reaching a certain pitch level at a particular point in time is the important thing, not the movement (rise or fall) itself. (...) The rises and falls are often – at least partly – being executed during consonant segments, which can be voiceless and consequently cannot signal a pitch change. Instead the pitch change has to be inferred from a comparison of pitch levels in successive vowels, which are assumed to carry the primary intonational information. (1977:132)

[Not all current models take this step; some prefer to leave the pitch accents un-analyzed, i.e. as configurational wholes (e.g. 't Hart/Cohen 1973, Crompton 1980).]

Second, the pitch levels employed are no longer assumed to correspond to constant, discrete $f_0$ domains in the speaker's voice range. Ceteris paribus, a tone assigned the feature [ + High] is higher than a [ + Low] tone. But the high and low levels are subject to contextual influences – typically of a positional or a temporal nature – which may require their ultimate $f_0$ values to be readjusted in one way or another (cf. Bruce 1977:137, 146; Pierrehumbert 1980:74). Thus a [ + High] tone might ultimately be realized by lower $f_0$ than a [ + Low] tone without thereby invalidating the system.[14]

What the majority of these recent models have in common is (i) the desire to establish not only an adequate *phonological representation* of intonation for a given language but also rules for the *phonetic implementation* of these abstract structures, ultimately in terms of actual $f_0$ values; and (ii) the aim to provide an adequate description of the attested intonational contours of a language as well as a principled account of the *possible intonational contours* of a language. Because of this predictive claim, the validity of such models can be tested by synthesizing intonations based on them and verifying acceptability with listener testing. On the grounds of (i) and (ii), such models can rightly be called 'generative' in the sense this term is given in modern linguistic theory.

---

[14] This development is an approximate parallel to the abandonment of the biuniqueness condition in segmental phonology.

# 3.    The basic unit

Just as approaches to intonation vary, so do the views of what the basic structural unit of intonation is and how it should be defined.

## 3.1    Physiological accounts

Perhaps the earliest attempt this century at identifying a prosodic unit was made by Sweet, who wrote:

> The only division actually made in language is that into 'breath-groups'. We are unable to utter more than a certain number of sounds in succession without renewing the stock of air in the lungs. (1906:45)

Some sixty years later Sweet's insights were to find support in the physiological/ acoustic research of Lieberman.

Lieberman (1967) asserts that human beings produce and perceive intonation in terms of unmarked and marked *breath-groups*, which result from the interaction of the respiratory and laryngeal muscular systems. The unmarked breath-group, said to be present in the cries of newborn babies and therefore innately determined, is characterized by a terminal fall in subglottal air pressure, which occurs automatically when the volume of air in the lungs is exhausted (Ch. II §1.3). Lieberman hypothesizes that as a rule laryngeal tension in the vocal cords remains constant during the breath-group, the natural fall in fundamental frequency towards the end thus resulting solely from a drop in subglottal air pressure. In the marked breath-group, on the other hand, the laryngeal muscles work to increase tension, it is hypothesized, thereby counter-ing the final drop in subglottal air pressure and producing non-falling fundamental frequency.

Lieberman's claims are controversial, however, especially with regard to the supposedly predominant role played by subglottal air pressure in the modulation of $f_0$. Counterevidence has been produced by Ohala/Hirano (1967), who were able to show via electromyography that laryngeal muscles are *actively* involved in the control of pitch during phonation, so that changes in subglottal air pressure can only account for a small part of pitch variation. A tentative conclusion might be that although some prosodic divisions are accompanied by breath-taking, they do not necessarily all arise this way. The breath-group is therefore hardly a reliable prosodic unit.

## 3.2    Semantic/grammatical accounts

Many researchers have posited a structural unit of intonation which corresponds to the *sense-group*, defined by Kingdon as "groups of words that have a semantic and grammatical unity – not necessarily complete" (1958b:162f.). Klinghardt, for instance, advanced the theory that since intonation serves, much as pauses do, to make meanings clear, we should speak of an 'intonational sense-group' ("intonatorischer Sinntakt", 1920:32). With this term Klinghardt of course implied that the basic intonation unit and the so-called sense-group overlap, indeed that one is dependent on the other (Scherer/Wollmann 1972:230). Armstrong/Ward likewise posit a one-to-one correlation between intonation unit and sense-group:

> Connected speech consists of sense-groups (either one or a series), each of which is an intonation group. (1926:25)

Yet, although we may indeed encounter correlation between sense-group and intonation group, particularly in the reading aloud of formal written English, there is little systematic overlap in natural spoken English, as more recent research into spontaneous speech has shown. This is because placement of rhythmic stress and accent depends to a certain extent on speech tempo and on speaker attitude (Ch. II §§3.2, 3.3). A person speaking slowly or deliberately tends to make more pauses and increase pitch variation within sense-groups, whereby the number of intonation groups also increases. By way of illustration, consider the following examples:

(a)  ‖ I think it would be ‖ uh entirely inconsistent ‖ (E3/CCB$_4$)
(b)  ‖ in terms of a partnership if there's a mistake ‖ (A1/EP$_1$)

In (a) one sense-group is realized as two intonation units; in (b) two sense-groups are realized in one intonation unit.

Moreover, a speaker may plan poorly and suddenly need to take a breath in the middle of a sense-group; a new intonation group will almost automatically result. For example:

(c)  ‖ I've never found that popular ‖ analysis very convincing ‖ (B/B)

Aside from the problem of the exact determination of sense-groups, it should be clear that intonation group and sense-group can hardly be said to correspond in any systematic manner when spontaneous speech is considered.[15]

Yet although intonation specialists no longer attempt to define the tone group as a function of the sense-group or any other semantic/grammatical entity, most are reluctant to view it as altogether unrelated to some sort of grammatical unit. It has been claimed that the intonation group and the *clause* are co-extensive to a certain degree, a clause being understood to consist minimally of subject-predicator (Quirk et al 1972). According to Halliday, "one clause is one tone group unless there is *good reason* for it to be otherwise" (1970a:3). In Crystal's corpus, however, less than one in every two clauses was co-extensive with a tone-unit, and less than one third of the tone-units were co-extensive with a clause (1969:258). Crystal concludes that it would make better sense to view the tone-unit in relation to *elements of clause structure*, since 80% of all tone-units can be said to contain minimally one element of clause structure (1969:260).[16] Whether clause or clause element is seen as the

---

[15] Of course, if a sense-group is defined, say, as those words a speaker chooses to treat as one unit, then a greater correspondence to the intonation group can be established. However, this view of the sense-group would result in circularity if it were used to account for the intonation group.

[16] Elements of clause structure include Vocative, Subject, Predicator, Complement and Adverbial (Crystal 1969:279f.).

typical grammatical counterpart to the tone group, however, the placement of tone-unit boundaries can arguably never be accounted for wholly in grammatical terms (Ch. VIII §3.1).

## 3.3   Phonetic/phonological accounts

Given the limitations of semantic and/or grammatical criteria in defining the basic unit of intonation, it has been argued that we must establish a phonological entity whose boundaries can be determined on phonetic/phonological grounds (Crystal 1969:205). This unit is the *tone-unit*, a stretch of utterance which has at least one prominent syllable with major pitch movement (the *nucleus*; Ch. V §1.1). At least one nucleus is necessary by definition; but under certain conditions a tone-unit may have two nuclei, simple or complex.

The boundaries of a tone-unit, according to Crystal, can be established with the help of a number of phonetic cues. For one, they are frequently accompanied by a short pause (although this is not an obligatory feature). Furthermore, there may be other articulatory cues such as phonetic lengthening or aspiration at the end of a tone-unit. Finally, since each speaker reportedly has a more or less constant pitch level at which s/he starts new tone-units (the *onset*; Ch. V §1.2.1), there is typically an audible step-up or step-down in pitch at the boundary, depending on the nature of the preceding nucleus. If a tone-unit ends on a falling pitch, the voice will move up to reach its onset level for the next tone-unit; if a tone-unit ends on a rising pitch, the voice will move down to the next onset.

Crystal does not claim that all tone-unit boundaries will be readily and non-ambiguously identifiable according to these criteria alone. Instead, he adds that phonetic/phonological cues are usually present "in normal (... meaning mainly 'not too hurried') speech" (1969:205). In rapid spontaneous speech, tone-unit boundary identification may become more difficult.[17] It is precisely the difficulty of boundary identification in spontaneous speech which has motivated Brown/Currie/Kenworthy (1980) to abandon the traditional tone-unit divisions and rely on *pause-defined units*, 'chunks' of speech delimited by pauses of more than 0.6–0.8 seconds (1980:56). Such divisions are undoubtedly highly reliable scientifically. However, they are vulnerable in one important way. If the aim of linguistic investigation is to discover the system of intonation and how it relates to other parts of the grammar of the language, i.e. if we are interested in establishing a competence model of intonation, then pause-defined units are notoriously ill-suited for this purpose. Many pauses have a performance-related origin – a pause for breath, a pause to search for a word or to plan speaking strategy, etc. Accordingly, the intonation chunks which result may not necessarily reflect the (competence-based) intonational structure of speech. In light of the ambiguity of pause phenomena, it seems wiser – in spite of admitted

---

[17] In cases of doubt, Crystal suggests, we should "have recourse to grammatical or semantic criteria to place the boundary" (1969:207). But this makes the establishment of correlation between intonation and grammar/semantics circular.

difficulties − to persist in the search for tone-units and tone-unit boundaries based on phonological/phonetic criteria, making allowance for cases of indeterminacy.[18]

In conclusion, the lack of consensus on what constitutes the basic unit of intonation has led to a plethora of competing terms: *breath group, phonemic clause, tone group, tone unit, tune, intonation group, intonation contour, intonation chunk*, etc. Whether any or all of these refer to the same thing, however, is a matter for careful consideration. Depending on what defining criteria are set forth, quite different units may result. In particular, semantically or grammatically based definitions often yield different results from phonetic/phonological ones. But even among phonetic/phonological definitions, a pause-based definition will produce different units from a nuclear-tone-based one. Whether breath-groups correspond fully to the latter is also an open question. Finally, which if any of these correspond to that "unit of neurolinguistic pre-preparation" which Laver (1970:68f.) claims is instrumental in the preparation and execution of a speech program also remains to be established.[19] In the meantime, due caution is recommended.

## References

Armstrong/Ward [2]1931
*Bolinger 1951
Bolinger 1958b
Bolinger 1961b
Bolinger 1970
Brazil/Coulthard/Johns 1980
Brown/Currie/Kenworthy 1980 (Ch. 3)
Bruce 1977
Bruce/Gårding 1978
Crompton 1980
*Collier 1974
Cohen/'t Hart 1967
Crystal 1969 (§§5.4, 5.5)
Crystal 1980
Crystal/Quirk 1964
Currie 1981
Dene 1959
Gårding 1983
Gårding/Abramson 1965

Gibbon 1976
Hadding/Studdert-Kennedy 1964
Halliday 1967a
Halliday 1970a
't Hart/Cohen 1973
*'t Hart/Collier 1975
Hirst 1979
Hirst 1983
Jassem 1952
Jassem 1978
Jones [9]1976 (§1007−1044)
Kingdon 1958b
Klinghardt 1920
*Ladd 1983a
Ladd 1983b
Ladefoged 1962 (Ch. 6)
Laver 1970
Lea 1977
Liberman 1975

---

[18] Without denying the importance of the tone-unit as such, Brazil/Coulthard/Johns (1980) argue that *"tone unit boundaries are not in fact of great importance"*. Pre-heads and tails do not contain prominent syllables and frequently there is pitch concord between them anyway (1980:46).

[19] According to Laver, "... the preparation and articulation of a speech program is not performed on a sound-by-sound, or even on a word-by-word basis. It is much more likely that neural elements corresponding to much longer stretches of speech are assembled in advance, and then allowed to be articulated as a single continuous program" (1970:68). This unit of neural assemblage, he speculates, may be the 'tone-group'.

Liberman/Sag 1974

*Lieberman 1965

Lieberman 1967

O'Connor/Arnold [2]1973

Ohala 1970

Ohala 1977

Ohala/Hirano 1967

Palmer 1924

Pierrehumbert 1980

Pike 1945 (§§3.1−3.5)

Sag/Liberman 1975

Scherer/Wollmann [2]1977

Schubiger 1958

Sledd 1960

Sweet [2]1906

Thorsen 1978

Trager 1972

Trager/Smith 1957

Vanderslice/Ladefoged 1972

Wells 1945

Chapter V
# A system of intonation

The preceding chapters have presented a survey of three major areas of English prosody. Although this by no means exhausts the field, the remainder of this book will be devoted to a closer examination of one of these areas, intonation proper, and to a critical evaluation of the role which it has been claimed to play in language communication. Prior to a discussion of *function*, however, the relevant *forms* capable of assuming functions must be identified. Such will be the aim of the present chapter.

We assume as basic descriptive unit the *tone-unit* defined according to the phonetic/phonological criteria described above (Ch. IV §3.3); its boundaries will be marked in notation by double vertical bars /‖/.

## 1. Internal tone-unit organization

The tone-unit can be viewed on an abstract level as consisting of one obligatory constituent, the *nucleus*, and a number of optional constituents, the *head*, the *pre-head* and the *tail*. The optional elements may occur in any combination with each other and the nucleus, but only in a specified order. The following are conceivable types of tone-unit:

|          |      | nucleus |      |
|----------|------|---------|------|
|          | head | nucleus |      |
|          | head | nucleus | tail |
| pre-head | head | nucleus |      |
| pre-head |      | nucleus |      |
| pre-head |      | nucleus | tail |
|          |      | nucleus | tail |
| pre-head | head | nucleus | tail |

Diagrammatically this could be represented as follows (with parentheses signalling optionality):

tone-unit → (pre-head) (head) nucleus (tail)     (Ashby 1978: 327)

## 1.1 Nucleus

### 1.1.1 Definition

Broadly speaking, the nucleus is the most prominent syllable in a tone-unit. If a tone-unit consists of only one syllable, it is by definition the nucleus (provided the tone-unit is complete). The prominence of the nuclear syllable is generally attributable to its pitch, although it tends to be loud and long as well. The nucleus is not, however, necessarily the loudest or the longest syllable in the tone-unit. The pitch prominence of a nuclear syllable may be due to its 'obtrusion', although it need not be the highest or the lowest syllable in a tone-unit. In general, nuclear prominence is due to the presence of noticeable pitch movement, either in the form of a *glide* on the nuclear syllable itself or in the form of a *jump* from the nuclear syllable to the following syllable or syllables.

### 1.1.2 Phonetic exponents

The various phonetic forms a nucleus can take are, phonologically speaking, intonational 'allotones'. That is to say, their occurrence is not accompanied by any perceptible change of meaning and is for that matter generally predictable in terms of the phonetic make-up of the syllable and the number of accompanying unstressed syllables in the rhythmic unit. Thus, in answer to the question *What does he do*? we might find

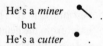

He's a *miner*
but
He's a *cutter*

[Large and small dots represent stressed and unstressed syllables respectively.]

The pitch jump in *cutter* is due to the short duration of the syllable *cut* (voiceless /t/ reduces the length of /ʌ/ considerably), whereas in *miner*, the diphthong /aɪ/ and the voiced /n/ provide enough duration for a glide to be realized. Likewise, in answer to the question *How many did you buy?* we might have

Six
but
Sixty

The fact that the falling nucleus does not take the form of a glide on the first syllable of *sixty* can be explained by its shorter duration, relatively speaking, in the rhythmic unit. Whereas *six* fills out its time interval alone, *six-* must share the unit with *-ty* and is consequently reduced in length.

A rising nuclear pitch movement is almost always spread over the following syllables, unless the syllable which constitutes the nucleus is final in the tone-unit. Thus:

| | |
|---|---|
| Sixty? | ● ˙ |
| Miner? | ● ˙ |
| Cutter? | ● ˙ |
| but | |
| Six? | ╱ |

In notation, however, we would mark the fall or the rise in all these cases with a /ˋ/ or /ˊ/ over the syllable marked in the lexicon as potential bearer of stress or accent:

| | |
|---|---|
| MÌNer | MÍNer |
| CÙTter | CÚTter |
| SÌX | SÍX |
| SÌXty | SÍXty |

It is important to realize that what the pitch of the voice does on the syllable before the prominent syllable or in order to get to the starting point for pitch movement on the prominent syllable is of no relevance in determining whether the nucleus is falling or rising. For instance, in the utterance *and this is something which I think* ... (C/AJ), the melodic line would look approximately as follows:

Fig. V/1

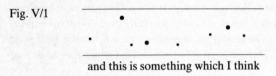

and this is something which I think

It is the syllables *this* and *I* which are prominent here (due to their obtrusion). The following syllables *is something* and *think* descend in pitch or level out from the height of *this* and *I*, respectively. We can therefore conclude that *this* and *I* are falling nuclei. It is true that the voice moves up in pitch from *and* to *this*, as well as from *which* to *I*, but in determining type of nuclear movement this is irrelevant. The decision as to whether a nucleus falls or rises depends solely on what the voice does on the prominent syllable itself and on any stressed or unstressed syllables following it which belong to the tone-unit. Based on the phonetic/phonological criteria for tone-unit identification outlined in Ch. IV §3.3, there would be a tone-unit boundary between *-thing* and *which* (due to the step-up in pitch after *-thing*). Therefore our notation so far would look as follows:

and THÌS is 'something ‖ which Ì think ‖

### 1.1.3 Kinetic tones and the nucleus

The fact that it is pitch movement which is typically associated with the nucleus is reflected in Kingdon's dichotomy between *kinetic* and *static* tones (Ch. II §2.3). Only kinetic tones may form the nucleus of an intonation group, according to Kingdon.

However, a number of considerations speak against the simple equation of kinetic tones and nuclei. For one, there is the phenomenon of level nuclei. According to Crystal, "... there is often (...) clear evidence of a tone-unit boundary, but no audibly kinetic tone preceding" (1969:215). In these cases, he argues, it is the most prominent *static* tone which must be considered the nucleus. On the view that level nuclei exist, pitch movement is obviously a sufficient but not a necessary condition for nuclear status.

However, not only must the equation of kinetic tones and nuclei be doubted because some static tones are nuclei: there are also kinetic tones which are non-nuclear. In so-called 'glissando' intonation (§2.4), for instance, every stressed syllable has pitch movement; in this case the nucleus must be defined as that stressed syllable with the greatest pitch movement. Kingdon's kinetic criterion is thus at once too narrow and too broad to distinguish all nuclear from non-nuclear tones.

### 1.1.4 Position

According to Kingdon, the nucleus "will be associated with the last fully stressed syllable of the (*sc.* intonation) group" (1958b:6). However, in both Crystal's and Halliday's systems the nucleus may come anywhere in the tone-unit and be followed by an unspecified number of *stressed* or *unstressed* syllables following the nucleus. This apparent contradiction stems from the fact that the systems in question recognize differing degrees of stress. Kingdon, for instance, distinguishes three degrees of stress: full stress, partial stress and non-stress. Only partially stressed syllables (in addition to unstressed syllables) may appear after the nucleus. For example, in

|I happen to be the 'one who's ↑↑ TÀLKing at the 'moment you 'see ‖ (A1/BD$_2$)
I $^h$|wouldn't SÂY that a'bout you ‖ (A1/EP$_2$)
|CÀRE for that 'child ‖ (A1/EP$_3$)

Kingdon would mark all of the stressed syllables following the nucleus by definition as partially stressed syllables or Low Level Static Tones. Crystal and Halliday, on the other hand, would mark the same post-nuclear syllables as stressed, since they recognize only two degrees of (non-emphatic) stress: stress and non-stress. Consequently, in their systems the nucleus cannot be equated with the last fully stressed syllable of the tone-unit; it is, however − because of conventions governing the tail − the last stressed syllable with any kind of noticeable pitch modulation.

## 1.2   Head

Tone-units which contain, in addition to the nucleus, at least one rhythmically stressed syllable before the nucleus are said to have a *head* (sometimes also called 'body'). The head extends from (and includes) the first stressed syllable of the tone-unit up to (but not including) the nucleus. It may encompass an unspecified number of stressed and/or unstressed syllables.

### 1.2.1 Onset

The first rhythmically stressed syllable of the head is sometimes called the *onset*. [Kingdon, however, refers to it as 'head' (1958b:22): *caveat lector*.] The onset, if present, establishes the general level (or *key*; Brazil 1975a) at which the tone-unit will be pitched with respect to other tone-units (§3.1).[1] At the same time it serves as a reference level for establishing the pitch of the other syllables within the tone-unit. This is possible, so Crystal (1969) hypothesizes, because each and every speaker has a typical pitch level at which they begin tone-units.[2] Indeed this is what is implied by the every-day phrase 'normal speaking voice'. Naturally, there can be some variation: a speaker may choose to use an unusually high or an unusually low pitch at the beginning of a tone-unit. If so, however, this is done for some linguistic purpose and these onsets are 'marked'.

In the following, onsets will be notated with a single vertical bar / | / preceding the syllable in question.

## 1.2.2 Relative pitch height and declination

Because unmarked onsets are more or less constant for a given speaker, the pitch height of other syllables in the tone-unit can be determined relative to it. As psycho-acoustic research has shown, the human ear is better able to determine pitch height in relation to surrounding pitches than with respect to an absolute scale. Thus the pitch height of each rhythmically stressed syllable in the tone-unit is assumed to be judged with respect to that of the preceding stressed and/or unstressed syllable, and ultimately with respect to the onset.

One additional assumption is made, however. This is that the natural tendency of syllables in a tone-unit is to descend gradually in pitch. Pike described the phenomenon in the following terms:

> The general tendency of the voice is to begin on a moderate pitch and lower the medium pitch line during the sentence. A long "level" contour, therefore, might gradually have its syllables pronounced on a lower pitch; this can be called DRIFT. (1945:77)

More recently, the phenomenon of 'drift' has come to be known as *declination*, and acoustic analysis-synthesis experiments have substantiated Pike's observations: the general tendency of average $f_0$ in an utterance is gradually declining.[3] Although we may not always perceive declination consciously, listening tests using synthesized material have shown that speech without declination sounds very unnatural indeed (Cohen/Collier/'t Hart 1982). The conclusion appears to be that hearers make un-conscious adjustment for declination in their perception of intonation.

---

[1] In tone-units without heads, this function is presumably taken over by the nucleus (Brazil 1978:9).

[2] This hypothesis is partially substantiated by evidence from Swedish, according to which speakers have 'favorite' frequency regions which they regularly employ and which remain constant over time (Hadding-Koch 1961).

[3] Despite general consensus on this fact, there is still a certain amount of debate on (i) whether two declination lines must be posited, a bottom line connecting $f_0$ valleys and a top line connecting $f_0$ peaks; (ii) what the domain of declination is, i.e. how often it must be 'reset' [note that if resetting and tone-unit boundaries could be shown to coincide, this would offer an additional means of identifying tone-units]; and (iii) whether declination and resetting of the declination line are linguistically significant phenomena. [Initial evidence from Danish, for instance, suggests that declination slope is greater in statements than in continuations or questions (Thorsen 1980).]

Declination has been attested in a wide variety of unrelated languages and is undoubtedly a universal tendency of physiological origin. It has been thought to be related to the gradual decrease in sub-glottal pressure which occurs automatically during the exhalation phase of respiration regulated for speech. But recent studies have suggested that there may be some laryngeal control as well (cf. discussion in Cohen/Collier/'t Hart 1982). However this may be, declination is incorporated into the system proposed here by virtue of the fact that syllables which are only slightly lower than the preceding ones receive no special marking at all.

Other notation conventions for pitch height in the body include the following: a syllable which drops noticeably in pitch below the level associated with declination is marked with a small arrow pointing downwards / ↓ /. A syllable which is at the same height as a preceding syllable is marked with a small horizontal arrow / → /. A syllable which is slightly higher in pitch than the preceding syllable has a small arrow pointing upwards / ↑ /. And a syllable which is noticeably higher than a preceding stepped-up or boosted syllable (i.e., one which has an upward arrow) or noticeably higher than the onset has a double arrow / ↑↑ /.[4]

The difference between a single arrow and a double arrow can be seen in the shape of the overall contour. A step-up which is higher than the preceding step-up changes the whole slope of the contour, whereas a step-up which is only higher than the preceding syllable but not higher than the preceding step-up does not alter the contour significantly. For example, in:

Fig. V/2

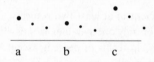

     a       b       c

(b) is slightly higher than the preceding syllable (which in this case is unstressed) but its effect on the overall contour is merely to produce a minor peak. Syllable (c), on the other hand, is not only higher than the preceding unstressed syllable but also higher than the preceding step-up; its effect on the overall contour is to produce a major peak:

Fig. V/3

By way of illustration, the reader is invited to compare the intonation of the following passages on the accompanying cassette with the transcribed versions:

---

[4] In Crystal's system, provision is made for three types of *booster*: (i) slightly higher than the preceding syllable / ↟ /, (ii) much higher than the preceding stepped-up syllable / ↑ /, and (iii) very much higher than the preceding stepped-up syllable / ↑↑ /. In addition, provision is made for two types of *drop*: (i) lower than descent due to declination / ↓ /, and (ii) very much lower than descent due to declination / ↓↓ /. However, we believe that two degrees of booster and one degree of drop (beyond declination) are in general sufficient for the notation of significant intonational contrasts.

I've |strongly ↑ÀLways taken the view (E1/SW₁)
and let to|morrow take ˈ↑↑care of it↑↑SÈLF (A3/EP)
and |so are the ˈ⁻ˈvast maˈ⁻ˈjority of the ˈ⁻ˈBritish PÈOple (F)
I'm |always ↓GRĀTEful (A3/BD)

## 1.2.3 Types of head

The typical head, according to Kingdon, consists of "a slowly descending series of
level tones usually starting at or near the top of the normal voice range and finishing
at or near the bottom" (1958b: 3). Only 30% of the heads in Crystal's data, however,
fit this description. He concludes that the ideal 'stepping' head which Kingdon
describes may be characteristic of written English read aloud or isolated example
sentences used in a pedagogical context; but in terms of statistical frequency, it cannot be considered in any way representative of a norm for spoken colloquial English
(cf. also Ch. VI §2.1).

Crystal identifies four basic types of head in British English. Generalizing somewhat, these can be described as follows:

I    falling heads (descending series of stressed syllables unmarked or marked with /↑/, /→/
     or /↓/);
II   rising heads (ascending series of stressed syllables marked with /→/ or /↑↑/);
III  falling−rising(−falling) heads  }
IV   rising−falling(−rising) heads    } combinations of I and II               (1969: 229ff.)

This classification, however, is insufficient in at least two respects. First, it automatically excludes heads which consist of only one syllable. Monosyllabic heads do
not fit into categories which are defined in terms of descent/ascent.[5] Second, the
classification cannot handle level heads in an unequivocal way. Stressed syllables
marked with /→/ are viewed as possible substitutes in both falling and rising heads
− but no provision is made for a series of /→/ stressed syllables as such. Yet level
heads *are* encountered in British English as well as in other varieties.[6] For instance, in

Fig. V/4

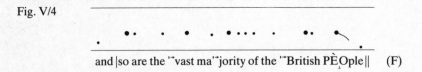

and |so are the ˈ⁻ˈvast maˈ⁻ˈjority of the ˈ⁻ˈBritish PÈ⌋Ople||   (F)

the head, extending from *so* to *people*, would have to be classified as a rising head
according to the scheme above, although the effect of a real rising head such as

---

[5] The same applies to bisyllabic heads if the second syllable is unstressed, since the head
categories are defined in terms of a series of *stressed* syllables.
[6] O'Connor/Arnold (²1973), for instance, provide for a *low* head (all syllables said on the
same low pitch) and a *high* head (all syllables said on some rather high pitch).

Fig. V/5

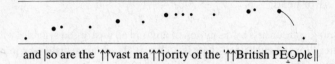

and |so are the 'ʔʔvast ma'ʔʔjority of the 'ʔʔBritish PĘOple||

would surely be quite different. Consequently, a category for *level* heads must be added to account for cases of 'monotone' pitch-range.

Level heads may be defined as series of rhythmically stressed and/or unstressed syllables on a level pitch. [The level pitch may or may not include the onset and other stressed syllables.] Several subcategories can be identified:

(ai) Onset and all stressed syllables up to nucleus are level (as are unstressed syllables)

Fig. V/6

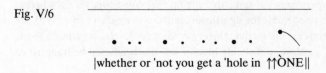

|whether or 'not you get a 'hole in ʔʔÒNE||

(aii) Only stressed and unstressed syllables between onset and nucleus are level

Fig. V/7

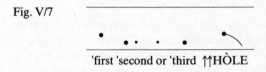

'first 'second or 'third ʔʔHÒLE

(b) Only unstressed syllables are level; stressed syllables proceed from this baseline

Fig. V/8

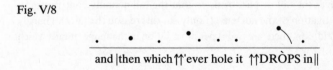

and |then whichʔʔ'ever hole it ʔʔDRÒPS in||

The level heads in *so are the vast majority of the British people* and *its rights must be respected* (F) belong in category (ai). Category (b) is typical of some American accents.

Note that these head classifications are wholly independent of nuclear type. One can conceivably find any type head with any type nucleus.[7] This is contrary to tune-based analyses, e.g. O'Connor/Arnold ([2]1973), according to whom a low head occurs only before a low rise, a falling head only before a fall–rise, a rising head only before a high fall and a high head before any type nucleus except a fall–rise. However, it is fully compatible with a feature-based approach to intonation (Ch. IV §2.4).

---

[7] *Pace* Crystal, according to whom a 'substantially pitch-prominent nucleus' must accompany falling head type C (1969:229).

## 1.3    Pre-head

The pre-head consists by definition of any and all unstressed syllables which precede the head (or the nucleus, if there is no head). These are usually few in number, the maximum being approximately five (Crystal 1969:233). In principle, pre-head syllables may be pitched anywhere in the voice range. Crystal establishes categories for high $/^-/$, extra-high $/^=/$, mid $/\_/$ and extra-low $/\_/$ pre-heads, the norm – not marked in notation – being considered pre-heads pitched at a level slightly below onset.[8] However, there is some evidence that the pitch of unstressed syllables may be influenced by *tonal sandhi*, "the tendency for the pitch of a syllable at one level to be assimilated to the pitch of a syllable at another level" (Brown/Currie/Kenworthy 1980:37). If so, then it is conceivable that pre-head height is at least partially determined by the following onset. In sum, there is no real consensus yet on whether pre-head pitch level is responsible for significant contrasts in English or not. We shall assume that if pre-heads are distinctive, then two 'marked' levels, in addition to the norm, will suffice. Therefore, noticeably high or low pre-heads will be transcribed here with $/\text{h}/$ or $/\text{l}/$.

## 1.4    Tail

The tail, defined as any rhythmically stressed and/or unstressed syllables following the nucleus, has long been considered the least significant part of the tone-unit, because the pitch contour of its syllables is said to be determined by the type of nucleus to which it is attached: syllables following a falling nucleus automatically continue the fall; syllables following a rising nucleus automatically continue the rise. However, this ignores the fact that nuclei – unless they are monosyllabic – are more often than not 'spread' over the tail or part of it, so that the tail actually contributes to the shape and identification of the nucleus. If only for this reason the tail can hardly be ignored. But, in addition, there are two types of variation in the shape of tails which are significant.

### 1.4.1 Slope

The prolongation of the nuclear movement may entail a relatively steep slope $/\setminus/$ or $//$ / with tail syllables moving *sharply* away from the nucleus or its starting point (and often reaching the upper or lower limits of the voice-range). Or the tail syllables may form a more gently slanting slope $/\diagdown/$ or $/\diagup/$ with final pitches moving *gradually* away from the nucleus or its starting point. Finally, tail syllables may have little or no slope, levelling out the nuclear movement instead $/\diagdown\_\_/$ or $/\frown/$. These are sometimes called 'flattened' tails.

(i) *Steep slope.* This is most perceptible in a long tail accompanying wide nuclear movement:[9]

---

[8] Hence the slight step-up in pitch which generally characterizes onsets.

[9] Obviously length of tail interacts with slope. A very steep descent (or rise) on a lengthy tail

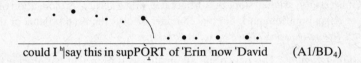

could I ʰ|say this in supPǪRT of 'Erin 'now 'David     (A1/BD₄)

Steep slope is characteristic of (though not restricted to) so-called 'contrastive stress' (Ch. VII §2.2.2.2). Thus:

Fig. V/10

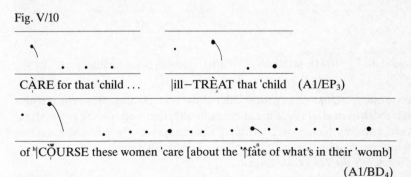

CÀRE for that 'child ...     |ill−TRÈ̤AT that 'child    (A1/EP₃)

of ʰ|CǪ̈URSE these women 'care [about the '↑fàte of what's in their 'womb]

(A1/BD₄)

The same utterances with gradual slope in the tail would 'mean' something else, in that they would no longer be appropriate in these contexts. Since steep slope (often in conjunction with low endpoint, §1.4.2) distinguishes contrastive from non-contrastive intonational contours, it should be marked in notation. We propose to indicate steep slope by a short vertical prolongation line immediately under or over the falling or rising notation mark / ˥ /, / ˩ /, e.g. *CÀRE for that child ... ill-TRÈAT that child; of CǪURSE these women care about the fate of what's in their womb.*

(ii) *Gradual slope.* This could be considered the unmarked variant, or the norm for tails. Examples include:

Fig. V/11

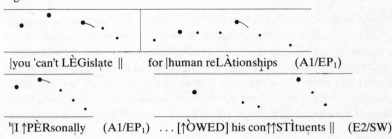

|you 'can't LÈGislate ||     for |human reLÀtionsḫips    (A1/EP₁)

ʰ|I ↑PÈRsonaḷly    (A1/EP₁)  ... [↑ỌWED] his con↑↑STÌtuęnts ||    (E2/SW)

will often mean that the final syllables level out, because the limits of the voice-range have been reached. Levelling of this pre-determined sort, however, does not function semantically like the independently chosen flattened tail described in §1.4.1 (iii).

If necessary, gradual slope may be notated with a vertical prolongation of the falling or rising notation mark but placed under or over the final syllable of the tail, e.g. *PÈRsonally, conSTÌtuents, reLÀtionships.*

(iii) *Flattening.* This may occur automatically if a speaker has already reached the limits of his/her voice-range before completing a tone-unit. However, level or flattened tails are also available for conscious linguistic exploitation. Examples include:

Fig. V/12

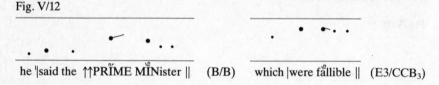

he |said the ↑↑PRĬME MĬNister ||   (B/B)   which |were făllible ||   (E3/CCB₃)

In these examples, flattening occurs with narrow nuclear tones. However, it is also possible with normal and wide nuclei. Semantically, flattened tails are said to signal sarcasm, boredom, monotony, etc. (Ch. X). Flattened tails can be indicated in notation by a horizontal prolongation of the falling or rising notation mark / ⌣ /, / ⌢ /. Thus: *I didn't say THAT Mr Powell.*

In conjunction with falling tones, flattened tails approximate to what Ladd (1978) has called *stylized falls.* These are "stepping-down sequence(s) of two level pitches" (1978:266) which, he claims, function as a signal of routineness, predictability or stereotype. For instance:

Fig. V/13

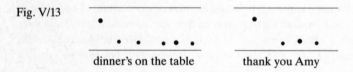

dinner's on the table     thank you Amy

Such falls may be stylized even more by the use of appropriate rhythmic patterns, fixed pitch intervals and/or sing-song voice quality, the result being vocal *chants.*

### 1.4.2 Endpoint

In addition to slope, the pitch level which the endpoint of a tail reaches is significant.[10] Recent research into the perception of tone has shown that the human ear easily distinguishes a pitch contour with an extreme endpoint from one with a non-extreme endpoint (Gandour 1978). In speech, these extremes are provided by the upper and lower limits of the voice-range. With respect to tails, we can distinguish those which descend or rise to the outer limits of the voice-range from those which stop short of these limits. And the difference between the two has distinctive function in English. Compare, for example:

---

[10] We thus second Trim in his opinion that "both the starting point and end point (of nuclei) are variable". In his view, "the higher the starting point, the greater the degree of emotional involvement. The lower the end point, the greater the degree of definiteness and conclusiveness" (1970:265).

Fig. V/14

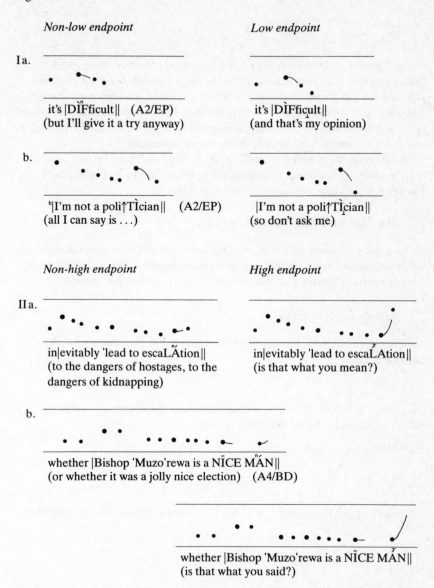

*Non-low endpoint*

Ia.

it's |DÌFficult|| (A2/EP)
(but I'll give it a try anyway)

*Low endpoint*

it's |DÌFfiçult||
(and that's my opinion)

b.

ʰ|I'm not a poli↑TÌcian|| (A2/EP)
(all I can say is . . .)

|I'm not a poli↑TÌçian||
(so don't ask me)

*Non-high endpoint*

IIa.

in|evitably 'lead to escaLÃtion||
(to the dangers of hostages, to the
dangers of kidnapping)

*High endpoint*

in|evitably 'lead to escaLÃtion||
(is that what you mean?)

b.

whether |Bishop 'Muzo'rewa is a NĪCE MÃN||
(or whether it was a jolly nice election) (A4/BD)

whether |Bishop 'Muzo'rewa is a NĪCE MÃN||
(is that what you said?)

Notice that a non-extreme endpoint cannot necessarily be equated with narrow pitch movement. Although they overlap in (Ia), the non-low endpoint in (Ib), for instance, accompanies normal pitch range. And non-low endpoint can also co-occur with wide pitch-range.

This view represents a departure from Crystal (1969:214), where it is argued that in order to describe the movement from pitch level A to pitch level B

89

Fig. V/15     A ----\
                    \
                     \
                      \----B

it is sufficient to know the *height* of A and the *width* of the movement (three widths being permitted, wide – normal – narrow). But even a so-called wide pitch movement may stop short of the extreme. Seen the other way around, a narrow pitch movement may have an extreme endpoint, which is different from a non-extreme one. In light of the fact that extreme vs. non-extreme endpoint has contrastive function in English, its recognition appears not only desirable but indispensable.[11]

In notation, we propose to indicate an extreme endpoint by adding a small horizontal line representing one extreme of the voice range to the nuclear mark, e.g. *I'm not a poliTĬcian, inevitably lead to escaLÃtion.*[12]

## 2.    Nuclear and non-nuclear tones

We turn now to a closer examination of nuclear tones and those non-nuclear tones which most closely resemble nuclei, in particular glissandos. Nuclear tones fall into three categories depending on their shape: simple, complex, and compound.

### 2.1   Simple nuclear tones

These are single pitch 'movements' exclusively in one direction: down (*fall*), up (*rise*) or straight ahead (*level*).

### 2.1.1 Fall

Simple falls are characterized by a downward pitch movement on or starting on a nuclear prominent syllable. Examples include:

Fig. V/16

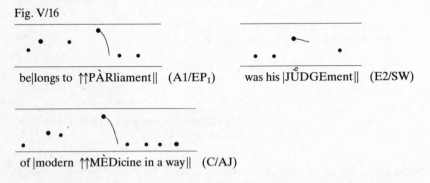

be|longs to ⇈PÀRliament‖   (A1/EP₁)          was his |JÛDGEment‖   (E2/SW)

of |modern ⇈MÈDicine in a way‖   (C/AJ)

---

[11] Cf. also Liberman (1975), who points out contrasts such as *cover your EARS* (with non-low termination, a jocular admonition) and *cover your EARS* (with low termination, 'I've told you a thousand times') (1975: 156ff.). Cf. also Bald 1979/80.

[12] These examples illustrate the frequent combination of steep slope and extreme endpoint. However, gradual slope and extreme endpoint are also conceivable: ' ⌐ , ⸳ ᵀ .

Phonetically speaking, these falls may differ somewhat. For example, the fall on *Parliament* is ⟍ , whereas the fall on *judgment* is more ⟍ . However, much as the 'tadpole' representation suggests, they all have in common a point of maximal intensity, usually perceived as loudness, initiating the descending pitch movement. Simple falls are indicated in notation by placing a / ˋ/ mark above the prominent syllable.

Traditionally some analysts have subdivided the category of fall into *low fall* and *high fall* (e.g. Schubiger, O'Connor/Arnold). Others, however, have not thought it necessary to establish two separate categories (e.g. Palmer, Kingdon). In Kingdon's words, for instance, the fall begins "according to its tonetic context, anywhere from the top to near the bottom, and finishes on the bottom, of the normal voice range" (1958b: 9).[13]

A prosodic feature approach to intonation (Ch. IV §2.4) avoids this problem and at the same time allows for greater delicacy of description. In keeping with the convention of judging the pitch height of syllables in the tone-unit with respect to the preceding syllable(s) and ultimately with respect to onset level, Crystal proposes to determine the height of the starting point of nuclear movement similarly. Thus, the system of arrows /↑/, /↑↑/, /→/, /↓/ is extended to nuclear syllables as well. This has the advantage of economizing on notation symbols as well as increasing descriptive adequacy.

In addition to specifying from what pitch level nuclear falls begin their descent, it is also necessary to specify how far they go. In order to do this, Crystal proposes to use *width* of pitch movement as a measure. Thus a nuclear fall may be very narrow (in which case a small /n/ is placed above the /ˋ/ mark), or it may be very wide (a /w/ is placed above the /ˋ/), or it may simply have normal pitch width (in which case no additional marking is necessary).[14] Together, pitch height and pitch width provide for a total of fifteen different types of fall, as the following table indicates:

Fig. V/17  Pitch width

|  | ˋ | ˋn | ˋw |
|---|---|---|---|
| ↑ | ↑ˋ | ↑ˋn | ↑ˋw |
| ↑↑ | ↑↑ˋ | ↑↑ˋn | ↑↑ˋw |
| ↓ | ↓ˋ | ↓ˋn | ↓ˋw |
| → | →ˋ | →ˋn | →ˋw |

(row labels above are under "Pitch height")

Phonetically, the number of falls is much greater, since nuclear pitch height is relative to the height of the preceding syllable, which itself may vary greatly.

---

[13] Kingdon thus makes no provision for arrested falls, i.e. falls with non-low endpoint.
[14] It could be argued that given the specification of the end-point (§1.4.2) and that of the starting point of a nuclear glide, it is superfluous to distinguish the *width* of the pitch glide. Until this point is clarified, however, we prefer to err on the side of over-specification.

Pitch height and pitch width together are referred to as *pitch range*. [All nuclear contrasts are assumed to be describable in terms of pitch range and pitch direction, or *tone*.] Describing nuclei in terms of these two features is justified by the fact that pitch height and pitch width are 'externally motivated', i.e. also found to be necessary elsewhere in the descriptive system. Pitch height, for instance, is needed for the specification of other stressed syllables in the tone-unit, and both pitch height and pitch width can be used to describe contrasts over wider stretches of utterance (§3.2).

Phonetically speaking, the fall may take on different configurations depending on 'subphonemic' factors such as presence of an on-glide, position of the point of maximal intensity in the contour, and accompanying increase or decrease of intensity. Palmer and others have noted, for instance, that a fall may be preceded by a slight rise in pitch: ⌐\ . This is known as *on-glide*.[15] The point of maximal intensity, represented by the tadpole's head, may also vary, coming early or late in the falling contour: e.g. \ or \ .[16] Likewise, perceptually different kinds of fall can be produced depending on whether the level of accompanying intensity increases or not. A concomitant increase of intensity will result in a convex fall (blocks representing intensity, a straight line representing frequency):

Fig. V/18

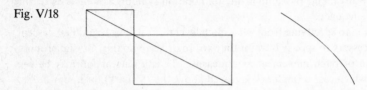

A concomitant decrease of intensity will result in a concave fall:

Fig. V/19

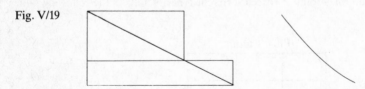

These two types of fall have been documented for French and may have a phonological function there (Rossi 1978). Whether or not they are functionally distinct in British English has yet to be determined (cf., however, Pilch 1980).

Phonetic exponence of the type sketched above may account for some of the identifying characteristics of the intonation of different socio-regional varieties (e.g. Liverpudlian vs. RP) or of different languages (e.g. French vs. English).

### 2.1.2 Rise

Rises are typified by upward pitch movement on or beginning on a prominent syllable. For example:

---

[15] If the on-glide is extensive ⌐\ , then the nucleus becomes a complex rise–fall (§2.2.2).
[16] The latter of these is said to be typical of Liverpudlian English (Knowles 1982).

Fig. V/20

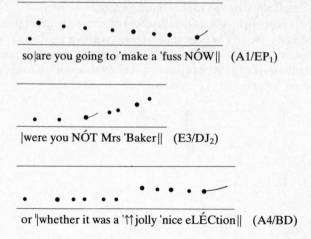

so|are you going to 'make a 'fuss NÓW‖   (A1/EP₁)

|were you NÓT Mrs 'Baker‖   (E3/DJ₂)

or '|whether it was a '↑↑jolly 'nice eLÉCtion‖   (A4/BD)

In RP there may be a short falling on-glide ![glide], but the point of maximal intensity comes relatively early in the contour. Rises are particularly likely to be 'spread' unless they occur on final monosyllables. In notation, rising nuclei have a / ′/ mark above the prominent syllable.

   Traditionally intonation specialists have distinguished *low rises* from *high rises*. However, the phonetic specifications of these two subcategories have often been at odds. According to Palmer, for instance, a low rise starts low and rises only slightly, whereas a *high rise starts low* and rises high (i.e. higher than a low rise). Halliday too has a tonic which rises (often from mid-low) to a high pitch and another which rises (from low) only to mid-low. On the other hand, according to Kingdon, Schubiger and O'Connor/Arnold, the low rise starts low and rises to approximately the middle of the voice-range, whereas the *high rise starts at mid level* and rises almost to the top of the voice-range. In other words, for Palmer it is the ending point of the glide which determines its categorization, whereas for others it is the starting point (Schubiger 1958:11).

   Just as with falls, a prosodic feature approach avoids this dilemma. Rises are characterized in terms of two pitch-range features, height and width, which produce a matrix of fifteen possible types:

Fig. V/21          Pitch width

| | ′ | ⁿ′ | ʷ′ |
|---|---|---|---|
| ↑ | ↑′ | ↑ⁿ′ | ↑ʷ′ |
| ↑↑ | ↑↑′ | ↑↑ⁿ′ | ↑↑ʷ′ |
| ↓ | ↓′ | ↓ⁿ′ | ↓ʷ′ |
| → | →′ | →ⁿ′ | →ʷ′ |

Pitch height (vertical label on left side)

Here too actual phonetic variation is much greater.

The phonetic configuration of rises depends on features similar to those mentioned for falls. An on-glide may be present (if it is too extensive, however, a fall−rise will be perceived); the position of the point of maximal intensity may vary; and depending on whether the level of accompanying intensity decreases or increases, a convex or concave curve may result:

Fig. V/22

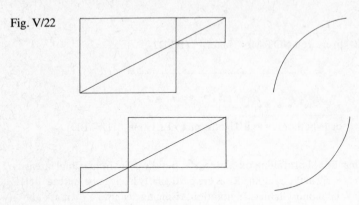

### 2.1.3 Level

Level nuclei are obviously not characterized by pitch movement. However, they can be distinguished from non-nuclear static tones by virtue of their greater length and loudness. Within a pre-established tone-unit, they are the most prominent of all the static syllables. For example:

Fig. V/23

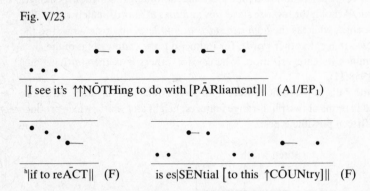

|I see it's ↑↑NŌTHing to do with [PĀRliament]||   (A1/EP₁)

ʰ|if to reĀCT||   (F)        is es|SĒNtial [to this ↑CŌUNtry]||   (F)

Many of these level nuclei could be replaced by rising tones. In fact, sometimes it is hard to determine auditorily whether a nucleus is strictly level or slightly rising; whether we choose one or the other or transcribe both /‹/ is, however, of only secondary importance, since they are functionally equivalent in these instances.[17]

---

[17] Sweet, too, sees an identity between rising and level tones in terms of function (³1900:32) (cf. also Gibbon 1976:102f.).

On the other hand, level tones may be functionally equivalent to (non-low) falling tones, judging from examples such as the following, where they appear to substitute for interrupted falls in enumerations:

Fig. V/24

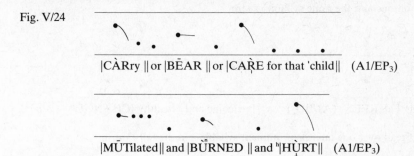

|CÀRry || or |BĒAR || or |CAR̀E for that 'child||   (A1/EP₃)

|MŪTilated|| and |BŪRNED || and ʰ|HÙRT||   (A1/EP₃)

Here too it may be difficult to determine auditorily whether the tone is strictly level or narrowly falling. Rather than decide the issue arbitrarily, it may be preferable to transcribe / ⤙/.

Because level tones sometimes function similarly to rising and to falling tones, we cannot call them variants of one or the other category exclusively. We could treat them as variants of both categories, but this would imply that they establish no significant contrasts on their own. Yet according to Crystal, level nuclei may communicate a meaning of boredom or sarcasm (1969:216), and according to Brazil/Coulthard/Johns (1980), they are used by speakers/readers 'oriented towards the language', i.e. concerned to transmit information about the linguistic organization of the utterance − to mark breaks in the message which are not potential completion points, syntactically speaking (1980:88ff.). There thus appears to be good reason for making level tones an independent category.

On the other hand, it must be admitted that level tones are often hard to identify, particularly in hesitant speech, where lengthening and pausing tend to render non-nuclear static syllables prominent in spite of themselves, so to speak. However, hesitant speech presents special problems of its own, not only in the recognition of nuclear tones (Currie 1981) but also in the recognition of tone-unit boundaries (Brown/Currie/Kenworthy 1980:41ff.), and it would be inconsistent to bar level tones (and only level tones) for this reason.

## 2.2   Complex nuclear tones

These are pitch movements first in one direction and then in the other on or beginning on a single nuclear prominent syllable. The most common types are the bidirectional fall−rise and rise−fall, but polydirectional movements may also be observed, e.g. fall−rise−fall, rise−fall−rise, etc.[18]

---

[18] Cf., for instance: |very limited fórm|| (E1/HW₅).

### 2.2.1 Fall–rise

The fall–rise is probably the most common of the complex nuclear tones. It is characterized by a phonetically prominent fall followed by a phonetically less prominent rise on one and the same syllable, as in:

Fig. V/25

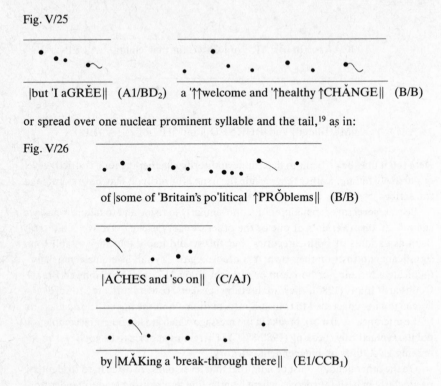

|but 'I aGRĚE‖   (A1/BD₂)   a '↑↑welcome and '↑healthy ↑CHĂNGE‖   (B/B)

or spread over one nuclear prominent syllable and the tail,[19] as in:

Fig. V/26

of |some of 'Britain's po'litical ↑PRŎblems‖   (B/B)

|AČHES and 'so on‖   (C/AJ)

by |MĂKing a 'break-through there‖   (E1/CCB₁)

The notation mark for fall–rise nuclei /ˇ/ is placed above the syllable with the prominent fall.

Although it is the first part of the complex fall–rise which is phonetically the more prominent, the second part, the rise, determines its functional category. Given two major classes of tones, falling and rising, it is to the latter that fall–rises belong.

There has been some confusion in the past concerning the difference between a *complex* fall–rise and a *compound* fall + rise (§2.3.1). As Crystal points out, however, the two are quite distinctly different (1969:220); compare, for example:

  he WĂNTS to (but can't)   vs.   he WÀNTS TWÓ (so he can't throw them all away)
                                                      (Sharp 1958:141)

---

[19] The longer the tail, the greater the number of phonetic realizations. In *by mǎking a break-through there* the rising portion could conceivably start anywhere from *-ing* to *there* (cf. also Jassem 1972). It is in cases like these that the notational system begins to break down, since a non-ambiguous reconstruction of the melodic line is no longer assured.

Fall–rises must therefore be distinguished from falls + rises. The criteria according to which this distinction is made are discussed in §2.3.

### 2.2.2 Rise–fall

Similar to its fall–rise counterpart, the rise–fall is characterized by a bidirectional movement on or beginning on the nuclear prominent syllable. Examples of rise–fall on one syllable include:

Fig. V/27

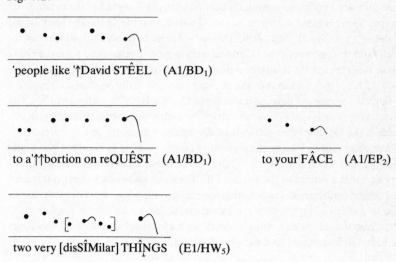

'people like '↑David STÊEL    (A1/BD₁)

to a'↑↑bortion on reQUÊST    (A1/BD₁)          to your FÂCE    (A1/EP₂)

two very [disSÎMilar] THÎNGS    (E1/HW₅)

Examples of rise–fall spread over the tail include:

Fig. V/28

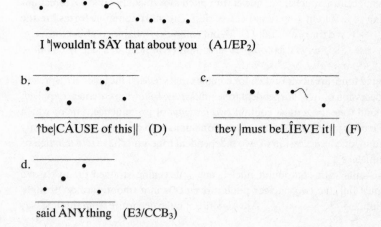

a.

I ʰ|wouldn't SÂY that about you    (A1/EP₂)

b.

↑be|CÂUSE of this‖    (D)

c.

they |must beLÎEVE it‖    (F)

d.

said ÂNYthing    (E3/CCB₃)

As the above examples illustrate, a rise−fall with following tail may be of two phonetic types. In type I, the rise−fall occurs as a glide on the stressed syllable, with the center of maximal energy coming late in the contour, e.g. (a) or (c). In type II, the center of maximal energy comes early; the rise is a pitch glide or jump upwards from the stressed to the following unstressed syllable, with the fall occurring between the next two unstressed syllables as in (b) and (d) (cf. also Kingdon 1958b:133ff. and Schubiger 1980). All rise−fall nuclei, however, are indicated in transcription with a / ˆ / mark above the stressed syllable.

According to Crystal, the first element of all complex tones is phonetically the more prominent. Yet there is some indication that the rise−fall may deviate from this norm. There is general agreement, for instance, that the unmarked form of the rise−fall is ⌒\ (Crystal 1969: 218). This would seem to imply that, at least as far as pitch range is concerned, the falling element is more pronounced than the rising element. It is perhaps for this reason that rise−falls are frequently interchangeable with /↑`/. According to Crystal, the two are "not normally confused" because a rise−fall has a somewhat delayed maximum of loudness: ⌒\ rather than •\ and because its on-glide is more pronounced: ⌒\ rather than •\ . However, in our experience the two are often difficult to distinguish (unless the rise is 'spread').

These observations lend support to more recent views (e.g. Gunter 1972, Ladd 1978, Schubiger 1980) that the rise−fall is actually not a distinctive tone itself but simply a phonetic variant of the nuclear fall. The contrast between the two is indeed more gradient (reflecting degree of involvement, say) than discrete. The same cannot be said of the fall−rise, which plays an important functional role in English quite distinct from that of the rise. But we are left with a lopsided system of nuclear tones if the rise−fall is demoted to a variant of the fall.


## 2.3  Compound nuclear tones

The major defining feature of this category as opposed to that of complex tones is the presence within one and the same tone-unit of *two* maxima of prominence with so-called 'endocentric' nuclei, i.e. nuclei with pitch movement in opposite directions or belonging to different functional categories. The most common forms are the fall + rise /`+´/ and the rise + fall /´+`/, but complex + simple combinations, e.g. rise−fall + rise /ˆ+´/ as well as complex + complex combinations, e.g. rise−fall + fall−rise /ˆ+ˇ/ may also be observed.

Compound tones are not mistaken for complex tones (even if the latter are 'spread') nor for a succession of two independent tone-units if the following criteria are applied:
(i) Compound tone-units must contain *two maxima* of prominence, one of which is typically *more prominent* than the other. Tone-units with complex nuclei have only one maximum, and a succession of two independent tone-units have two maxima of equal prominence.
(ii) In tone-units with compound nuclei, any intervening stressed or unstressed syllables must link the two nuclear pitch movements in a smooth arc or 'trough' configuration; e.g. \ . . . . . / . Any significant pitch departure from this line, say

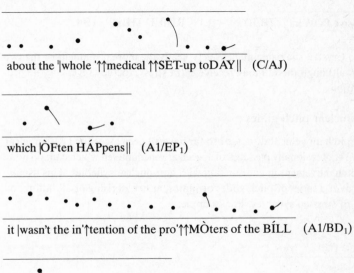 signals the presence of a tone-unit boundary before the step-up in pitch and a compound tone-unit is excluded by definition.

(iii) There should be no other evidence of a tone-unit boundary between the two nuclei of a compound tone-unit. Pauses and rhythmic breaks are, for instance, excluded in this position. If they do occur, then the nuclei must be interpreted as belonging to two separate tone-units.

### 2.3.1 Fall + rise

In this type of compound tone-unit the first nuclear prominent syllable bears a fall and the second a rise. There may or may not be intervening stressed or unstressed syllables. For example:

Fig. V/29

about the ⁾|whole '↑↑medical ↑↑SÈT-up toDÁY‖ (C/AJ)

which |ÒFten HÁPpens‖ (A1/EP₁)

it |wasn't the in'↑tention of the pro'↑↑MÒters of the BÍLL (A1/BD₁)

col|"LÈCtive de'cision-MÁKing‖ (B/B)

The fall is usually more prominent phonetically than the rise. The rise, however, determines the functional category to which this compound nucleus belongs.

### 2.3.2 Rise + fall

Here the first nucleus is a rise, the second a fall. For example:

Fig. V/30

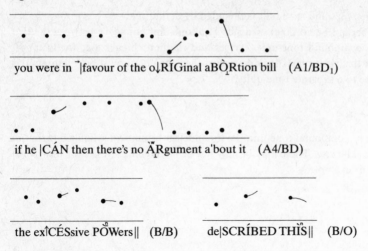

you were in ⁻|favour of the o↓RÍGinal aBȮRtion bill    (A1/BD₁)

if he |CÁN then there's no ÄRgument a'bout it    (A4/BD)

the ex↑CÉSsive PŎWers‖    (B/B)        de|SCRÍBED THĬS‖    (B/O)

According to Crystal, the rising nucleus is typically the more prominent of the two phonetically, although the fall may receive extra stress, thereby reversing the prominence relation.

## 2.4   Non-nuclear pitch glides

The types of pitch movement discussed so far have all been associated with nuclear prominence. Yet occasionally passages of speech are encountered which contain quite noticeable pitch movement in conjunction with non-nuclear syllables. This usually takes the form of a series of pitch glides or jumps, either all rising or all falling, on a succession of stressed syllables. For example:

Fig. V/31

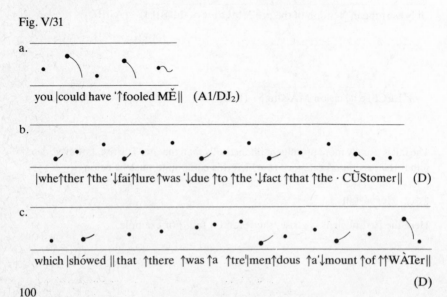

a.

you |could have '↑fooled MĚ‖    (A1/DJ₂)

b.

|whe↑ther ↑the '↓fai↑lure ↑was '↓due ↑to ↑the '↓fact ↑that ↑the · CŬStomer‖    (D)

c.

which |shówed ‖ that ↑there ↑was ↑a ↑tre'|men↑dous ↑a'↓mount ↑of ↑↑WÀTer‖

(D)

d.

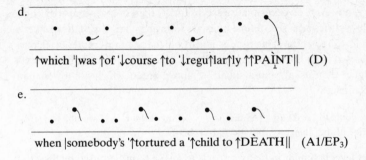

↑which '|was ↑of '↓course ↑to '↓regu↑lar↑ly ↑↑PAI̞NT|| (D)

e.

when |somebody's '↑tortured a '↑child to ↑DÈATH|| (A1/EP₃)

In cases such as (e), where all the pitch movements in the tone-unit are similar, the nucleus is defined as that syllable whose movement is maximally prominent.

Crystal proposes to call this phenomenon either *glissando* or *spiky* depending on whether glides or jumps are used, respectively. However, since pitch glides and jumps are not distinguished elsewhere in the system (§1.1.2), it hardly seems necessary to do so here. We shall therefore refer to both types of non-nuclear pitch movement as 'glissando'. In notation, single quotation marks will be used to mark that part of the utterance demonstrating glissando and the type will be noted in the margin:

'falling
glissando'      'you 'could have 'fooled MĔ'


## 3.  External tone-unit organization

The categories described so far have been internal tone-unit categories — and indeed most intonation analysts have restricted their attention to these. Yet tone-units rarely occur in isolation; most often they appear in succession, forming strings of varying length. Naturally it is conceivable that such strings consist of unrelated tone-units in temporal juxtaposition. If so, there would be little use in extending intonational description beyond the single tone-unit. However, judging from what we know, for instance, about the interrelatedness of sentences in texts, this is not very likely. Indeed, listening to strings of tone-units and comparing them to one another will convince any careful observer that there is intonational structure beyond the tone-unit.

Very little is known as yet about external tone-unit organization, but at least three aspects appear to be important: relative onset level, polysyllabic pitch-range features, and tonal subordination.


### 3.1  Relative onset level

In §1.2.1 we pointed out that most speakers have a preferred pitch level at which they tend to begin tone-units, usually somewhere around the middle of the voice range. This level is assumed to be constant for a given speaker and is unmarked in notation.

Speakers may, however, on occasion use exceptionally high or low onsets. By comparing onset levels in a succession of tone-units, we form an impression of the speaker's normal onset level and at the same time establish which tone-units represent departures (up or down) from this norm. In notation, a small $/h/$ is placed above onsets which are higher than usual, and a small $/l/$ above onsets which are lower than usual. For example:

that |you're going to ↑TĔND up || (A1/EP₁)    ʰ|I don't think ↑MỲ womb|| (A1/EP₁)
who was ˈ|one of the ˈ↑biggest proMÔters|| (A1/BD₁)

Relative onset level is similar in many respects to *key*, a term first used by Sweet at the beginning of this century: "each sentence, or sentence group, has a general pitch or key of its own" (³1906:70). Recently the term has been reintroduced by Brazil (1975, 1978) to refer to the choice of three possible onset levels: high, mid and low. However, whereas onsets in Crystal's system are discrete levels in the speaker's voice-range and are constant for a given speaker, for Brazil onset, or key, is wholly relative:

> ... mid key is not defined as the *norm* for the speaker − instead key choices are made and recognized with reference to the comparable pitch choice of the immediately preceding tone unit. (Brazil/Coulthard/Johns 1980:24)

There are both advantages and disadvantages to adopting a wholly relative scale for onset level. One of the advantages is that in contrast to a system with fixed levels, perceptible differences in onset height can be recorded more accurately. Consider, for instance, a sequence of tone-units with the following onsets:

Fig. V/32

In a relative system if onset A is high, onset B would be mid. In a system of fixed levels, however, both these onsets would probably represent the 'norm', since neither is extreme enough to justify $/h/$ or $/l/$. That is, in a system with fixed levels, one may be forced to put an onset which is perceptibly higher or lower than the preceding onset in the same category with it, if their differential happens not to cross category boundaries.

On the other hand, there are also a number of problems connected with a wholly relative approach to onset:

(i) If every level is determined with respect to the preceding onset level, how do we establish the height of the very first onset? A strictly relative system which refers backwards makes this a theoretical impossibility.

(ii) It is difficult to know how successive onsets at the *same* pitch level can be handled unequivocally with the three categories high, mid, low. Consider, for instance, the following succession of onsets:

Fig. V/33

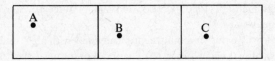

If A is high, B would presumably be mid, whereas if A is mid, B would be low. Assuming the latter, what would onset level C be? If we call it low, do we not imply that it is low with respect to B, i.e. lower than B? Cf:

Fig. V/34

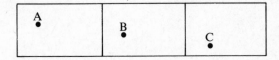

If so, we find ourselves putting two perceptibly different onset heights (one equal to, the other lower than the preceding onset) into one and the same category; yet this was precisely the problem with the fixed-level system.

(iii)  One of the consequences of adopting a wholly relative approach to onset is that skips of two levels, say from high to low, or from low to high, must be excluded on theoretical grounds. [If they were allowed, there would be no way to distinguish a high-to-mid switch from a high-to-low switch.] Consider, however, onset sequences I and II below:

Fig. V/35

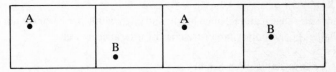

If A were high, B *in both I and II* would be termed mid, although phonetically speaking their levels are quite different. In fact B in I is closer to /ɪ/ (low) in terms of voice-range.

Of course, this latter point would not convince supporters of a strictly relative approach. They would simply claim that such differences are not linguistically significant and therefore need not find expression in the system. But as we have seen elsewhere, there is a good deal to be said for making phonological categories reflect phonetic reality as much as possible (Ch. I §3.2.3). It might therefore be more satisfactory to allow for relativity of onset level but within a minimally fixed framework, say that provided by individual voice-range. Working from the concept of 'normal speaking voice', it would be possible, for instance, to ascertain the level of the first onset with respect to voice-range and describe subsequent fluctuation in terms of 'higher than', 'lower than' or 'the same as' with respect to the preceding onset. [The system of arrows could perhaps be adopted here as well.]

If we do relax onset conventions and allow for more variation, then the way is open to describing the sequences which successive tone-units appear to form in speech. Brazil (1978) and Brazil/Coulthard/Johns (1980), for instance, posit a phonological unit above the tone-unit termed *pitch sequence*, which "begins immediately following a tone unit with low termination and includes all succeeding tone units until the next one with low termination'' (1980:61). [Low termination refers to a nuclear pitch glide with low starting point.[20]]

A pitch sequence on this view may theoretically *start* with high, mid or low onset; however, it must always *end* with low termination. For instance, the following would be examples of pitch sequence (for economy of space, only onset and nucleus are notated):

Fig. V/36 (A1/EP₁)

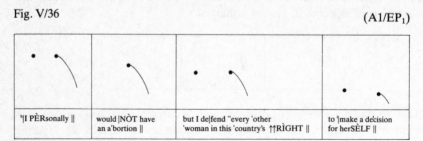

| | | | |
|---|---|---|---|
| ᵸ|I PÈRsonally \|\| | would \|NÒT have an a'bortion \|\| | but I de\|fend "every 'other 'woman in this 'country's ↑↑RÌGHT \|\| | to '\|make a de'cision for herSÈLF \|\| |

We return to pitch sequences and other units of intonational organization beyond the tone-unit in Ch. XI §2.1.

## 3.2 Polysyllabic pitch-range features

The pitch-range features, pitch height and pitch width, are pertinent not only to single syllables but to polysyllabic stretches of utterance as well.

### 3.2.1 Polysyllabic pitch height

Stretches of utterance, and frequently a succession of tone-units, may be set off from surrounding tone-units by the use of *extra high* or *extra low* pitch. In notation the stretch of utterance affected is enclosed in single quotation marks and tagged as either 'high' or 'low' in the margin. For example:

'low'  and I 'thinking that there was a very minor problem and she was probably you know one of the few people this had ever happened to' (A3/EP)

'high'  'I didn't say that Mr Powell' (E3/CCB₃)

Note that polysyllabic 'high' or 'low' is not equivalent to high or low onset. In the latter case only the pitch height of the first stressed syllable is affected. 'High' or 'low', on the other hand, imply that the whole tone-unit or succession of tone-units has shifted up or down in pitch-range. This is closer to what we mean musically when we say a melody has 'changed key'.

---

[20] There is some confusion as to whether the 'low' of low termination is to be understood relatively (if so, in relation to what? preceding prominent syllable? preceding key? preceding termination?) or absolutely (say, in terms of speaker voice-range). In the following we shall rather arbitrarily assume that 'low' means low with respect to preceding key choice, or, in the absence of a separate onset, with respect to preceding termination choice.

The polysyllabic contrasts mentioned so far are similar in that they may equally as well occur within the tone-unit. The assumption is, however, that if they do span two or more tone-units, these are 'bound' together in a way that other tone-units are not.

A second set of polysyllabic contrasts, however, is encountered only over a series of tone-units. As frequently attested, tone-units may form sequences which *descend* or *ascend* in terms of pitch height. Consider, for instance:

'descend'   'of wise leaders have been unable to bring the nation to its senses' (B/B)

'descend'   'it's Tuesday July the seventh it's the Daily Express and that's David Jack who reported it' (E3/DJ$_3$)

In both these instances, each tone-unit is somewhat lower than the preceding one with respect to over-all pitch height, so that a descending sequence is formed.

### 3.2.2 Polysyllabic pitch width

In addition to pitch height features, stretches of utterance may also display an over-all widening or narrowing of pitch contrasts. The extreme of narrowing is monotone, which may also be encountered over a succession of tone-units. For instance:

'wide'       'I didn't have anything to do with Parliament
             I'm taking no issues in it at all' (A1/EP$_2$ – BD$_2$)

'narrow'     'was to open a small community center for mothers and children with toddlers who were very lonely and isolated like I'd been when I was bringing up children especially in London' (A3/EP)

'monotone'   'and its rights must be respected' (F)

Similar to polysyllabic pitch-height features, 'wide', 'narrow' and 'monotone' consolidate the series of tone-units which they affect by setting them off from surrounding tone-units.

## 3.3   Subordination

Just as the discovery of compound tone-units was a major step towards the recognition of inter-tone-unit relations,[21] so is the theory of tonal subordination as propounded by Crystal/Quirk (1964) and Crystal (1969) a milestone. Developed to account for 'consolidating features' between tone-units, the theory recognizes a superordinate tone-unit (with a superordinate nucleus) which contains at least one subordinate tone-unit (and subordinate nucleus). The criteria which a sequence of tone-units must satisfy in order to qualify as subordination are as follows:
(i) There must be a sequence of at least two nuclear prominences.
(ii) The pitch contours must be 'exocentric', i.e. of the same major category, either rising or falling. [Level tones may substitute for either one.]

---

[21] Trim is to be credited with recognizing that "the fusion of the tail of the first [tone-unit] with the prehead of the second" constitutes a 'consolidating feature' in a sequence of tone-units (1959:27).

(iii) The nuclei must be of differing pitch width (and/or loudness and length).

(iv) There must be no rhythmic break or pause between the two nuclei.

Tone-units which meet these stipulations give the impression of forming a whole (much as compound tone-units do) but contain two *similar* nuclei, one of which is said to be subordinate to the other. Both simple and complex nuclei may enter into subordinate relationships. Thus the following pairs of 'exocentric' nuclei are possible:[22]

Fig. V/37

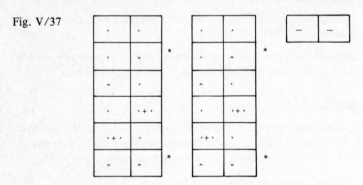

If we add to this list all the possible variants in terms of relative pitch height (the pitch range of the two nuclei may or may not overlap: e.g. ↘ ↖ or ↖ ↘ ), then we come up with at least 26 forms which subordination may take.[23] Some, however, are much more frequent than others.

The question of which nucleus is subordinate to which can usually be decided in terms of general prominence: one nucleus will be louder, longer and have wider pitch range than the other. However, if these three features do not coincide in one nucleus, then pitch width is considered to be the determining factor: the nucleus with the widest pitch movement is superordinate. In the case of level nuclei, loudness and length serve as criteria.

In transcription subordinate tone-units are placed in square brackets within the boundaries of the superordinate unit. There are, however, as yet few guidelines for determining how much material should be included in the subordinate unit (cf. also Crompton 1978). Sometimes, particularly in the case of post-subordination, there are clear phonological signs of the presence of a second tone-unit, e.g. a step-up in pitch at onset. In these cases, the marking of subordinate boundaries presents no difficulty. However, there may be no clear phonological cues at all and one is tempted to place subordinate boundaries in conjunction with lexical or grammatical structure. Potential circularity can perhaps best be avoided by systematically placing brackets around only the nuclear syllable or the word which contains it, in the absence of phonological cues.

---

[22] The pairs marked with / * / are indeed exocentric in that their directly adjacent members are parallel, although they belong to different functional categories.

[23] Crystal reckons 32 just for simple rises and falls by allowing for an 'extra high', 'high' or 'low' beginning point of the subordinate tone with respect to that of the superordinate tone (1969:247).

Examples of subordination include:

I |didn't uh plan ↑↑MẎ career [↑EÌther]|| (A3/BD)
it's ¹|almost im↑↑PÒSsible [to MǪVE them] (A1/BD₁)
¹[THÌNKing] that there was a↑↑VÈRy minor [↑PRÒblem]|| (A3/EP)
is the |LEŇGTH of 'time you have to 'wait for 'treatment [and for an ope↑RẠtion]||
(E3/SW₂) '

Intonational subordination is one of a number of cohesive devices which speakers
employ to link the tone-units of connected speech. We return to a general discussion
of these devices in Ch. XI §2.2.

## 4.   The system and its claims

In this chapter we have attempted to specify at a very basic level which aspects of
the melodic line are relevant for the functioning of the intonational system in English.
To review, if we encounter a melodic line such as

Fig. V/38

this would be analyzed as having four stresses or rhythmic beats, the first of which
is by definition the onset, and the last of which is by virtue of added length, loudness
and pitch movement the nucleus:

Fig. V/39

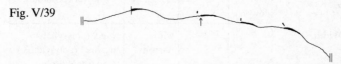

Other melodic lines – such as those below – would be analyzed differently:

Fig. V/40

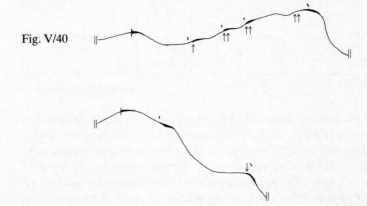

107

The major *categories* which we have found it necessary to postulate are stressed syllable (with a special subcategory for onset), nucleus, and tone-unit, based on the notions of rhythmic prominence, nuclear prominence, and intonational boundary. The stressed syllables constitute a frame for the melodic line; those which are more prominent than others (due to greater loudness, length and/or presence of pitch movement) are said to have nuclear prominence; nuclei are separated from one another by the presence of boundaries (signalled by pauses, rhythmic breaks, phonetic lengthening, etc.), which delimit the tone-units. [Beyond the tone-unit, as we shall see, further units will be necessary (Ch. XI §2.1).]

In addition to these categories, we have made use of two major *features*, pitch direction and pitch range, the latter encompassing height, width, slope and endpoint. The options offered by this descriptive system can be summarized in tabular form as follows:

Fig. V/41   Descriptive categories and features

| Category / Feature | Stressed syllable — Onset | Stressed syllable | Nucleus | Tone-unit | Tone-unit sequence |
|---|---|---|---|---|---|
| Pitch direction | * | * | ` ´ ˇ ˆ etc. | Rising/ falling/ level head | Ascending/ descending (polysylla-bic) |
| Pitch range — Height | high mid low | ↑ ↑↑ → ↓ | ↑ ↑↑ → ↓ | | 'high' (polysyllabic) 'low' (polysyllabic) |
| Width | * | * | wide narrow | | 'wide' (polysyllabic) 'narrow' (polysyllabic) 'monotone' (poly-syllabic) |
| Slope | * | * | steep gradual flattened | | * |
| Endpoint | * | * | low non-low | | * |

* inapplicable by definition

Note that there is a hidden claim behind the establishment of these categories and features, namely that these are the significant aspects of the English intonation system, and indeed *all* and *only* the significant aspects of it. [All phonological systems make similar claims − either explicitly or implicitly − for their categories and features.] By *significant* we mean, with respect to categories, that these are the ones which it is necessary to posit in order to provide an adequate account of the system: no relevant level of generalization has been overlooked nor any irrelevant level established. By *significant* with respect to features we mean that these are distinctive, i.e. the substitution of one for another or the omission of a feature produces a meaningful contrast (Ch. VI §1).

The notion of contrast is a central one in phonological theory. If an element can be replaced by another or omitted altogether in a given environment without producing a meaningful contrast, then that element is non-functional with respect to the phonological system, whose task it is to relate sound patterns to structured combinations of meaningful units in a language. That element belongs simply to the *etic* level of language, the level of material substance. If, however, the substitution of one element for another or its omission in a given environment does produce a meaningful contrast, then that element is functional in the phonological system; it belongs to the *emic* level of language, i.e. to the level of structure or organization. Language in this inherently structural model is seen as a system whose units exist by virtue of their relations to one another.

With respect to intonation, the categories and features posited here belong to the emic level of language. Presence or absence of pitch height, for instance, is considered to be potentially as significant as a falling (vs. a rising) tone. The claim is that with these four major categories and two features a system is formed which provides a motivated, economical and adequate description of the empirical facts. And in accordance with accepted scientific procedure, so long as this hypothesis is not falsified we are justified in proceeding on the basis of it.

## References

Ashby 1978
Bald 1979/80
Brazil 1975
Brazil 1978
Brazil/Coulthard/Johns 1980
Breckenridge 1977
Brown/Currie/Kenworthy 1980
*Cohen/Collier/'t Hart 1982
Crompton 1978
*Crystal 1969 (Ch. 5)
Crystal/Quirk 1964
Gandour 1978
Gussenhoven 1983c
Hadding-Koch 1961
*Halliday 1970a (§1.1–3.3)
Hultzén 1964
Jassem 1972
Kingdon 1958b

Knowles 1982
Ladd 1978 (Ch. 8)
Lee 1956b
Liberman 1975
*O'Connor/Arnold [2]1973 (Ch. 1)
Palmer 1924
Pierrehumbert 1980
Pilch 1980
Rossi 1978
Schubiger 1956
Schubiger 1958
Schubiger 1967
Schubiger 1980
Sharp 1958
Sweet [3]1906
Trim 1959
Trim 1970
Weinrich 1956

# Chapter VI

# Functions of intonation

## 1. Intonation and meaningful contrasts

Until now we have ignored the question of what a *meaningful* contrast is. This is one of the critical issues in prosodic phonology and indeed in linguistics in general. For our purposes, however, an informal understanding will suffice. A meaningful contrast between, say, two minimally distinct intonational configurations is established when native speakers associate different meanings (whether of a descriptive, expressive or social nature; Lyons 1977:50ff.) with different members of the pair, or when different contexts (in a broad sense) would be appropriate for different members of the pair. Contrastive elements usually do not occur in the same environment without a concomitant change of meaning.[1] If two elements do occur interchangeably in the same environment, they are normally not contrastive, unless it can be shown that they contrast in other environments (in which case they are contrastive but neutralizable under certain conditions).

The view of language that we have sketched so far is an inherently *functional* one. In Martinet's words: "... structure can be found in language only, as it were, as an aspect of its functioning" (1962:5). [The term *function* is to be understood here not in its mathematical sense but as an equivalent to 'role', 'the role (of a given element or system) in language communication'.] Logically, those elements which are responsible for the meaningful contrasts in a language system contribute to its functioning in communication, since it is they which transmit the information (with respect to the domain in question). [Whether an element or a system is the only agent which transmits this information as well as how frequently it does so determines its *functional load*, which may be 'heavy' or 'light'.] However, what kind of function a given element or system has in the over-all communicative process can only be determined by looking at the type of contrast which it is capable of establishing, that is at the kind of 'meaning' it is responsible for.

In the following we shall present examples of some of the types of meaningful contrast, and consequently of some of the functions which have been attributed to English intonation.

---

[1] Elements which always occur in different environments and are naturally similar are sometimes viewed as 'allotonic' variants in complementary distribution. For example, it has been suggested that the high level and low level intonation patterns used for 'parentheses' in French are in complementary distribution, since the former occur only after contours which end high and the latter only after contours which end low (Delattre 1969:11).

## 1.1 Informational

Compare:

    a) I saw a MÀN in the garden
        vs.
    b) I SÀW a man in the garden

Whereas (a) could conceivably answer the question 'What happened then?' or 'Who did you see?', (b) could only answer a question such as 'Did you hear a man in the garden?'. That is, (a) and (b) belong in contexts with different information structure. Utterance (a) could theoretically contain all 'new' information, but (b) suggests that *a man in the garden* is given and that *saw* is new (or contrastive) information for the hearer. This type of example has been used to substantiate the claim that intonation choice (here, position of the nucleus) functions to signal the information structure of utterances.

Compare:

    c) there's a MÀN ‖ in the GÀRden ‖
        vs.
    d) there's a MÀN in the garden ‖
        vs.
    e) there's a MÀN [in the GÀRden] ‖    (Crystal 1975a:27)

Here too it has been claimed that intonation (i.e. placement of tone-unit boundaries) contributes to information-related meaning. Whereas (c) clearly presents two bits of information, (d) presents only one, and (e) arguably presents one main and one subordinate bit of information.

## 1.2 Grammatical

Compare:

    (a) |John's going HÒME‖
        vs.
    (b) |John's going HÓME‖

    (c) |shut the DÒOR‖
        vs.
    (d) |shut the DÓOR‖

These are classic illustrations of the so-called grammatical function of intonation. The use of a rising contour as opposed to a falling contour appears to turn a statement (a) into a question (b), a command (c) into a request (d). [The term *grammatical* is used here in the traditional sense, intonational contrasts being related to the notion of sentence-type.]

Compare:

    (a) |George has directions to FÒLlow‖
        vs.
    (b) |George has diRÈCtions to follow‖

In (a) George has been told to follow someone or something; in (b), on the other hand, George must proceed according to a set of instructions. Here, it has been argued, intonation – i.e. position of the nucleus – has syntactic function. [*Syntactic* refers in the modern linguistic sense to the relations obtaining between grammatical categories such as Noun Phrase, Verb Phrase, etc.] That is, intonation is claimed to disambiguate what would otherwise be an ambiguous syntactic construction, *directions to follow* being derivable from either 'directions that George must follow someone' or from 'George must follow the directions'.

## 1.3 Illocutionary

Compare:

(a) <sup>h</sup>|WHỲ don't you 'move to CaliFÓRnia‖

      vs.

(b) <sup>l</sup>|why don't you '↑move to Cali↑↑FǪRnia‖    (Sag/Liberman 1975)

Whereas (a) is appropriate as a genuine inquiry, the intonation of (b) clearly renders it a suggestion (in spite of the interrogative form). It could occur, for instance, in a context such as 'You know, Henry, the climate here is really bad for you. I've got a suggestion ...' In contrast to (a), it need not be followed up by an informative answer such as 'Because it's too expensive there' but could evoke as a possible response 'That's a good idea' or 'I wish you'd stop trying to tell me what to do'. Evidence of this sort has given rise to speculation that intonation has an illocutionary function in English, i.e. that it signals the intentional force of an utterance in a given context.

## 1.4 Attitudinal

Compare:

(a) that's <sup>h</sup>|GRĔAT‖

      vs.

(b) that's <sup>l</sup>|GRÈAT‖

(c) <sup>h</sup>|good MÓRNing‖

      vs.

(d) <sup>l</sup>|good MÒRNing‖    (Gimson <sup>3</sup>1980:276f.)

Examples of this sort are usually cited to illustrate the attitudinal function of intonational choice. [In (a/b) the contrast is one of pitch range, in (c/d) one of pitch range and direction.] Whereas (a) might be appropriate if the speaker were excited, happy or pleased, (b) would be appropriate if the speaker were sad, reserved or being ironic. In greetings, (c) is cheerful and friendly, whereas (d) is routine or perfunctory.

## 1.5 Textual/discourse

Compare:

(a) the <sup>h</sup>|lecture was CÀNcelled ‖ the <sup>h</sup>|speaker was ÌLL‖
      vs.
(b) the <sup>h</sup>|lecture was CÀNcelled ‖ the |speaker was ÌLL‖

(Brazil/Coulthard/Johns 1980:31; cf. Ch. XI Note 13)

This example is illustrative of what could be called the textual function of intonation, *textual* referring to aspects of linguistic organization beyond the sentence and related to the message per se. Whereas (a) is a succession of two (a priori) unrelated propositions, in (b) the second proposition is 'linked' to the first. To put it somewhat differently, the second pair (b) cohere. Since the pairs of sentences are otherwise identical, the contrast must be attributed to intonation (specifically, to onset level).

Compare:

(a) Doctor: it's <sup>h</sup>|DRŶ skin‖ <sup>m</sup>|ÌSn't it‖
    Patient: |MM̀‖      (Brazil/Coulthard/Johns 1980: 75; cf. Ch. XI Note 13)
      vs.
(b) Doctor: it's <sup>h</sup>|DRŶ skin‖ <sup>m</sup>|ÌSn't it‖
    Patient: <sup>h</sup>|MM̀‖

Example (a), taken from an actual doctor–patient exchange, has been used to show the discourse function of intonation, *discourse* referring to the interactive aspects of linguistic organization beyond the sentence. In (a) the patient demonstrates 'compliant' behaviour as a discourse participant by answering 'in key' to the doctor's question (i.e. by using a mid onset following the doctor's mid termination; Ch. V §3.1). Example (b), which is fictive, would be said to illustrate 'non-compliant' behaviour on the part of the patient (a high onset following mid termination).


## 1.6 Indexical

There is evidence, furthermore, that intonation establishes contrasts which make it possible to identify speakers as individuals or as members of different social groups. This has been termed the indexical function of intonation.

For instance, it has been claimed that *sex-group* membership predisposes men to avoid certain intonation levels or patterns which women use (Brend 1972). Some intonations may be indexical for a particular *age-group*, as, for instance, in 'baby talk'. Speakers of many *socio-regional groups* can be identified by their intonation: Liverpudlian intonation has idiosyncratic features which differ from those of Tyneside intonation, for instance. And we may associate typical intonation patterns with certain occupational groups, e.g. preachers, street vendors, etc. (Crystal 1975c:88). Finally, each *individual* has his or her own intonational idiosyncrasies, a fact which makes speaker recognition − even at a distance − a common occurrence.

## 2. On establishing intonation functions

The existence of contrasting pairs such as those above, in which the commutation of one intonational feature with another produces a change in informational, grammatical, illocutionary, attitudinal, and textual/discourse content, suggests on a very general level that intonation may have a role to play in these respective domains. On the other hand, the case should not be allowed to rest on the existence of a few minimal pairs alone. Other stipulations can and have been made for the establishment of intonational function.

### 2.1 Co-occurrence

With respect to the grammatical function of intonation, for instance, some linguists would require not only that the substitution of one intonation for another produce a change in grammatical 'meaning' or function, but that a given intonation regularly accompany that grammatical structure in actual speech. Thus Crystal writes:

> ... grammatical considerations are relevant for the study of intonation in so far as it can be shown that a given grammatical structure has a *regular correlation* with a given intonational pattern, and that a change in intonation causes one to assign a different structural description to an utterance, no other morphological change being necessary. [emphasis added] (1969:254)

That is, depending on the interpretation of *regular*, we must expect to find a given intonation used with a given grammatical construction anywhere from 100% to, say, 50% of the time. If there is 100% co-occurrence (which, Crystal admits, is rare), then the function of intonation is highly grammatical; if there is only 50% co-occurrence, then intonation functions less grammatically. There is thus potential gradation (or varying 'degrees of exponence'), according to Crystal, in the grammatical role of intonation. [Needless to say, the same line of argumentation would apply to other intonational functions.]

It is, however, often unclear whether co-occurrence is intended as an additional or as an alternative criterion for intonational function. If a particular intonation pattern is distinctive with respect to a certain kind of meaning (based on minimal pairs) but does not invariably co-occur with the appropriate member of the pair in actual speech, can we still speak of intonational function?[2] What if a particular intonation pattern tends to co-occur regularly with a given grammatical, attitudinal, illocutionary, etc. 'meaning' but is not strictly distinctive?[3] These questions are part of a larger debate concerning the value and necessity of statistical frequency in determining linguistic norms.[4] We shall not try to settle the controversy here. Instead, in the

---

[2] This is, for instance, the case with the intonational distinction between restrictive and non-restrictive relative clauses, which is not consistently made in actual speech (Ch. VIII Note 4.)

[3] This is, for instance, the case with final direct speech markers, which are regularly post-nuclear (Ch. VIII §2.2.2, 3.2).

[4] Whereas Crystal (1969) appears to accept – and indeed require – statistical frequency as proof of an intonation norm, Wode (1971) counters that this is self-contradictory: from the

following we shall take both contrastive pairs and co-occurrence patterns into consideration in evaluating functional claims. If there is evidence of both sorts, then this will be considered support for a *strong* version of the claim that intonation has a particular function; if there is evidence of only one sort − i.e. only distinctive pairs or only co-occurrence patterns − then this will support only a *weak* version of the functional claim.

## 2.2 Range of function

In addition to the criterion of co-occurrence, the question of *range* must be considered in assessing intonational function. We shall use this term to refer (i) to how many of the categories and features of the intonational system are responsible for meaning contrasts of a particular sort, and (ii) to the 'pervasiveness' with which these intonational contrasts function within a given content domain.

(i) The term *intonational function* strongly suggests that *all* the categories and features of the intonation system are equally distinctive with respect to a certain type of meaning. Yet this is rarely the case. A contrast may be due in one instance to boundary placement, in another to position of the nucleus, and in a third to height of onset, etc. Or these features may be distinctive only in combination. How much of the intonational system need be involved in order to speak of an intonational function is clearly debatable. Whatever the outcome, however, the term *intonational function* remains at best only a vague descriptive label.

(ii) Similarly, phrases such as *grammatical function of intonation, attitudinal function of intonation*, etc. imply that intonational distinctions are responsible for *all* meaning contrasts in a given domain. Yet this too is rarely the case. One attitude may be signalled by intonation but another by lexical choice, for instance. One grammatical construction may have an intonational correlate but another, none. Thus here too the range of intonational distinctivity within a given content domain is likely to be limited in one way or another. Whether we are still justified in speaking of a particular function of intonation in cases of extremely narrow range is one of the questions which we will ultimately have to face.

## 2.3 Uniqueness

Finally, in determining intonational function, we must consider the question of *uniqueness*. Is intonation alone responsible for the contrasts we find? Are there no other correlative factors which might be doing the work instead? Similar to functional

point of view of information theory the norm as the most frequent intonation would be rather redundant. Furthermore, if the norm were based on frequency, it would vary depending on the corpus in which it was established. Finally, a norm based on frequency would not offer an explanation for how speakers and hearers are able to produce and interpret the intonation contours of new sentences (1971:191).

range, which is rarely extensive, uniqueness of function is likewise an ideal state of affairs rarely encountered in reality. The attitude of a speaker, for instance, is frequently communicated as reliably by the lexical content of the utterance as by its intonation. Textual relations between sentences may be indicated more explicitly by logical connecters than by intonational configuration. And a question is as likely to be signalled by an interrogative form as by its intonation, etc. It is for reasons such as these that Hultzén claims the function of intonation has been grossly overestimated:

> It is possible that we have been expecting a great deal more of intonation than we are justified in expecting. The signalling device may be very simple and nonspecifying. Whatever is specific in the interpretation may be got more from the text in its material and linguistic context than from the refined shape of the intonation. (1959:119)

Hultzén suggests that the role of intonation should be seen in relation to information theory, according to which the information value of an item depends on its probability of occurrence. The more likely an item is to occur, the less information it bears. So long as intonational shape and verbal content or text 'fit', little information is conveyed by intonation. But when there is a discrepancy between the two, then intonation functions as a signal that "some qualification is to be made regarding the whole utterance" (Hultzén 1959:109).

This more sober estimate of the role of intonation nevertheless provides some indication of its potential importance. When lexical content or syntactic/textual structure are at odds with intonation, it is often the meaning derived from intonation which prevails:

> ... we often react more violently to the intonational meanings than to the lexical ones; if a man's tone of voice belies his words, we immediately assume that the intonation more faithfully reflects his true linguistic intentions.... (Pike 1945:22)

Hence the well-known comment 'It wasn't what she said, it was the way she said it'. This puts a powerful tool into the hands of the speaker. S/he can *exploit* intonation to communicate meaning which 'objectively' may not be there.

On the other hand, as Ladd (1978) points out, words may also override intonation. Thus a stewardess who, instead of saying *I'm sorry, Sir, but I'll have to ask you to put away your pipe. FFA regulations only permit cigarette smoking*, says *Put that goddam pipe away* would have a hard time convincing the irate passenger that no insult was intended because she had spoken with polite intonation.[5] We must thus fully expect there to be some give-and-take of functional means in the various domains in which intonation plays a role.

## 3.  Universal functions of intonation

Before proceeding to a critical evaluation of the claims made concerning specific intonational functions in English, it would be wise to consider the general role of pitch in English as compared to that in other languages of the world.

---

[5] Ladd concludes: "When attitudinal signals of any sort are incongruent, we interpret the combination as best we can in the context" (1978:182).

Do all languages have pitch and/or pitch modulation? The answer is clearly yes, to the extent that they are spoken. But not all or nearly all languages use pitch the same way. It is customary to distinguish three types of linguistic use of pitch and consequently three types of language: (a) tone, (b) pitch- or word-accent, and (c) non-tonal languages.

(a) *Tone languages.* Over 50% of the world's languages are tonal (Fromkin 1978:1). These include (i) certain groups of American Indian languages, (ii) the vast majority of African languages, and (iii) almost all Sino-Tibetan and Southeast Asian languages (Wang 1967:93). In a tone language, pitch functions to distinguish lexical items one from another. That is, dictionary entries carry — in addition to the characteristic sequence of segmental phonemes — unique specifications for tone. In Mandarin Chinese, for instance, the sound sequence /ma/ has four different entries due to the fact that it can occur with four distinct lexical tones: (i) *mā* 'mother', (ii) *má* 'hemp', (iii) *mǎ* 'horse' and (iv) *mà* 'scold'. These lexical tones are realized as follows:

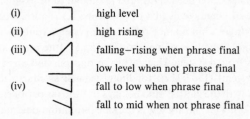

| (i) | high level |
| (ii) | high rising |
| (iii) | falling—rising when phrase final |
| | low level when not phrase final |
| (iv) | fall to low when phrase final |
| | fall to mid when not phrase final |

[In this notation, devised by Y. R. Chao (cited in McCawley 1978:120), the vertical line indicates pitch range; the horizontal and/or slanted line indicates pitch direction: level, rise or fall.]

It has been suggested that tone languages can be divided into those which utilize contour or gliding tones (e.g. Chinese) and those which utilize primarily level tones (e.g. most African languages) (Pike 1948). However, just as with the configurations of non-tonal languages, there is some debate as to whether contour tones should be described as unanalyzable wholes or as a sequence of level tone elements (S. R. Anderson 1978).

(b) *Pitch-accent or word-accent languages.* In these — among which Japanese and the Scandanavian languages Swedish and Norwegian number — pitch is also significant in differentiating (some) lexical meaning but the possibility of a pitch contrast is restricted to certain types of syllables or positions in the word. In Swedish, for instance, the word *búren* 'cage' is distinguished from the word *bùren* 'carried, borne' uniquely by the fact that the former has Accent 1, the latter Accent 2. In terms of phonetic realization, Accent 1 is realized by a high-low turning point which comes earlier with respect to the accented syllable than that for Accent 2. [The exact timing depends on the dialect; see Bruce/Gårding 1978 for details.] The Swedish and Norwegian accents, however, are distinctive only on sequences of one stressed syllable followed by at least one unstressed syllable (i.e. no contrast is possible on monosyllables and polysyllables with stress on the final syllable).[6]

---

[6] Since not only words but also parts of words and sequences of words may be contrasted by the accents, the term *word-accent* is actually somewhat misleading (Vanvik 1978).

(c) *Non-tonal languages.* These are languages in which pitch modulation functions at the level of utterance rather than at the level of word to create meaningful distinctions. For instance, in English, French, German and most other European languages, the use of a rising pitch on *yes* or an equivalent word will distinguish it from *yes* with a falling pitch. However, it is not two different lexical items which have been produced, but two different utterances instead.

Utterance-level pitch distinctions are also found in pitch-accent and tone languages, where they interact with the lexical tones or word-accents in various ways (Ladefoged 1971:87; Bruce 1977:74ff.).

## 4. Linguistic functions of intonation

However, in spite of the basic, if varying role of pitch in the languages of the world, the 'linguisticness' of intonation has often been in dispute. Although some assign it as central a role in the structure of language as that of phonemes (cf. Faure, who claims: "la structuration prosodique d'un énoncé relève d'un système tout aussi rigoureux et tout aussi économique que le système phonématique" [the prosodic structure of an utterance derives from a system which is just as rigorous and just as economical as the phonemic system] (1967:317), for linguists such as Martinet, intonation is mere "gesturing ... with the glottis" and belongs to "the far periphery of the field of language" (1962:28). This, he argues, is because intonation does not have 'double articulation': it is not organized at one level into a succession of minimal units which have meanings attached to them, and at a lower level into a sequence of distinctive segments which lack meaning. Such diverging opinions are due partly to the fact that linguists do not agree on the criteria according to which the linguistic nature of speech phenomena should be determined.

### 4.1 Defining linguistic phenomena

Most scholars would probably recognize minimally the following three criteria:

(a) *Systematicness.* A linguistic phenomenon is one for which there is an organized system of options or structural choices available.

(b) *Conventionality.* The options or choices which a linguistic system makes available are conventional, i.e. determined by cultural tradition rather than by human physiology alone.

(c) *Purposiveness.* A properly linguistic system is used consciously for the purpose of communicating.

However, there is less agreement on three supplementary criteria:

(d) *Arbitrariness.* According to Saussure, a linguistic sign is arbitrary as well as conventional. That is, there is no special relationship between a linguistic sign and the non-linguistic entity to which it refers which would make one particularly suited to signify the other. Those who adhere strictly to this school of thought would deny that intonation is a linguistic sign, since, as Bolinger so aptly put it many years ago, "the feeling determines the tune" (1947:70). That is, intonation is a 'symptom' of the psychological and physiological state of the speaker.

Yet to insist that all linguistic signs must be arbitrary may be overstating the case. In the first place, most languages have onomatopoeic words which either directly or indirectly reflect the nature of the entities to which they refer. Furthermore, choices originally 'motivated' or determined by physiological factors (e.g. relaxation of vocal musculature at the end of an utterance) may now be used conventionally in different ways in different linguistic systems. That is, "the arbitrary signs are necessarily conventional, but the conventional signs are not necessarily arbitrary" (Fónagy/Magdics 1963:298). Thus it may be more appropriate to speak only of the conventional, rather than the conventional *and* the arbitrary nature of linguistic signs.

(e) *Discreteness.* According to classical structuralist thought, linguistic contrasts must be of the all-or-none sort, with a meaning component either present or absent but not present/absent in degrees. Only speech phenomena which are organized into discrete units and related to one another in a system are considered linguistic; speech phenomena which are gradient or continuous are accordingly non-linguistic. Bolinger (1961b) makes a strong plea for allowing (some) gradient phenomena into the realm of linguistic enquiry. However, even he refers to intonation as "around the edge of language" (1972a:19). Crystal (1969), on the other hand, advocates a continuous scale of linguistic contrastivity for non-segmental speech phenomena, some of which are more discrete than others, more contrastive than others, etc.:

> At the 'most linguistic' extreme [of the scale] would be placed those *prosodic* features of utterance, describable in terms of closed systems of contrasts, which are relatively easily integrated with other aspects of linguistic structure, particularly grammar, and which are very frequent in connected speech (....) At the other, 'least linguistic' end would be placed those *paralinguistic* features of utterance which seem to have little potential for entering into systemic relationships, which have relatively little integrability with other aspects of language structure, are very infrequent in connected speech, and are much less obviously shared, conventional features of articulation ... [emphasis added] (1969:129).

On this scale, intonation is at the more linguistic end, although its contrasts may not always be strictly discrete (cf. also Quirk 1965).

(f) *Language-specificness.* If linguistic signs are said to be wholly determined by cultural convention, it appears to follow that they must also be language-specific. Martinet's dictum that "there is nothing linguistic in the proper sense which may not differ from one language to another" (1960:29) exemplifies this view. Yet it does not necessarily follow that any feature found universally in all languages is therefore non-linguistic; languages may have a universal infrastructure and still display the unique language-specific features which a structuralist would expect to find (Lyons 1977:249). Thus universal features need not be excluded per se from linguistic enquiry.

## 4.2   The linguistic status of intonational functions

Returning to intonational function, it is, needless to say, the linguistic nature of the attitudinal function which has most often been called into doubt. The justification has been that (a) the relation between intonation and attitude is not *arbitrary*; (b) the attitudinal contrasts which intonation establishes are not *discrete*; and (c) the psychological and physiological factors it depends on are *universal*. However, these are precisely the disputable criteria for determining the linguisticness of speech phenomena.

Martinet notwithstanding, it is quite possible that the speakers of a given language have an organized system of linguistic contrasts for expressing attitudes and that this system, although rooted in universal physiological and psychological processes, is in its elaboration a unique product of the culture which fashioned it. Furthermore, it is possible and indeed likely that since a speaker's inner state is as much a part of the reality s/he wants to communicate as the 'real' world, this system will be used purposively to communicate real or simulated attitudes. If these points are granted, then the attitudinal function meets the undisputed criteria (a) – (c) and can rightly be called linguistic.

We turn now to a critical appraisal of the purported functions of intonation in English (§1).[7]

## References

Anderson, S. R. 1978
Bolinger 1947
Bolinger 1961b
Bolinger 1964
Bolinger 1972a
Bolinger 1978
Brazil/Coulthard/Johns 1980
Bruce/Gårding 1978
Cruttenden 1981
*Crystal 1969 (§4.16)
Crystal 1975c
*Daneš 1960
Delattre 1969
Faure 1967
Faure 1970
Fónagy/Magdics 1963
Fromkin 1978
*Gibbon 1976 (§1.2.4)
Halliday 1970b
Halliday 1976a
Hultzén 1959
Hultzén 1962
Huttar 1968
Jakobson 1960
Ladd 1978 (Chs. V, VI §1)
Ladd 1981
Ladefoged 1971 (§9)
Lyons 1977 (§2.4)
Malmberg 1966
Martinet 1960
Martinet 1962
McCawley 1978
Pike 1945
Pike 1948
Quirk 1965
Rigault 1964
*Scuffil 1982 (§2.3)
Siertsema 1962
Vanvik 1978
Wang 1967
Wode 1971

---

[7] The indexical function will be omitted here, on the grounds that it is not strictly linguistic. Indexical intonational cues inform the hearer about who, or a member of what group, the speaker is – but they typically do so independent of speaker intention.

# Chapter VII

# Intonation and information

The theory of information structure in sentences and texts stems from the pioneering work of the Prague School linguists, e.g. Mathesius, Firbas, Daneš, etc., and in Britain from the work of Halliday. The latter in particular accords a central role to intonational choice: "In English, information structure is expressed by intonation" (Halliday 1970b:162). In the following we shall present what is claimed to be the informational function of intonation and then attempt to assess its validity in the light of recent studies.


## 1.    The informational function of intonation

'Be informative (but not more so than necessary)' – one of the tacit rules of conversational interaction (Grice 1975:45) – refers explicitly to what speakers typically do when they communicate, namely tell their interlocutor something s/he does not already know. In doing so, they are imparting information, enlarging the hearer's horizons, increasing his/her knowledge of the world or some aspect thereof.

To be effective, however, a speaker must present this information in an appropriate form, or – to borrow a term from Chafe – with the proper 'packaging'. That is, s/he must decide not only what the message is, but also how the message should be sent. This involves first of all chopping up the message into 'chunks', typically in such a way that each chunk has only one bit of new information. And this means structuring the material in each chunk in accordance with the hearer's state of knowledge. For instance, some of the material will be new to the hearer, some may be already 'known' or can be taken as 'given'. Furthermore, some material may be more accessible than other material. When we speak of the information structure of sentences and texts we mean the division of a message into chunks and the organization of these chunks in terms of given and new information.


## 1.1    Unit of information and tone-unit

According to Halliday, 'chunking' results from "the speaker's blocking out of the message into quanta of information or message blocks". Each of these quanta is a *unit of information* (Halliday 1967b:202). Units of information may or may not coincide with grammatical clauses. For instance, the clause *John saw the play yesterday* could be all one chunk (a) or less than one chunk (b) or several chunks (c–e):

a. [*John saw the play yesterday*]
b. [*John saw the play yesterday* you know]
c. [*John*] [*saw the play yesterday*]
d. [*John saw the play*] [*yesterday*]
e. [*John*] [*saw the play*] [*yesterday*]

The unmarked or neutral case, however, is (a), in which one information unit corresponds to one clause.

According to Halliday, it is through tonality, or division into tone groups, that the chunking of sentences and texts is achieved. That is, one information unit is realized as one tone-unit. It follows that the more information units there are, the more tone-units there are, and vice versa. Thus the difference between [*John saw the play yesterday*] and [*John*] [*saw the play yesterday*] in terms of information content would be realized intonationally as:

(a)  John saw the play yesterday ‖
(b)  John ‖ saw the play yesterday ‖

Conversely,

(c)  John ‖ saw the play ‖ yesterday ‖

would be considered informationally weightier than (a) or (b) because it has more tone-units.

Neither information structure nor division into tone-units is determined by constituent structure, according to Halliday (cf. however Crystal 1975; also Ch. VIII). Instead, whether the speaker uses few or many tone-unit divisions reflects a free choice as to what the information content of the message is. This means that the relation between tone-unit and information unit can also be exploited. For instance, it has been pointed out that some politicians make a point of multiplying the number of tone-units when speaking in public and thereby appear to be saying more (Gutknecht/ Mackiewicz 1977:111).

## 1.2   Information focus and the nucleus

In each unit of information, one or at the most two elements are selected as "points of prominence within the message" (Halliday 1967b:203). This/these form the *information focus* or *foci* of the unit:

> Information focus reflects the speaker's decision as to where the main burden of the message lies. It is ... one kind of emphasis, that whereby the speaker marks out a part (which may be the whole) of a message block as that which he wishes to be interpreted as informative. (1967b:204)

Because it is obligatory that the information unit have at least one information focus, there is a reciprocally contingent relation between unit of information and information focus. If the number of units increases or decreases, so must the number of foci; if the number of foci are increased or decreased, so the number of units is likely to multiply.

The choice of information focus in each unit of information, according to Halliday, is realized by the assignment of prominence in the tone-unit. That portion of the message which is most informative is realized by the tonic segment, i.e. the nucleus (and tail); that portion which is least informative is generally realized by the pre-tonic segment (i.e. head). In some cases, however, the focussed material may extend into the pre-tonic; in others the focussed material may be restricted to the nucleus, excluding the tail.[1] If there is only one focus, the nucleus will be simple; if there are two foci, then the nucleus is compound − or (presumably) subordination is present (Ch. V §3.3). Thus we might compare:

(a) there's a MÀN in the garden ||
(b) there's a MÀN || in the GÀRden ||
(c) there's a MÀN in the GÁRden ||
(d) there's a MÀN [in the GÀRden] ||      (Crystal 1975a:27)

The difference between (a) and (b) in terms of information is that (a) presents only one quantum of information, whereas (b) presents two: 'there is a man', '[the man is] in the garden'. Sentences (c) and (d) also present only one quantum of information each, but with two information foci, primary followed by secondary.

## 1.3   Information type and pitch height

The structure of the information unit in terms of focussed and non-focussed material relates to the different types of information which may be present in the message block.

### 1.3.1 New vs. given

The element which has information focus in the unit is typically said to be new information for the hearer. *New* may mean that the information is factually new or that it is new "in the sense that the speaker presents it as not being recoverable from preceding discourse" (Halliday 1967b:204). In Chafe's terms, it is new in the sense of being "what the speaker assumes he is introducing into the addressee's consciousness by what he says" (1976:30).

The counterpart to new information is typically called *given*, information which is recoverable from the preceding discourse or situation, or which the speaker assumes to be 'on stage' in the hearer's mind. For example, in the following hypothetical exchange:

A: You know John?
B: Yes.
A: He had an accident last week.

A's first question has the purpose of introducing John (*new*) into B's consciousness. Once A is assured that John is on stage (*given*), then information concerning the

---

[1] For example, respectively: 'I'm looking for *the caretaker who looks after this BLOCK*'; 'I've seen *BETTER* plays' (focussed material italicized, tonic capitalized) (Halliday 1967:207).

accident (*new*) can be added. This is indeed the usual way we proceed in comprehending. We understand by putting new information in relation to what we already know.[2]

Note that information need not necessarily have had prior mention in a discourse in order to be given. For instance, imagine the following interchange between two strangers looking at the same picture in an art gallery:

A: Know who did it?
B: Picasso I think.

A's utterance is structured to fit the expectation that B is thinking about the painting in front of them. However, this information is given only because of the situation and not because of any prior mention in the discourse.

Given information may also be information which is derivable from common beliefs or knowledge which the speaker and the hearer have about their world. For instance, if both A and B know that B has an important test in school that day, the following exchange could occur when B comes home from school:

A: How was it?
B: I passed.

Here the information as to what 'it' is does not occur explicitly in the discourse but is assumed to be 'on stage' due to common knowledge.

Although the given-new distinction is not a lexical or grammatical one per se, certain preferences with respect to word category and grammatical construction can be observed. For one, new information is typically carried by lexical items which form open classes (sets which have no natural or de facto boundaries). Given information is often associated with grammatical items, many of which form closed classes, e.g. personal pronouns (*I, you, she*, etc.), deictic adjectives, adverbs (*this, those, here, there*, etc.), definite articles, pro-forms (*one, do*), etc. In order to use such expressions properly, a speaker must assume that the hearer knows which referent is meant. New information and given information are, however, not restricted to lexical items and grammatical items, respectively. A lexical item may well represent given information, just as a grammatical item under some interpretations may be new (§1.3.2).

The notions of given and new likewise figure in the work of the Prague School linguists, although with different terminology. According to the theory of *Functional Sentence Perspective* (FSP), communication is an essentially dynamic process; it develops across the utterance or utterances. Linguistic elements contribute in varying degrees to this development or, technically speaking, they have different degrees of Communicative Dynamism, depending on the extent to which they "push(..) the communication forward" (Firbas 1966a:270). Those elements which contribute most to advancing communication form the *rheme* of the sentence or clause; those which contribute least, the *theme* of the sentence or clause.[3] The term *transition* is

---

[2] Cf. Haviland/Clark: "It is only when the listener finds (or constructs) the Antecedent in memory that he can attach the New information to it, thereby integrating the New information with what he already knows" (1974:513).

[3] Note that *theme* in FSP is not equivalent to *theme* in Halliday's system, where it refers to the element which comes first in the clause.

sometimes used to refer to elements (or an element) which mediate between the thematic and rhematic sections of the sentence. For instance, in the sentence *He was cross, he* might be viewed as theme, *cross* as rheme and *was* as a transition between them (Firbas 1972:78). To a certain extent, theme/rheme (FSP) and given/new (Halliday, Chafe) are equivalent. However, whereas Halliday views given/new as a binary choice, linguists working within the FSP tradition assign theme/rheme on a gradient basis with the possibility of intermediate degrees.

Intonationally the given/new dichotomy in English, according to Chafe (1974), is reflected in the use of low vs. high pitch respectively. Thus in a conversational opener such as *I just found some books that belong to Peter, I* is given and pronounced with low pitch, *Peter* is new and pronounced with high pitch, and *books* would have either low or high pitch depending on the speaker's judgment as to whether it is 'on stage' or not. Chafe admits, however, that this use of high vs. low pitch to distinguish new from given information functions more consistently with nouns than with verbs. If the verb is the only new element in the sentence, then it will have high pitch, as in:

he BROKE it

However, if a verb carrying new information is accompanied by a noun with new information, it may lose its high pitch if the noun precedes:

the BUTTER melted

but retain it if the noun follows:[4]

he's sitting in the CAR

We shall return to this point shortly.

### 1.3.2 Contrastive vs. new

In Halliday's view new information may be either "cumulative to or contrastive with what has preceded" (1967b:211). In particular, new information is contrastive when grammatical or closed-system items form the information focus, e.g. *he felt himSELF* ('not someone else'), *I put it ON the table* ('not under it') (1967b:206f.). According to Chafe (1976), however, contrastive information is qualitatively different from new information and belongs in a category of its own. This can be demonstrated by the following hypothetical dialogue:

A: I didn't know Susie could cook so well.
B: She can't. RONald made the hamburgers.

Three factors characterize contrastive sentences such as *RONald made the hamburgers*: (a) the speaker presupposes that someone made the hamburgers; (b) the speaker assumes that a limited set of candidates is available for the role of having made the hamburgers; (c) the speaker asserts that of all these candidates Ronald is

---

[4] This is no doubt another way of looking at the well-documented fact that certain intransitive verbs shun the nuclear accent; cf. Firbas (1966b) and §2.1.2.1.

the correct one (and the others, by implication, are not). These features are not present in a sentence which merely imparts new information. Compare, for instance:

A: Who made the hamburgers?
B: RONald made the hamburgers.

Here *Ronald* is new information but not contrastive: the speaker neither assumes that the hearer is entertaining a limited set of candidates, nor asserts that only one (as opposed to all the others) is correct. This is attested to by the fact that paraphrases such as 'not Tom/rather than Tom/instead of Tom' are inappropriate.

In Chafe's (1974) view, both contrastive and new items may have high pitch, but over-all pitch configuration in units containing them is different. This is particularly evident in sentences with two foci. Consider, for instance, the sentence *I brought Matthew a book*. Non-contrastively, provided *Matthew* and *book* are both new, the intonational pattern of this sentence would be:

Fig. VII/1

If, however, both *Matthew* and *book* are contrastive (i.e. opposed to, say, 'Tom' and 'toy'), then we would have this configuration:

Fig. VII/2

But even in sentences with only one focus, contrastive information can often be distinguished from new information in terms of pitch configuration. According to Armstrong/Ward (1926), for instance, if a final lexical item is contrastive in a sentence spoken with Tune I (Ch. IV §2.3.2), it will either have a fall from a higher than normal starting point, e.g.

Fig. VII/3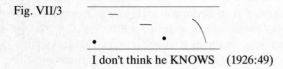

I don't think he KNOWS   (1926:49)

or a rapid fall[5] with all other surrounding syllables deaccented:

Fig. VII/4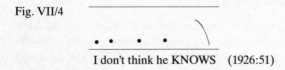

I don't think he KNOWS   (1926:51)

---

[5] A 'rapid' fall corresponds roughly to what we have called steep slope (Ch. V §1.4.1).

The same features will be present if some word other than the final lexical item has a contrastive accent:

Fig. VII/5

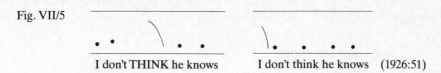

I don't THINK he knows     I don't think he knows     (1926:51)

In sum, combining Chafe's and Armstrong/Ward's views, pitch height and/or over-all pitch configuration are claimed to distinguish given from new information, as well as contrastive from new in the information- and intonation-unit.

## 1.4 Distribution of information and nucleus location

According to Halliday and the Prague School linguists, given and new information may be distributed in different ways in the sentence or clause:

a) *New* (no given).   An information unit may contain only new information. This is typically the case with opening sentences in fairy tales, e.g. *Once upon a time there was a king*, or with out-of-the-blue utterances such as *The pope's been shot* or *There's a fly in your soup*.

b) *Given-new*.   An information unit may present first given and then new information. For instance, a follow-up sentence in the fairy-tale mentioned above might be: *The king had three sons*. The fact that there is a *king* can be considered given by virtue of the first sentence, whereas the fact that he has *three sons* is being brought 'on stage' for the first time.

c) *New-given*.   New information may be presented first, with given following, viz: *John's the one you're thinking about, Peter did it*. This type of information distribution is also found in sentences with 'dislocated' subjects: *He's a good friend, John is* or *It starts so early, the movie*.

Since the information focus of a unit of information typically contains new (or contrastive) information and the nucleus marks information focus, it follows that the position of the nucleus in the tone-unit will depend on where new/contrastive information is located. Both Halliday and the Prague School linguists regard (b) *given-new* (FSP: theme-rheme) as the *unmarked* arrangement of information. Intonationally this means that the unmarked position of the nucleus is considered to be on the last lexical item of the unit (since it is typically lexical items which carry new information). If the nucleus falls elsewhere (i.e. on a pre-final lexical item or a final grammatical item), this is referred to as *marked* focus. Compare, for instance:

(a)   John painted the SHED yesterday
      vs.
(b)   JOHN painted the shed yesterday
(c)   John PAINTED the shed yesterday
(d)   John painted the shed YESTERDAY     (Halliday 1967b:207f.)

Sentence (a) would be an example of unmarked focus, since the nucleus falls on the final lexical item (*yesterday* is a reference item, i.e. it is interpretable only in relation to 'today'). Sentences (b), (c) and (d), on the other hand, all have marked focus — and, it might be added, contrastive meaning.[6]

## 2. Assessing the claims

If we were to list the functions which intonation is claimed to fulfil with respect to information structure, the list would include the following: (1) tone-units realize units of information; (2) the nucleus signals the presence of information focus; (3) high vs. low pitch marks new vs. given information; extra pitch height, steep slope and accompanying low level deaccented syllables mark contrastive information; (4) the position of the nucleus realizes unmarked vs. marked focus. We shall now attempt to assess the validity of these claims.

### 2.1 The concept of information

#### 2.1.1 What is information?

Theories concerning information structure have been notoriously evasive about one central question: What is information? Obviously, glossing it as 'relevance' or 'significance' is hardly satisfactory, since these notions are equally ill-defined. *Information* does have a very precise definition within the framework of information-theory, where it is viewed as a quantity whose value — expressable in bits — is inversely proportionate to the (statistical) probability of occurrence of an item. Yet most students of natural language tend to feel uncomfortable with this strictly mathematical notion.

Bar-Hillel/Carnap (1952) adapt the idea of information as statistical probability to a linguistically more relevant notion of *semantic information*, which can be described as "elimination of uncertainty ... as to what the message is" (Lyons 1977:49). The amount of information content in a proposition is said to be in inverse proportion to its degree of *logical probability*. But whether and precisely how this theory is compatible with that of information structure as posited by Halliday, Chafe, the Prague School linguists and others remains to be determined.

One point of divergence would seem to be the question of whether information relates to propositions or to sentence constituents. Bar-Hillel/Carnap, for instance, speak of the information content of propositions; but most linguists working with information structure in texts consider primarily clause constituents, e.g. NPs, Vs, etc., to be given or new (although whole clauses are not excluded). Yet whether we are talking about propositions or clause constituents can lead to different evaluations of information content. Consider, for instance:

---

[6] Contrastive meaning, however, cannot be restricted to marked focus, since it may also be present when focus is unmarked: *John painted the SHED yesterday* ('not the house') (Ch. II §4.3).

A: John likes Mary's husband.
B: He likes him too.

Here the constituents in B's response are all given (their referents having been introduced by A), but the propositional content that Mary's husband also likes John is new. Such disparity in the evaluation of information content is often due to a lack of agreement on what information is.

A second point of divergence is the following: if semantic information is viewed as equivalent to the reduction of uncertainty, this renders the notion of given information meaningless. On this interpretation, semantic information is always new; if it is not, it is not information. In order for the distinction given-new to be meaningful with respect to information, we must appeal to a more neutral sense of *information* as simply 'content'. The term *information* is thus inherently polysemic, with a meaning equivalent to unexpectedness and one equivalent to content. Unfortunately this polysemy is rarely made explicit and is consequently a source of misunderstanding in work on information structure.

A third point of divergence is that the theory of semantic information as it stands now does not provide for information of a pragmatic or social nature. Yet it is commonly acknowledged that information in language communication may not be purely factual. For instance, Halliday states: "the 'message' may be of any kind, such as *how do you do?* where the 'new information' is simply that the speaker is well-disposed and is acting within accepted social conventions" (1970a:41f.). Likewise Brazil et al (1980) point out that some intonation units, e.g. those containing only adverbials: *to tell you the truth*, *actually*, etc., typically communicate no new factual information but rather social information concerning the state of convergence/divergence between speaker and hearer (1980:51) (Ch. II §4.1.3). Until the theory of semantic information can be made sensitive to this kind of pragmatic and social information, it will be of only limited use for linguists investigating the information structure of texts and discourse.

### 2.1.2 What is an information unit?

But not only is *information* poorly defined: so also are the so-called *units of information*. How do we determine what they are? In the traditional view a unit of information is (realized as) an intonation unit. Yet equating the two units this way is patently circular if one of the functions of intonation is said to be the blocking of a message into quanta of information. A unit of information is further said to be a quantum of information and to include at least one point of information focus. But there is no clear statement as to (i) what constitutes a quantum of information and (ii) how to decide when more than one point of information focus is present. For instance, does a quantum of information contain only one new item or can it contain several new items? When does a unit of information contain a primary and a secondary bit of information? When should two bits of information be viewed as two quanta? In the present form of information-structure theory, there are no criteria — independent of phonological ones — which would make an answer to these questions possible.

### 2.1.2.1 Multiple accents and merging

The problem of what constitutes a quantum of information has recently cropped up in discussions of all-new sentences such as (a) *JOHNson died* and (b) *the PRESident's been assassinated*. Here, it will be recalled, the fact that the nuclear accent falls on the subject rather than the predicate presents a problem both for syntactically-based and for information structure-based accent rules, since according to both the unmarked position of the nucleus should be on the rightmost lexical item (§1.4 and Ch. II §4). If we assume, however, that every new item constitutes a quantum of information and should therefore receive an accent, then the unmarked form of these all-new sentences becomes (a') *JOHNson DIED* and (b') *the PRESident's been asSASsinated*, i.e. they have multiple accents (Fuchs 1980) and are presumably realized with more than one intonational group.[7] The question then becomes, what principles condition the merging or integration of two quanta of information into one, as in (a) and (b)?

A number of recent studies have addressed themselves to this point. The picture that is emerging is one in which both syntactic and semantic factors play a role. Syntactically speaking, it appears that in order for constituents to merge they must not be overly complex nor contain quantifying or anaphoric expressions (Fuchs 1980; Gussenhoven 1983a). Furthermore, it appears that predicates and adverbials are less likely to merge than are predicates and subjects or objects. Thus we could expect merging in ('What does he do?') *He teaches linguistics* but not in ('What does he do?') *He teaches in Ghana* (Gussenhoven 1983a).

But there are also important semantic constraints. According to Allerton/ Cruttenden (1979), for instance, merging takes place (with subsequent accenting of the subject) in three instances:

(i) with 'empty' verbs, i.e. those which Bolinger (1972) calls predictable, e.g. *the SUN'S shining, the KETtle's boiling*;

(ii) with verbs of (dis)appearance — these often involve little activity; instead the NP-referent is conspicuous by virtue of sudden presence or absence, e.g. *my KEYS have disappeared, the proFESsor called round*;

(iii) with verbs denoting a misfortune, e.g. *the CAR broke down, the TRAIN'S late* (1979:51f.).

With exception of the third criterion, which has since been criticized as being neither unique nor determining (Fuchs 1980:452), the common denominator of these semantic constraints appears to be that the merging constituents must denote some kind of unit (Fuchs 1980, Gussenhoven 1983a). Not surprisingly it is the latter type of condition which offers insight into the semantic notion of information unit. Chafe's (1974) comment that accents may merge only if the corresponding notions are "coalesced to form a conceptual unit" points in the same direction.[8] It is along these lines that research must continue.

---

[7] This can be done either with two wholly independent tone-units: the PRESident's ‖ been asSASsinated ‖, or (conceivably) with subordination: the PRESident's [been asSASsinated] ‖.

[8] With respect to *the BUTTER melted*, for instance, Chafe writes: "one might say that there is a single concept 'butter-melt', an instance of which is said to have occurred" (1974:115).

### 2.1.2.2 Primary vs. secondary information

In the classical information-structure model, a unit of information must contain at least one point of information focus but may contain two, one primary and the other secondary (Halliday 1967b:203). As was the case with the information unit, however, the distinction between uni-focal and bi-focal information units is based on phonological criteria — the secondary point of information focus being realized by the low-rising tone of a compound falling + rising nucleus.[9] Consequently linguists who, for theoretical reasons, do not recognize compound nuclei must claim either that all nuclei realize separate but equal points of information focus (as do Brazil/Coulthard/Johns 1980, for instance) or that nuclei may realize points of information focus with differing degrees of importance (e.g. Leech/Svartvik 1975:174f.). The latter, for instance, state that in

> I saw your BRÒther ‖ at the game YÉSterday ‖

the first (falling) nucleus marks 'main' information and the second (rising) nucleus marks 'subsidiary' information. However, no distinction is made between this kind of subsidiary information (which would undoubtedly be realized with a compound nucleus in a model recognizing such a category) and information added as an afterthought (which would be realized as two separate units in such a model): *she'll do ÀNYthing ‖ if you ask her NÍCEly ‖*.

Allerton (1978) also implies that quanta of information may not be equal when he distinguishes degrees of newness. He claims, for instance, that in:

> (a)  I saw MARy ‖ in a BOOKshop ‖

*a bookshop* clearly represents wholly new information, whereas in:

> (b)  I saw MARy ‖ in the BOOKshop ‖

*the bookshop* implies that the addressee will remember that there is a bookshop but may not have this bit of information on stage at the moment. It is consequently only 'semi-new' (Allerton 1978: 146f.). To the extent that main and subsidiary information or degrees of newness can be distinguished, it appears that not all quanta of information are equal. However, whether two information foci with differing newness value may occur within one and the same information unit is a theoretical question which must be clarified on strictly informational grounds.

## 2.2  The prosodic marking of focus

### 2.2.1  Nuclear prominence

From the claim that information focus is realized by the tonic or nucleus and that it consists of either new or contrastive information, it can be inferred that presence of nuclear prominence will signal new information, while absence of nuclear

---

[9] Crystal implies that primary and secondary points of information are also present in subordination (1969:248 and 1975a:27).

prominence will signal given information. Yet counter-evidence here has never been lacking.

### 2.2.1.1 Accented given material

Gunter (1966) points out that whereas absence of (nuclear) accent may indeed mean that an item is not new, presence of (nuclear) accent does not automatically mean that an item is new. For instance, in the following hypothetical dialogue:

A: the man can see the BOY
B: the man can see the BOY      (1966, 1974:35)

speaker B recapitulates A's statement using the same wording and accent placement. In this case, the second accent on *boy* does not signal strictly new information.

Empirical studies of pitch level and stressing in spoken discourse point in the same direction. Yule (1980a) finds that given items are often realized with high rather than low pitch and concludes that this may be in order to emphasize one particular aspect of a topic, or in order to re-establish the topic after a digression. Lehman (1977), investigating the use of primary stress in spontaneous conversation, likewise finds that given material may be stressed to 'bracket' off digressions. However, she also emphasizes that speakers may stress given material in order to control the mechanics of conversation. For instance, if there is some competition from an interlocutor for the floor, a speaker may repeat the same phrase with the same prosodic contour until a turn is secured, although the items are formally given after first mention. Or if a speaker's point has been acknowledged by an interlocutor's response, the first speaker may attempt to regain the floor by stressing a previously mentioned item (cf. also Abdul-Ghani 1978).

Such evidence appears to argue against the claim that given material is marked by absence of nuclear prominence. However, the possibility should not be overlooked that this apparent 'counter-evidence' is due to lack of agreement as to what information is. If information is thought of as propositional rather than constituent-oriented and if it may be pragmatic as well as factual, then one could argue that the repetition of formally given items with nuclear prominence, as reported by Yule and Lehman, is communicating new information of a pragmatic sort. For instance, the new information in the dialogue above may be that speaker B agrees with speaker A. Nevertheless, given such an interpretation of information, it would still be necessary to account for the exact location of the accent when new, pragmatic information is not reflected as such in lexical/syntactic form.

### 2.2.1.2 Unaccented new material

But there is also counter-evidence to the claim that what is new information will have nuclear prominence. For instance, when new information is carried by a complex syntactic constituent, only the last lexical item takes the accent: e.g. *I'm looking for the caretaker who looks after this BLOCK*. Here not only *block* but also *the caretaker who looks after this* are new, but only the former has nuclear prominence.

New information is likewise non-prominent in all-new sentences, in particular those whose new elements have merged so that the accent falls on only one. Thus:

(a) What's up?
   *the KETtle's boiling*

(c) What does he do?
   *he teaches linGUIStics*

(b) What happened?
   *the PRISoners have escaped*

(d) What is the nature of your business?
   *we repair RAdios*

(b,c,d from Gussenhoven 1983b)

In these examples, *boiling, escaped, teaches* and *repair* are all new but unaccented.

### 2.2.1.3 Newsworthiness and degrees of given/new

It is due to such counter-evidence that some linguists have proposed the introduction of a new dimension, independent of given/new, to account for the presence or absence of nuclear prominence. Allerton (1978) and Allerton/Cruttenden (1979), for instance, claim that it is the subjectively perceived "newsworthiness" of an item which ultimately determines whether it is accented or not.[10] In a sentence such as *the TAP'S leaking*, they suggest, "both the tap and its leaking are in some sense new, but the important thing in the speaker's mind is to get the attention of the listener focused on the tap" (1979:53).

However, it is doubtful whether the introduction of a new notion, itself not properly defined on independent grounds, will improve matters. What does seem called for is a more precise definition of what information, and in particular new information is. If the notion of formal constituent-level newness is abandoned, then *newsworthiness* is perhaps one way of describing what constitutes new propositional information. Whether it can be extended to pragmatic and social information is another question.

If, on the other hand, the notion of formal, constituent-level newness is maintained, then it must surely be acknowledged that the traditional given/new dichotomy provides an insufficient account of nuclear prominence. It is for this reason that some linguists have found it helpful to distinguish *degrees* of givenness and/or newness.[11] For instance, Allerton (1978) points out that several variables may interact in establishing relative information value: use of a pro-form, use of the definite vs. indefinite article, denuclearization and "separate group" intonation. Thus compare:

(a) I was offered ↑HÈLP ‖ by a poLÌCEman ‖
(b) I was offered ↑HÈLP ‖ by the poLÌCEman ‖
(c) I was offered ↑HÈLP by the poLÍCEman ‖
(d) I was offered ↑HÈLP by the policeman ‖
(e) I was offered ↑HÈLP by him ‖   (1978:145)

---

[10] Cf. also Esser (1983), who speaks of an item being more or less "foregroundworthy".

[11] Cf. Allerton (1978) and Prince (1981). These independently developed classificatory systems differ primarily in that the former makes use of both syntactic and intonational variables, whereas the latter has, broadly speaking, only semantic variables.

In these examples we can distinguish a totally unknown item [*policeman* introduced with an indefinite article as in (a)] from a number of known items [*policeman* with a definite article (b–d) or as the pro-form *him* (e)]. The latter is obviously wholly known, whereas (b), (c), (d) illustrate *policeman* with differing degrees of givenness depending on intonational configuration. With "separate group" intonation (b), the speaker implies that the item is known to the hearer but is not immediately accessible, i.e. it is offstage.[12] If *policeman* is integrated into the first tone-unit but has a secondary (rising) nucleus (c), this implies that the item is known and relatively accessible, i.e. it is on-stage: the hearer needs only a gentle reminder. With denuclearization, (d) and (e), the item is wholly given. The interaction of syntactic and intonational variables makes it possible then to distinguish four different kinds of information: new (indefinite, "separate group"), semi-new (definite, "separate group"), semi-given (definite, secondary rise) and given (denuclearized and/or pro-form). Thus, according to this model, not only presence or absence of nuclear prominence is significant with respect to given/new, but also intonation boundary placement. The importance of this variable, long underestimated, is just beginning to emerge both in studies on the given/new distinction and in work on focus assignment (Gussenhoven 1983a, Ladd 1983c).

## 2.2.2 Pitch height and configuration

So far we have considered only those aspects of the purported informational function of intonation which are related to tone-unit division and the location of the nucleus. We turn now to other tonal features within the tone-unit to which information-structure models have laid a claim. These include (i) the use of pitch height to distinguish given from new information, and (ii) the use of extra pitch height, steep slope and surrounding deaccentuation to distinguish contrastive from new information.

A considerable amount of counter-evidence has amassed concerning the claim that high pitch signals new information and low pitch, given information. To the extent that high pitch is co-occurrent with nuclear prominence, the evidence presented in §2.2.1.1 militates against it. And there is the well-documented fact that nuclei may be low-pitched, as evidenced by Bolinger's B-accent or Crystal's ↓` and ↓´; furthermore, that non-nuclear syllables may be high-pitched, as, for instance, in rising tails (Ladd 1978:79). In fact, the matter is much more complex than a simple high–low dichotomy would suggest.

## 2.2.2.1 Falls vs. rises

One recent investigation of intonation (Brazil/Coulthard/Johns 1980) claims that it is nuclear type rather than nuclear prominence which distinguishes given from new information. [Given information is defined as that which is *referred to*, i.e. which is already present as part of the common ground between speaker and hearer; new information is defined as that which is *proclaimed*, i.e. which is intended to enlarge the common ground between speaker and hearer.] Compare, for instance:

---

[12] Cf. Prince's (1981) category "Unused", which, however, is classified as a kind of New.

a) when I've finished MĬDdlemarch ‖ I shall read Adam BÈDE ‖
b) when I've finished MĬDdlemarch ‖ I shall read Adam BĔDE‖     (1980:13)

These two sentences would be appropriate in wholly different contexts: (a), in case the hearer knows that the speaker is reading *Middlemarch*; (b), in case the hearer knows that the speaker intends to read *Adam Bede*. However, what is common to both is that it is the falling tone which is used to proclaim new information [i.e. in (a) that the speaker intends to read *Adam Bede*, in (b) that the speaker will do so after finishing *Middlemarch*] and the falling–rising tone which is used to refer to information already known. Brazil et al's point is that it is the choice of a falling vs. a falling–rising tone which signals the information value of an item.

The claim is appealing in its simplicity – yet it is perhaps somewhat too simple to be an adequate reflection of the complexity of intonational form and function in speech. Esser (1983), for instance, points out that falls and rises also have attitudinal function and that these could theoretically obscure the given-new distinction completely. Furthermore, a (falling–)rising tone in a separate intonation group may sometimes signal an afterthought, i.e. subsidiary but new information. For instance:

it was SNÒWing ‖ when we arRÍVED ‖

Although *arrived* has a rise, a variant of the fall–rise in Brazil's system, it cannot be interpreted as given or referred to. In other words, the utterance would be wholly inappropriate as an answer to *What was the weather like when you arrived?* (Esser 1983:126). A similar point could be made with respect to the fall–rise used with so-called negative implication:

A:  did you feed the animals?
B:  I fed the CĂT

Here the fall–rise marks new information but has the additional function of implying that none of the other members of the presupposed set of animals was fed. If only for these reasons, Brazil's theory is not wholly satisfactory. We must conclude then that neither the choice of high or low pitch nor the choice of falling or falling–rising tone corresponds systematically to information type. The search for pitch correlates of given/new thus continues.

## 2.2.2.2 Contrast and emphasis

The claim that pitch distinguishes contrastive from new information has been rejected by a number of linguists. According to Bolinger, for instance: "… as far as we can tell from the behavior of pitch, nothing is uniquely contrastive" (1961a:87). This statement is based on evidence such as the following:

(i) How was the job?          (ii) Was the job hard?
    Oh, it was EASy               No, it was EASy

Here, Bolinger argues, there is no difference between the contours used on *easy*, although (ii) is contrastive and (i) is not. But remember that *contour* for Bolinger means 'pitch accent' (Ch. II §2.2). While it is true that in terms of pitch accent a

135

contrastive and a non-contrastive accent may not differ, phonetically speaking they often do. This is obvious in two of Bolinger's own examples:

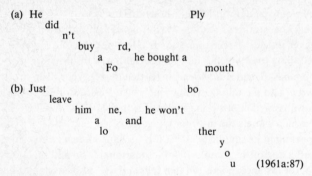

In (a), where *Plymouth* is contrastive, the fall has steep slope, while in (b), where *bother you* is non-contrastive, it has gradual slope. In other words, the following unstressed syllables fall gradually away from the accented syllable in (b) rather than descending immediately to the baseline. The distinction is of course obscured if there is only one syllable following the accent, as in (a). But consider what happens when *Cadillac* is substituted in the same context:

```
(a′) He                        Cad
        did
           n't
              buy    rd,
                 a       he bought a
                 Fo                   illac
```

Similarly if *bother you* occurred in a contrastive environment, it would be realized as:

```
(b′)   don't                              bo
     I
            think
                he                   he wants to
                   wants      you,
                        to
                          help            ther you
```

Based on this analysis it appears that a case can be made for recognizing a typical pitch configuration associated with contrastivity, although intonational features realizing other functions may be superimposed on it (Couper-Kuhlen 1984).

Other linguists also recognize intonational differences between contrastive and new. In the data analyzed by Brown/Currie/Kenworthy (1980) contrastive information regularly has higher pitch than new information. But "there also appear items raised high in the speaker's pitch range which can be interpreted either as in non-specific contrast or, more straightforwardly, as being *emphasized* by the speaker" (1980:29). For example:

(i)   I *don't* think – *especially* after the *war* you know ...
(ii)  they were quite happy where they were if they'd built houses in the town – *which* they're *doing now*
(iii) *that's* what I regret *especially*     (1980: 66f., 74)

136

Indeed, whether contrastive intonation is identified with extra pitch height or with steep slope, it cannot be denied that the pattern occurs in sentences where no strict semantic contrast (§1.3.2, Ch. II §4.3) is present.

Brazil/Coulthard/Johns (1980) note a similar phenomenon. In their model it is choice of high key (Ch. V §3.1) which signals contrastivity. However, they remark, in a sentence such as

as soon as he'd finished EĂTing ‖ he changed into $^h$| TÈNnis gear ‖

(1980:27; cf. Ch. XI Note 13)

the speaker's choice of high key on *tennis gear* may not signal any specific contrast such as changing into tennis gear as opposed to, say, washing the dishes, but rather a particularization: changing into tennis gear as opposed to doing anything else worthwhile. In other words the speaker could have added "... of all things".

Whether we call this a kind of contrast (as Brazil et al do) or *emphasis* (as would Brown et al), the phenomenon is well attested and constitutes counter-evidence to the claim that pitch height or configuration distinguishes contrastive from new information − if we mean *contrastive* in its strictest sense. This indeed was Bolinger's point when he wrote:

In a broad sense every semantic peak is contrastive. Clearly in *Let's have a picnic*, coming as a suggestion out of the blue, there is no specific contrast with *dinner party*, but there is a contrast between picnicking and anything else the group might do. (1961a:87)

But it is doubtful whether we need be this extreme. First, strict semantic contrast can be identified relatively well and is systematically accompanied by a distinctive pitch configuration (which may of course be neutralized in certain contexts, or modified by intonational features realizing other functions). Second, there is a sense in which the absence of contrastive pitch configuration in the presence of clear semantic contrast is a speech error (Couper-Kuhlen 1984). This constitutes the strongest evidence for its linguistic function. Third, even if the pitch configuration typically associated with contrastivity is extended to non-specific contrast or emphasis, a case can still be made for considering these as distinct from new information. Both specific and non-specific contrast make, loosely speaking, additional presuppositions. With specific contrast, the speaker chooses one candidate and simultaneously implies that all the other possible candidates are not the right ones: *JOHN ordered the tickets* ('it wasn't Tom'). With non-specific contrast, the speaker presupposes that a particular candidate has a low degree of expectability but chooses that candidate anyway: *JOHN ordered the tickets* ('of all people', 'I wasn't expecting him'). Nothing similar is presupposed or implied with new information. In sum, if we recognize that contrast/emphasis are distinct from new information, then it can be argued that there are distinctive pitch configurations which correspond to these two broad categories.

In conclusion, in spite of the inherent problems and inadequacies exposed so far, we need not be wholly pessimistic about the possibility of establishing an informational function for certain aspects of intonation. However, the model that it will be necessary to posit will doubtless look quite different from classical information-structure and involve a much greater degree of complexity than previously envisaged.

## References

Abdul-Ghani 1978
Allerton 1978
*Allerton/Cruttenden 1979
Armstrong/Ward [2]1931
Bar-Hillel/Carnap 1964
*Bolinger 1961a
Bolinger 1972b
Brazil/Coulthard/Johns 1980 (Chs. 1, 4)
*Brown, G. 1983
Brown/Currie/Kenworthy 1980
    (pp. 27ff., 34ff., 72ff.)
Chafe 1974
Chafe 1976
Couper-Kuhlen 1984
Crystal 1969
Crystal 1975a
Currie 1981
*Daneš 1967
Esser 1983
Firbas 1966a
Firbas 1966b

Firbas 1972
Fuchs 1980
Grice 1975
Gunter 1966
*Gussenhoven 1983a
Gussenhoven 1983b
Gutknecht/Mackiewicz 1977
Halliday 1967b
Halliday 1970a
*Halliday 1976b
Haviland/Clark 1974
Hultzén 1959
Ladd 1983
Leech/Svartvik 1975
Lehman 1977
Lyons 1977 (pp. 32–50)
Prince 1981
Schubiger 1964
*Taglicht 1982
*Yule 1980a
Yule 1981

# Chapter VIII
## Intonation and grammar

It has long been an article of faith that intonation and grammar go hand in hand. Indeed references to their interdependence can be found as early as the 16th and 17th century in manuals of English orthography and pronunciation. Butler (1634), for instance, in his discussion of the proper use of punctuation marks, tacitly assumes that sentence-type (e.g. statement, question, exclamation, etc.) and tune (falling, rising) go together:

> §3.1 Period is a point of perfect sens, and perfect sentence: *which, in the last word, falleth the Tone of the voice* below its ordinari tenour, with a long paus ...
>
> Comma is a point of more imperfect sens, in a simple axiom, or in either part of a compound: *which continueth the tenour of the voice* to the last, with the shortest paus.
>
> §3.2 Erotesis [question mark], if it be pure, *raiseth the common Tone or tenour of the voice* in the last word; unless Emphasis draw it: but if it begin with a word interrogative; as *who, what, how, where, when* &c. *it falleth* as a Period ...
>
> Ecphonesis [exclamation point] *falleth as a period, and raiseth the tone* in the particle of Exclamation, *o, oh, ah, alas, fi upon, out upon* .... [emphasis added] (cit. Danielsson 1963:49)

This traditional view of the interdependence of sentence-type and tune has in fact persisted to our day. For instance, according to Armstrong/Ward ([2]1931), Tune I [final falling contour] is used in:

1. Ordinary, definite, decided statements
   *We did what we were bid.*
2. Questions requiring an answer other than 'yes' or 'no'
   *Where? What for?*
3. Commands
   *Open the door.*
4. Exclamations
   *What a cold day!*     ([2]1931:9f.)

On the other hand, they continue, Tune II [final rising contour] is used

1. In sentences in which the statement is not so definite as in the case of Tune I
   *It seems rather a pity.*
2. In questions requiring the answer 'yes' or 'no'
   *Are you quite sure?*
3. In requests
   *Don't trouble to answer it.*
4. In incomplete groups
   *When they arrived at the station*, they found that the train had gone.     ([2]1931:20ff.)

139

Not all modern-day linguists or phonologists would wish to make such categorical statements; however, the claim that intonation and grammar are somehow related is still being debated today.

## 1. The definition and scope of grammar

Any attempt to determine the exact nature of the relation between intonation and grammar depends crucially on the definition and scope of grammar. Needless to say, previous investigations of intonation and grammar have differed widely on this point.

Traditionally grammar has been understood as that complex formed by *inflection*, the form words take in grammatical categories (e.g. gender, person, number; or tense, mood, voice, etc.) and *syntax*, the ways these words combine with one another in the construction of sentences (Lyons 1981:102). In addition to inflected form and syntactic construction, however, traditional grammar has also typically been concerned with the functions which grammatical classes perform in the sentence (e.g. certain parts of speech function as subjects, others as predicates, etc.) and with the functions which certain types of sentence are said to fulfil (e.g. a declarative sentence makes a statement, an interrogative sentence asks a question, an imperative sentence gives a command, etc.). In this traditional view of grammar, intonation appears to relate primarily to the grammatical category of mood (declarative, interrogative, hortative, exclamative), or in functional terms to sentence-type.

With the advent of modern linguistics, however, scholars have begun to suspect that intonation and grammar may relate in more ways than just the traditional sentence-type/tune correlations. With immediate constituent analysis, for instance, came the hypothesis that intonation is related to surface phrase-structure (e.g. Lee 1956, Wode 1966, Crystal 1969, 1975a), and with generative grammar, the claim that prosodic contrasts (in particular, position of primary stress) reflect differences in deep syntactic structure (Bresnan 1971).

Not all linguists, however, would subscribe to a view of grammar based on constituent or phrase structure. Among those holding other views the most significant is Halliday. According to him, "grammar is that level of linguistic form at which operate closed systems," whereas "any part of linguistic form which is not concerned with the operation of closed systems belongs to the level of lexis" (1961; 1976:54f.).[1] Grammar and lexis being the only two kinds of formal patterning which are said to exist in language, the domain of 'grammar' is consequently very broad. In Halliday's sense 'grammar' encompasses phonological, morphological, syntactic and even semantic phenomena to the extent that they can be reduced to closed systems. Intonational contrasts are thus also an integral part:

> English intonation contrasts are grammatical: they are exploited in the grammar of the language. The systems expounded by intonation are just as much grammatical as are those, such as tense, number and mood, expounded by other means. (1967a:10)

---

[1] 'Closed systems', according to Halliday, are sets of terms which have the following characteristics: "(a) The number of terms is finite …, (b) Each term is exclusive of the others …, (c) If a new term is added to the system this changes the meaning of all the others" (1961; 1976:54).

In Halliday's model, English intonation expounds (inter alia) the following 'grammatical' distinctions: information distribution, information focus, sentence structure, clause structure, sentence function, reservation, agreement, commitment, involvement, force, etc. (1967a:31ff.). Within the framework established here, however, distinctions such as information distribution or information focus belong to the informational function of intonation, whereas those such as reservation, agreement, force, etc. belong to the attitudinal function. Setting these aside, we are left with distinctions which are strictly grammatical in that they concern inflection and syntax. It is this traditional sense of the term that we shall employ here.[2]

## 2. The case for a grammatical function

The following represents a compilation of some of the evidence which has accumulated to date in support of a grammatical function of intonation. For greater clarity, contrasts and correlations are grouped according to the primary intonation feature at play. In each case the grammatical relation or structure expounded by intonation figures as heading. Grammatical terminology has been unified based on Quirk et al (1972).

### 2.1 Location of tone-unit boundaries

#### 2.1.1 Contrastive pairs

The placement of tone-unit boundaries has been attributed *distinctive* function with respect to the following grammatical structures:

(a) Ellipsis vs. non-ellipsis of direct object in clausal coordination

   i.  he washed and brushed his hair ‖
      ('he washed [his hair] and he brushed his hair')
         vs.
   ii.  he washed ‖ and brushed his hair ‖
       ('he washed and he brushed his hair')    (Halliday 1967a:36)

In (i) two verbal elements with co-referential objects are conjoined, whereas in (ii) two whole clauses are conjoined. The tone-unit boundary between *washed* and *and* signals the clause boundary.

(b) Clausal apposition vs. simple sentence + postmodifying relative clause

   i.  that's aNOther thing ‖ I don't KNOW yet ‖
         vs.
   ii.  that's another thing I don't KNOW yet ‖[3]    (Halliday 1967a:36)

---

[2] Few if any significant intonational regularities have been reported for word or form-classes (cf. Crystal 1969:266f.), so that in effect we shall be concerned with correlations between intonation and syntactic structure and/or function. Prosodic regularities in morphological derivation will also be excluded from consideration here under the assumption that these involve above all lexical stress and are more appropriately treated within the lexicon.

[3] The additional contrast in tonicity is contingent on the number of tone-units present.

The relation between the clauses in (i) is paratactic, between those in (ii) hypotactic. [An explanation in terms of information structure is also possible.]

(c) Restrictive vs. non-restrictive postmodifying relative clause

   i.  that's from my brother who lives in PARis ‖
       vs.
   ii.  that's from my BROther ‖ who lives in PARis ‖[4]    (Schubiger 1958:103)

The first sentence implies that the speaker has several brothers but is singling out the one in Paris, whereas the second implies that the speaker has only one brother. Consequently the information that the brother lives in Paris is coincidental to his identification.

(d) Subordinate clause of reason inside the scope of negation vs. outside

   i.  he didn't go to Holland because his DUTCH was weak ‖
      ('he went for some other reason')
       vs.
   ii.  he didn't go to HOLland ‖ because his DUTCH was weak ‖[5]
      ('he didn't go')   (Lee 1956a:350)

In (i) it is the main clause + adverbial clause of reason which is negated (*not* [*he went to Holland because his Dutch was weak*]), whereas in (ii) only the main clause is negated (*not* [*he went to Holland*]).

(e) Manner adjunct vs. attitudinal disjunct

   (i)  he speaks English NATurally ‖
       vs.
   (ii)  he speaks ENGlish ‖ NATurally ‖    (Schubiger 1958:91)

Whereas in (i) *naturally* describes the manner of *x*'s speaking English, in (ii) it expresses the speaker's evaluation of the fact that *x* speaks English. [According to Allerton/Cruttenden (1974), final sentence adverbials or disjuncts such as *naturally* can also be part of the preceding tone-unit − provided they are non-nuclear. In this case the distinction between manner adjunct and attitudinal disjunct would depend on tonicity.]

---

[4] These distinctive intonation patterns are, however, not consistently used in actual speech. For instance, we find *make the point* ‖ *that you're trying to make to Erin* (A1/DJ₁), *anybody* ‖ *who has the temerity...* (A1/EP₁), *this is one issue* ‖ *in which I would have no hesitation ...* (E1/CCB₁), etc. Further study would be required to determine whether variables such as length of the elements involved and/or presence of the relative pronoun influence boundary placement on restrictive relative clauses.

[5] A tone contrast is also involved here. Note that this distinctive intonation is not maintained by SW on the accompanying tape: [*that's the basic principle of the National Health Service*] *is that one shouldn't seek specialized treatment* ‖ *because one is in a privileged position* (E3/SW₁).

### 2.1.2 Co-occurrence patterns

In the following cases, boundary placement does not function distinctively for the most part. However, in frequency analyses of large quantities of spoken data certain regularities between the placement of tone-unit boundaries and sentence structure have appeared. According to Crystal (1975), for instance, one clause generally has one tone-unit provided (i) the clause consists maximally of Subject (S) + Verb (V) + Complement (C) and/or Object (O), with one optional Adverbial (A); *and* (ii) each of the clause elements S, C, O or A consists of a simple nominal group. A simple nominal group is defined as a noun modified by *a, the, this, his,* etc. (e.g. *that hog*); a pronoun (*it*); or a proper name (*Henry*), with maximally one adjectival premodifier (*that heavy hog*) and/or prepositional phrase postmodifier (*that [heavy] hog on the farm*) (Quirk et al 1972:933, Crystal 1975a:16). For example, the following sentences would normally have only one tone-unit:

the big boy kicked the ball yesterday (S V O A)
we gave him a lift in the car (S V O O A)
go away (V )
I asked him (S V O)
he spoke (S V)      (Crystal 1975a:16ff.)

Crystal's model predicts that additional tone-unit boundaries above and beyond this minimal set will occur only if (a) there is more than one clause, (b) clause structure is complex, i.e. contains more than four elements (S, V, O, C) and one optional A, or (c) nominal group structure is complex, i.e. there is more than one adjective premodifier and/or prepositional phrase postmodifier.

### 2.1.2.1 Multiple clauses

If a sentence has *more than one clause*, then additional tone-unit boundaries will be added for the following (illustrations, so far as possible, from the accompanying recordings):

(1) Structural parallelism

... don't care ‖ you don't understand ‖ you don't mind (A2/EP)

(2) Coordinate clauses

it's no use your setting yourself up on a pedestal ‖ and lecturing to them in this way (A1/BD₄)

(3) Subordinate clauses

  i. Adverbials (initial, medial, final)
    if I had known what I'd known ‖ I'd have probably put down my paint brush and run (A3/EP)
    it's like wallpaper ‖ until you actually get there (A2/EP)
    I've always been grateful for the accidents in life ‖ because they are wonderful (A3/BD)
  ii. Nominal clauses as subject
    whether the election ... was free or fair ‖ is rather irrelevant (A4/BD)
    what on the whole you get ... ‖ is precisely what Enoch Powell said (E1/HW₁)

iii. Non-restrictive relative clauses[6] (§2.1.1)

   ... movement ‖ which is world wide now ‖ having never planned ... (A3/EP)
   ... the famous Walter Mitty complex ‖ which people still have in this country (A4/BD)
   ... who gets caught up in a cog ... ‖ which is actually goes back to what you said (A3/EP)

iv. Nominal clauses as complements[6] (§2.1.1)

   one of the problems is ‖ the woman ... who doesn't want to carry ... that child (A1/EP₃)
   the fact is ‖ many of those people do not want children ... (A1/EP₃)

## (4) Medial parenthetic clauses

   I went over to Belfast ‖ uh it was last week ‖ to do a television programme (A2/EP)
   but the best thing you can do ‖ I think ‖ is to wake up every day ... (A3/EP)

## (5) Direct speech markers[7]

   somebody asked ‖ why did they recognize ... (A4/BD)
   what ‖ people ask ‖ do you make of him

## (6) Comment clauses

   and she was probably ‖ you know ‖ one of the few people this had ever happened to (A3/EP)

## (7) Tag questions

   it's bullying ‖ isn't it (A1/EP₂)
   it's not quite fair ‖ is it (E1/HW₅)

An independent statistical frequency analysis carried out by Bald (1980) corroborates (7) in the case of reversed-polarity tag questions such as the ones above. However, identical-polarity tags such as *John went home, did he?* are apparently more often than not part of the preceding tone-unit (1980:268).

### 2.1.2.2 Complex clause structure

If a sentence does not meet condition (i) that the clause structure not contain more than four clause elements (S, V, O, C) and one optional A, additional boundaries are inserted for:

### (1) Initial vocative

   Teddy Taylor ‖ put that question (A4/DJ)
   Conor ‖ would you assume ... (E3/DJ₄)

---

[6] The placement of these boundaries also has distinctive function.

[7] The tone-unit boundary comes directly after the direct speech marker and any complements which modify it. Thus a distinctive function is also possible, as in: *Have you a motorcycle ‖ she asked ‖ to gain time* vs. *Have you a motorcycle ‖ she asked to gain time* (Schubiger 1958:99).

(2) Sentence adverbials (conjuncts or disjuncts) in initial, medial, final position[8]

> on the other hand || there was this feeling (A2/EP)
> probably || sanctions will be lifted || inevitably (A4/EP)
> so Sir Freddy Laker || with great respect Conor || is in a rather different market
> (E1/SW$_1$)

(3) Adverbial sequence

> than if we were simply doing it || piecemeal || with odd pains ... (C/AJ)
> I mean he's undoubtedly || enormously enterprising (E1/HW$_1$)

### 2.1.2.3 Complex nominal group

If condition (ii) is not fulfilled, i.e. if a clause element contains *more than a simple nominal group*, tone-unit boundaries must be inserted for:

(1) Structural parallelism

> everybody || people who drove the taxis || people who were carrying bags || everybody
> around us (A2/EP)

(2) Multiple heads

  i. Separate pre- or postmodification [cf. Note 6]
     in that shop you'll find some very nice chairs || and tables
     the man || and the woman dressed in black
  ii. Non-restrictive apposition
     we should be talking about contraception || not abortion || contraception for men ||
     not women (A1/EP$_3$)
     what I object completely to is his attitude || his self-righteous attitude (A1/BD$_4$)

(3) Multiple modification

  i. Premodifying, general adjectives
     for a very definite || very limited form (E1/HW$_5$)
     you are putting yourself in a wholly different || supplicant kind of position to the man
  ii. Postmodification in subject, passive agent or non-final object
     the hotel I was in || had been completely bombed out (A2/EP)
     ... was to open a small community center || for mothers and children with toddlers
     (A3/EP)
     they have an absolute right || to make a decision over their own lives (A1/EP$_1$)
     the people who can afford private treatment || ... (E3/HW)

---

[8] A detailed study of English conjuncts and disjuncts by Allerton/Cruttenden (1974, 1976, 1978) indicates that the choice of intonation for adverbials depends not only on syntactic but also on illocutionary, thematic and attitudinal factors. The rules here, however, have been set up to account for the 'norm', so that such results do not necessarily jeopardize the model.

(4) Medial non-restrictive phrases

> and I would say ‖ as strongly as may be ‖ that I do not think that that would be right (E3/SW₁)
>
> I suppose if I was absolutely compelled to buy a share ‖ at the point of a gun ‖ I'd buy his (E1/SW₁)

These tone-unit divisions represent the norm, the unmarked patterns which Crystal's model would predict, provided there is no interference due to sociolinguistic or stylistic variation, idiosyncratic variation, performance factors such as lack of concentration or false starts, or attitudinal colouring (1975a:21).[9]

## 2.2 Placement of the nucleus

### 2.2.1 Contrastive pairs

In the following minimal pairs intonation appears to expound different syntactic structures and/or grammatical functions:

(a) Covert passive vs. active voice in postmodifying infinitive clause

> (i) George has PLANS to write ('to be written')
> vs.
> (ii) George has plans to WRITE     (Newman 1946: 179f.)

Here, it has been argued, intonation (i.e. placement of the nucleus) distinguishes between (i) in which *plans* is the direct object of *write* [i.e. George must write plans], and (ii) in which *write* is the complement of *plans* [i.e. George intends to write something]. Similarly, intonation would create two possible readings for: *George has directions to sign, George has instructions to prepare, George has orders to obey,* etc.

(b) Alternative vs. *yes—no* question

> (i) may I offer you some TEA or COFfee?
> vs.
> (ii) may I offer you some tea or COFfee?     (Schubiger 1958:105)

Whereas (i) offers either an unlimited or a limited choice of specific drinks (§2.3.1) and requires the name of one of them as an answer, (ii) asks in general whether the hearer wants a warm drink or not and requires a yes—no answer.

(c) Positive vs. negative implication

> (i) I THOUGHT it would rain ('and it did')
> vs.
> (ii) I thought it would RAIN ('but it didn't')

---

[9] In a corpus containing over 12,000 tone-units, Crystal reports that only 100 did not conform to his rules of boundary placement, i.e. required this type of explanation (1975a:21).

(Cf. Nash/Mulac 1980.) [A theory of information structure could also account for this distinction.]

(d) Adverbial clause of condition vs. indirect question

(i) please WIRE if I am to come
vs.
(ii) please wire if I am to COME     (Schubiger 1958:106)

In (i) *if* is construed as signalling the dependence of one circumstance on another ('If I am to come, [then] please wire'), whereas in (ii) *if* is understood to be introducing a yes–no question 'Am I to come or not?'. [An explanation in terms of information structure is also possible here.]


### 2.2.2 Co-occurrence patterns

In addition, there are co-occurrence patterns between grammatical structure and presence of the nucleus, or lack of it (illustrations, so far as possible, from the accompanying recordings):

(a) *Final vocatives.* These normally do not have nuclear prominence, but occur post-nuclearly in the tail instead:[10]

were you NÓT Mrs Baker (E3/DJ$_2$)
I didn't say THĀT Mr Powell (E3/CCB$_3$)

Sometimes a final vocative does have tonal movement, but only as the second, rising half of a compound fall + rise nucleus:[11]

it's an old Yorkshire CÙStom you see ĒRin (A1/BD$_2$)
well exCÙSE me Énoch (E3/DJ$_2$)

(b) *Final direct speech markers.* These too normally appear in the tail:

he WĀNTed he said ...

(c) *Final disjuncts.* These occur post-nuclearly, but may also have a low rise as part of a fall + rise compound nucleus:

(you've given a fair description) of modern ↑↑MÈDicine in a way (C/AJ)
(you get different levels) of THRÈSholds as it WÉRE (C/AJ)

(d) *Final conjuncts of time, place, manner and condition*

(goes to the heart) of what our ↑↑PRǪblem is today (C/AJ)
but we're not an ↑↑ĘMpire anymore (A4/EP)
(one of the sad things) about the whole medical ↑↑SÈTup toDÁY (C/AJ)

---

[10] According to O'Connor, this rule is rarely broken, even when ambiguity may result. Cf.: *I choose to igNORE that, Sally* vs. *I choose to igNORE that sally* (cit. Schubiger 1958:96).

[11] Firbas' category *shade*, which encompasses the final rise of compound F + R nuclei as well as nuclear tails, is thus appropriate here (1980:126).

According to Halliday, final conjuncts of this sort generally do not receive major tonicity if they present 'secondary' information, defined as being "subsidiary to the main point" (1970a:38). This is corroborated by Firbas' distinction between the *setting* and the *specification* of the proposition at hand (1980:130). The former presents concomitant information; the latter belongs to the core of the message. [Compare, for instance: 'I haven't finished my essay yet' *it's supposed to be IN by toMÓRrow* vs. *it's supposed to be in by toMÒRrow*.] An explanation in terms of information structure may, however, be preferable here.

## 2.3  Nuclear type

### 2.3.1  Contrastive pairs

(a) Statement vs. question

> (i) JÒHN has
>      vs.
> (ii) JÓHN has      (Halliday 1967a:41)

This is surely the most frequently cited evidence for the grammatical function of intonation. As Schubiger puts it: "Intonation can turn any sentence or fragment of a sentence into a question" (1958:39). Notice, however, that the term *question* is not used here in its strict grammatical sense of 'interrogative form'. Sentence (ii) is not a grammatical question − if it were, it would have subject-operator inversion − but a pragmatic one instead: its intention is to elicit some answer from the addressee.

(b) *Yes−no* question vs. exclamation

> (i) isn't he SÚRE of himself
>      vs.
> (ii) isn't he SÙRE of himself

Whereas (i) is typically said to be a genuine question requiring a *yes−no* answer, (ii) has the force of an exclamation and requires acknowledgement or agreement.
  A similar distinction is found with tag questions:

> (iii) he likes his JÒB ‖ DÓESn't he
>       vs.
> (iv) he likes his JÒB ‖ DÒESn't he      (Quirk et al 1972:391)

With a rising tag the speaker is uncertain of the answer himself, whereas with a falling tag s/he knows or expects a certain answer and wants confirmation from the hearer (cf. also Ch. IX §3).

(c) *Wh*-question vs. echo question

> (i) WHÈRE are you going
>      vs.
> (ii) WHÉRE are you going      (Halliday 1967a:43)

An echo question, defined as "a request for repetition of something unheard, forgotten or disbelieved" (Halliday 1967a:43), is typically accompanied by a high rising tone.

(d) Command vs. echo question

    (i)  tell him the TRÙTH
        vs.
    (ii)  tell him the TRÚTH     (Halliday 1967a:46)

In (i) the imperative is used for a command; in (ii) it is given questioning force by the rising intonation.

(e) Alternative vs. list question

    (i)  would you like TÉA or CÒFfee
        vs.
    (ii)  would you like TÉA or CÓFfee     (Halliday 1967a:44)

Whereas (i) implies that there are only two choices, (ii) leaves the matter open. The addressee is thus likely to infer that other drinks are available.

(f) Negative statement vs. negative implication

'Do you think I should take a few Dutch lessons before going to Amsterdam?'

    (i)  it isn't esSÈNtial
        vs.
    (ii)  it isn't esSĔNtial ('though very useful')    (Schubiger 1958:46)

    (i)  they don't admit ÀNy students
        vs.
    (ii)  they don't admit ĂNy students (= just any students)    (Lee 1956a:346)

In each case (i) is a straightforward negation, whereas (ii) strongly implies some kind of reservation ('but ...') or even the opposite ('but rather ...').[12]

(g) Adverbial clause of concession vs. adverbial clause of time

    (i)  he keeps on TÀLKing ‖ when he knows it anNÒYS us
        vs.
    (ii)  he keeps on TÀLKing when he knows it anNÓYS us[13]    (Schubiger 1958:97)

(h) Adverbial clause of concession vs. adverbial clause of condition

    (i)  I'll make her do the flowers herSÈLF ‖ if I have to stand over her all MÒRning
        vs.
    (ii)  I'll make her do the flowers herSÈLF if I have to stand over her all MÓRning[13]
                                    (Schubiger 1958:98)

---

[12] Tone is thus partially responsible for the contrast in negative sentences with subordinate clauses of reason, viz. *I didn't come because of the FÒOD* vs. *I didn't come because of the FÓOD* ('I came for some other reason') (Schubiger 1958:95) [§2.1.1(d)].

[13] Tone-unit boundary placement is also involved.

(j) Conditional vs. imperative

    (i)  give him that TÓY (and) he will break it at ÒNCE

        vs.

    (ii)  give him that TÒY (and) he will break it at ÒNCE    (Schubiger 1953:269)

The imperative form with rising intonation is interpreted as the protasis of a conditional sentence in (i), whereas in (ii) with a fall it has the force of a command.

### 2.3.2 Co-occurrence patterns

Typical correlations between grammar and tone which have been documented in the literature include (illustrated to the extent possible with examples from the accompanying recordings):

(a) *Non-restrictive apposition.* Clauses and phrases in non-restrictive apposition tend to have the same nuclear tone as their antecedent noun or phrase:

    people like David STÊEL ‖ who was one of the biggest proMÔters (A1/BD$_1$)
    the Chairman of ↑ÒXfam ‖ Sir Geoffrey ↑WÌLson (B/O)
    two hundred and twenty MÌLLion ‖ the population of AMÈRica

(b) *Lists.* These are likely to have one of the following patterns, depending on whether they are complete or incomplete:

*Complete*
    (i)
    (ii)
    (iii)

    (i)   there are hundreds of RÚSSian ‖ CÚBan ‖ and East German [SPÈCialists] and adVÌSors ‖
    (ii)  the horses were NÈIGHing; the oxen were BÈLlowing; the cows were LÓWing; and the pigs were GRÙNTing    (Schubiger 1958:72)
    (iii) and they're about to die ‖ MŪTilated ‖ and BŪRNED ‖ and HÙRT (A1/EP$_3$)

*Incomplete*
    (iv)
    (v)              (Schubiger 1958:72f.)

    (iv) if you ask people to speak about their LÁWyers ‖ or their WÁSHer repairman ‖ or their CÁR mechanic
    (v)  it's like FLŪoride ‖ it's like [CĀPital] PÙN̊ishment ‖ it's ONE ... (A1/BD$_1$)

(c) *Non-final syntactic groups.* Long and/or syntactically complex sentences, especially with heavy modification, are typically broken up into several groups or tone-units (§2.1.2). As non-final tone-units in a sentence we find (rise−)falls, levels and rises. For example:

    (i)   has said the [CHĀRity] raised a ↑RĒCord ‖ (B/O)

        or

    (ii)  two million pounds MÔRE ‖ (B/O)

        or

    (iii) Sir GÉOFfrey ‖ speaking to the Oxfam annual MÈETing ‖ (B/O)

150

According to Schubiger, the choice is "a matter of style, of personal speech habits" (1958:69). In spite of this apparent free variation, however, we would be unlikely to find a fall-to-bottom on any but a final group. This has led some linguists (e.g. Hultzén 1964) to posit two major classes of intonation contour: non-low ending (or 'open') and low ending (or 'closed'). The former would include all rises and arrested falls, the latter falls-to-bottom (cf. also Couper-Kuhlen 1983).

(d) *Subject displacement.* A subject displaced to the end of a sentence typically has a low rise:

>    (i) it's a real NÙIsance that DÓG     (Halliday 1970a:38)

As the contrastive pairs above demonstrate, intonation does have the potential to function distinctively with respect to certain grammatical categories and structures. But when the intonation of actual speech is investigated, it becomes evident that grammatical constructions rarely show 100% consistency as to intonational configuration. The degree of co-occurrence may vary anywhere from 'almost always' to 'only sometimes'. This is just one consideration which militates against a strong version of the grammatical claim.

## 3. The case against a grammatical function

Arguments against a grammatical function of intonation maintain, in a nutshell, that "encounters between intonation and grammar are casual, not causal" (Bolinger 1958c:37). The claim is that grammar does not determine intonation nor intonation, grammar; any attested overlap is merely *derivative* (e.g. dependent on more general 'meanings' of the tones; Cruttenden 1970) or *coincidental* (both intonation and grammar are expounding the same meaning; Barry 1981a).

### 3.1 Boundary location

According to Cruttenden, three facts argue against attributing a grammatical function to tone-unit boundary placement:
>    (i) disambiguation by tone-unit boundary placement is relatively infrequent
>    (ii) there are a large number of exceptions to the high correlation between tone-units and clauses
>    (iii) division into tone-units is in many cases optional.     (1970:184)

Cruttenden's first objection addresses the question of functional load (Ch. VI §2): how often is intonation called upon to disambiguate utterances, and how often does it really do so? The likelihood of the contrastive pairs cited above actually occurring in speech is relatively small indeed, one might argue, and even if a potentially ambiguous structure did occur, the context would probably resolve the ambiguity. However, similar arguments have been advanced against all structuralist analyses based on minimal distinctions. For instance, the phonemic contrast /ʃ/ vs. /ʒ/ is documented in very few minimal pairs in English. How likely is it that, say, *Asher*

/ˈæʃə/ and *azure* /ˈæʒə/ might ever occur in the same environment? And even if they did, would hearers really rely on the phonemic contrast to disambiguate the utterance? Nevertheless there is general consensus that /ʃ/ and /ʒ/ are distinct phonemes in the English sound system. Objections such as (i) above must thus be placed in the context of a more broadly based criticism of structuralist procedures in general, and alternative models must be developed. At present, such arguments need not affect the validity of claims pertaining to the structure of linguistic systems.

Cruttenden's second and third objections, however, are of a different nature. They address the question of how much regularity there is in the grammatical placement of boundaries. Crystal's (1975) model, introduced subsequent to Cruttenden's critique, implies that there is a great deal. It lays down explicit rules for the association of clause and tone-unit and accounts for instances of non-overlap in terms of type and degree of clause and phrase structure complexity. Since 99% of the tone-unit boundaries in a large corpus examined by Crystal and his co-workers can be explained by this model, one might assume that Cruttenden's objections are thereby invalidated.

However, a brief application of Crystal's model to selected material from the accompanying recordings reveals a number of inadequacies. In addition to the fact that the rules need some elaboration,[14] there are two major problems:

(1) Although it may be possible to account for the majority of tone-unit boundaries which *occur* using these rules (this is what Crystal claims with respect to his own corpus), it is not possible to account for the *non-occurrence* of tone-unit boundaries when requisite syntactic structure is present. Thus we find, for example:

   i.   let her in and said of course I'll take care of you ‖ (A3/EP)
   ii.  I'd have probably put down my paint brush and run ‖ (A3/EP)
   iii. if he can then there's no argument about it ‖ (A4/BD)
   iv. after one hopes considering ‖ what has been said in a debate ‖ (E2/SW)

The rules would have predicted the insertion of tone-unit boundaries after *in* and *said* in (i), after *brush* in (ii), after *can* in (iii), and around *one hopes* in (iv). How do we explain their non-occurrence?

(2) Even the implicit claim that the overwhelming majority of tone-unit boundary *occurrences* in speech can be accounted for by these rules is not confirmed in our material. The relative frequency of unpredictable tone-unit boundaries casts doubt on such a high rate of predictability. Consider, for instance,

   (i)    they feel like they're a forgotten bit ‖ of a war ‖ that nobody really wants to solve (A2/EP)
   (ii)   they'll leave it alone ‖ till it splatters out ‖ to a deadly end (A2/EP)
   (iii)  so here I am ‖ in the middle of the most enormous ‖ movement (A3/EP)
   (iv)  as if the whole world ‖ is hanging waiting on our decision (A4/BD)

---

[14] In particular the rules appear to miss a certain amount of regularity in the area of sentence complementation, for example: *there's no doubt at all* ‖ *that when the original abortion bill came into Parliament* (A1/BD₂) or *many people don't realize* ‖ *that British Airways has to fly routes…* (E1/SW₁).

(v) which I found one of the most fascinating and most interesting || times of my life (A3/BD)
(vi) you can't legislate || for human relationships (A1/$EP_1$)
(vii) I personally || would not have an abortion (A1/$EP_1$)
(viii) a Member of Parliament || makes a judgment (E2/SW)

As Crystal himself points out, such unpredictable boundary placement can usually be explained in terms of sociolinguistic or stylistic variation, speaker idiosyncrasy, performance errors and/or emotional colouring. Thus examples such as (ii) and (v) can perhaps be attributed to performance errors, whereas (iv), (vi), (vii) and (viii) may be due to the emphatic attitude which the speaker is using at the time. However, this is doing little more than explaining away exceptions after the fact. In short, it is virtually impossible to *predict* where boundaries will come as a result of performance error or emotional colouring.

The major point which is overlooked by rules such as these is the *apperceptive* nature of boundary placement. In discussing the intonation of lists, Schubiger (1958) remarks that with patterns such as 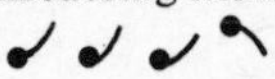 or 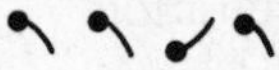 "apperception is comprehensive; from the beginning the speaker has all the items he is going to mention in mind". On the other hand, with a pattern such as  "the speaker's apperception is gradual. That is why *and* mostly introduces each item; for each might be the last and in this case have a low fall" (1958:72). But the fact is that apperception is crucial in more than just the intonation of enumerations.

From past and present research into the processes of speech production we know that speakers do plan ahead. The planning appears to encompass not simply one word at a time, but larger 'chunks' of organized structure. Boomer (1965) hypothesizes that these chunks overlap with 'phonemic clauses', a term used by American structuralists to refer to the expanse from one primary stress up to but not including the next – i.e. for all practical purposes, the equivalent of what we have been calling a simple tone-unit. If this is so, then it follows that phonemic clause or tone-unit boundaries will mark the extremities of what is conceived of as an integral unit in the speaker's mind. The fact that these boundaries do not always coincide with points which seem syntactically appropriate is simply proof that human beings do not necessarily plan speech this way. We may find that a simple nominal group is given separate intonation if it is planned as a single unit, or that more than one clause is put in one tone-unit if they are integrated in planning. [Obviously tempo plays a concomitant role, undoubtedly interacting with physiological constraints on breathing.] The point is, however, that boundary placement rules which rely solely on syntactic structure – no matter how subtle the analysis is – will never be able to account fully for speech data, even if performance errors and the like are set aside. This is because the tone-unit is a unit of speech planning which is not fully sensitive to syntactic criteria.

Yet this should not be taken to mean that syntactic constituents are wholly irrelevant for the placement of tonal boundaries. On the contrary, there is a strong tendency for the latter, should they occur, to coincide with syntactic boundaries, in particular major ones. This observation – on which models for boundary placement such as Crystal's are founded – is also supported by instrumental data. Experimental evidence indicates, for instance, that both clause and phrase boundaries are typically accompanied by a fall–rise pattern in $f_0$ (Cooper 1980), and that structurally ambiguous sentences may have different $f_0$ contours. Lehiste (1973a) investigated a number of these experimentally and concluded that in particular ambiguity based on bracketing, e.g. *old (men and women)* vs. *(old men) and women*, is disambiguated by prosodic means. However, her results indicate that temporal features – segment lengthening and pause – are used more systematically than pitch features. To the extent that segment lengthening and pause interact with pitch configuration in the realization of tone-unit boundaries, we can conclude that intonation is instrumental in this disambiguation process. But it is important to remember that there is no obligation for a speaker to mark syntactic boundaries with intonation. In the words of Collier/ 't Hart, it depends "to what extent the speaker cares to provide the listener with syntax-linked intonational cues" (1975:120).

## 3.2 Nuclear position

The evidence for a grammatical function here is meagre to begin with. Most counter-arguments center around the fact that the apparent contrasts are just as readily explained in terms of information content (e.g. Bolinger 1972b). The one set of examples where this is not immediately evident is *George has directions to follow* and the like. But even this distinctive intonational configuration is at best merely a norm, in the sense that it is only found consistently in the absence of a special context. Under appropriate conditions, information structure overrides syntactic structure in determining nuclear placement. Consider, for instance:

(i)  A: (to a policeman): What if pursuing a criminal places you in mortal danger?
     B: I have no choice. I have diRECtions to follow ('directions to follow the criminal')

                    or

(ii) A: Why didn't John's model plane turn out?
     B: He had directions to FOLlow – he just didn't look at them ('directions to be followed')

Thus the intonation of these syntactic constructions must also be ultimately explained in terms of information structure and a *distinctive* grammatical function of tonicity appears dubious indeed.

Nevertheless, there are important *correlations*, if only negative ones, between tonicity and grammatical structure which cannot be explained by information content. Indeed, if information structure were involved, say, in the case of final direct speech markers, we might expect complex, heavily modified NPs to attract the nucleus – but this does not happen:

no THANK you said the exceptionally plump young man in blue standing near the window

In fact, even when the direct speech marker introduces a new development in the plot, the nucleus does not alter its position:

no THANK you he said raising his hand and firing three deadly shots

Thus there seems to be some justification for recognizing a weak version of the grammatical claim with respect to nuclear position, based on negative correlations of this sort.

## 3.3 Nuclear type

It is with respect to choice of tone and its relation to sentence-type that the so-called grammatical function of intonation has come in for the most criticism. There are two major objections: (1) the difficulty of separating grammatical from attitudinal variables, and (2) the confusion of grammatical category with pragmatic function.

### 3.3.1 Separating grammatical from attitudinal variables

Implicit in the traditional view of intonation and grammar is the hypothesis that each major sentence-type is associated with a given tune or tone in *neutral* or 'matter-of-fact speech' (Schubiger 1958:40).[15] Any other nuclear choice is said to carry a connotation which is expressive of the speaker's attitude. Thus, commands generally have falls; if a rise is used, then the command becomes a (more polite) request.[16]

One of the numerous problems with this view, however, is that it is virtually impossible to distinguish grammatical from attitudinal function. Why is a fall on a (neutral, matter-of-fact) statement an instance of the grammatical function of intonation, but a rise on a (non-neutral questioning) statement an instance of the attitudinal function? In the former the fall may distinguish a grammatical statement from a grammatical question, but at the same time it also distinguishes a neutral, matter-of-fact attitude from a non-neutral, questioning attitude. How can we draw the line between a grammatical question and a questioning attitude?[17]

### 3.3.2 Confusion of grammatical category with pragmatic function

It has often been concluded, for instance, from the fact that rising intonation turns a statement into a *yes–no* question that all *yes–no* questions therefore have rising intonation. Yet this conclusion is scarcely borne out by the facts. Fries (1964), for

---

[15] In Halliday's model, for instance, the neutral tone for the major speech functions 'statement', '*wh*-question' and 'command' is tone / 1 / (falling) and for the major speech function '*yes–no* question', tone / 2 / (low rising). The neutral tone for the minor speech functions 'response', 'exclamation' and 'call' – to the extent that they can be said to have one – is tone / 1 / (1970a:26).

[16] Note that the dichotomy between neutral vs. non-neutral intonation begins to lose its meaning when the marked variant becomes the norm and the original unmarked variant takes on an added connotation. This has happened, for instance, with the originally 'neutral' fall for a command, which has been replaced by the 'neutral' rise; it is now the fall which carries a note of abruptness (Schubiger 1958:41).

[17] Crystal proposes to restrict the term *grammatical* to "only those uses of intonation which can be shown to expound categories *already required* by a grammar" (1975:35). But is the following a grammatical distinction according to this criterion? YÈS ‖ it ÌS (response signalling agreement) vs. YÈS ‖ it ÍS (response signalling opposition) (1969:273).

155

example, analyzed the intonation of *yes–no* questions used by panelists in the TV quiz game "What's My Line?" and found that more than half of the 2561 questions asked (62%) had falling rather than rising intonation. [Obviously these results are valid only for this very special situation; nevertheless they disprove the above claim as a generalization.]

In fact, not all interrogatives have rising intonation:

(a) do you mind closing the DÒOR
would you beLIÈVE that
is this water CÔLD
can you TÈLL me something about your dream

nor do all rises accompany interrogative forms or signal questions:

(b) I didn't say THÁT
tell me your NÁME
I'm WÀRNing YÓU

Thus the simple equation of *yes–no* questions and rising intonation is misguided indeed. In fact, many questions do not even have interrogative form to begin with:

(c) you've been there beFORE I assume
it's over by three o'CLOCK you say
I'm not sure I know where you LIVE

We must thus make a three-way distinction between *intonational* shape – rising or falling tone, etc.; *grammatical* form – declarative, interrogative, imperative, etc.; and *pragmatic* function – question, statement, command, etc. While there appears to be little relationship between choice of tone and grammatical form in this strict sense,[18] on the other hand linguists have begun to suspect that there may be important correlations between intonational shape and pragmatic function.

In conclusion, the so-called grammatical function reduces on closer analysis to very modest proportions indeed. Only a weak version can be maintained for most intonational distinctions due to boundary placement, and even this only to the extent that apperception and speaker planning strategies do not interfere. Intonational distinctions due to nuclear position are rarely of a grammatical nature; a few co-occurrence patterns can be established but these are highly limited in range (Ch. VI §2.2). Nuclear tone distinctions are more often than not pragmatic/illocutionary rather than strictly grammatical. Thus only a weak version of the functional claim can be maintained here too – and it is further restricted by narrow range.

---

[18] "... there seem to be no intonation sequences on questions as a whole that are not also found on other types of utterances, and no intonation sequences on other types of utterances that are not found on questions" (Fries 1964:250f.).

# References

Allerton/Cruttenden 1974
Allerton/Cruttenden 1976
Allerton/Cruttenden 1978
Armstrong/Ward ²1931
Bald 1980
Barry 1981a
Bing 1979
Bolinger 1958c
Bolinger 1972b
Boomer 1965
Boomer 1978
Bresnan 1971
Butler 1634
Collier/'t Hart 1975
Cooper 1980
*Cruttenden 1980
Crystal 1969
*Crystal 1975a
Danielsson 1963
Firbas 1980

Fries 1964
Halliday 1961
Halliday 1967a
Halliday 1970a
Hultzén 1964
Kingdon 1958b (§J)
Lee 1953
Lee 1956a
Lee 1980
Lehiste 1973a
Nash/Mulac 1980
Newman 1946
O'Connor 1955
Quirk/Duckworth/Svartvik et al 1964
Quirk/Greenbaum/Leech/Svartvik 1972
Schubiger 1953
Schubiger 1958
Scuffil 1982
Wode 1966

# Chapter IX

# Intonation and illocution

"What we have to study," Austin once said, "is *not* the sentence but the issuing of an utterance in a speech situation" (1962:138). When speakers use a sentence in a given situation, they inevitably do so with a purpose. For instance, the proverbial wife who says to her husband at a cocktail party *It's really quite late* may intend to *state* a fact or *object* to a previous remark that it is early or *suggest/request* that the couple now leave or even *warn* of the consequences if they don't (Searle 1969:70f.). Our utterances are thus verbal actions and constitute *speech acts*, which are ultimately the basic categories of linguistic communication.

## 1.   Locution – illocution – perlocution

Austin distinguished three senses in which we 'do things with words':

(a) First, we perform a *locutionary* act when we utter words in a particular combination with a particular meaning.

(b) Second, we perform an *illocutionary* act in using the utterance with a particular intention. The illocutionary *force* of an utterance issued in context depends on the way the speaker intends it in the given situation. For instance, the locution *Shut the door* may be intended in one context as a plea, in another as a piece of advice, and in yet another as a command.

Since locutionary and illocutionary acts are not mutually exclusive – every illocution has a locution and every locution has illocutionary potential as part of its meaning – Searle (1971) has argued that we need actually only distinguish the propositional content ($p$) of an utterance from the illocutionary force ($F$) of that utterance. For example, the proposition of *Shut the door* involves reference to an actor (unnamed) and to an object (*door*), as well as the predication of an action (*shutting*). These remain constant regardless of what illocutionary force is attributed to the utterance.

Frequently the illocutionary force of an utterance will be explicitly marked by so-called *illocutionary force indicating devices*. For instance:

I $\begin{cases} \text{urge} \\ \text{advise} \\ \text{order} \end{cases}$ you to shut the door

In cases like these we say that illocutionary force is signalled by the *performative* use of a verb. This means – with reference to a certain class of verbs – that the verb is used not to describe an act but to perform the act itself. One well-known example is the verb *do* as used in wedding vows:

> When I say, before the registrar or altar, etc., 'I do', I am not reporting on a marriage: I am indulging in it. (Austin 1962:6)

Other examples of the performative use of verbs include:

> I christen you Matilda
> I accept your offer
> I nominate Ludwig for president
> I bet you ten dollars
> I forbid you to stay
> I acknowledge receipt of your letter
> I congratulate you on your success

On the other hand, the illocutionary force of an utterance may be signalled grammatically by the mood of the verb or by word order – and prosodically, most linguists claim, by tone of voice, stress and/or intonation. At times, however, there may not be any overt marker at all: the context of the actual speech situation makes it clear what the illocutionary force is (Searle 1969:30).

(c) Third, we may perform a *perlocutionary* act by using an utterance in such a way that the feelings, beliefs or actions of another person (or of the speaker) are affected in some way. If we are successful in urging, advising or ordering someone to shut the door, then this may have the perlocutionary effect of convincing, persuading or inducing that person to shut the door. Other typical perlocutionary acts include eliciting an answer (by asking a question), frightening someone (by stating, warning, etc.), deterring someone, amusing someone, etc. However, whereas all locutions used in context have some kind of illocutionary force, not all illocutionary acts have a perlocutionary effect.[1] Promising, to name one, does not necessarily bring about consequential effects on the feelings, beliefs or actions of the persons involved (Austin 1962:102, Searle 1969:71).

## 1.1    Felicity conditions for illocutionary acts

As Austin was first to observe, an illocutionary act may come to naught or be invalidated for a number of reasons. With respect to marriage vows, for instance, the priest may be an imposter or a mistake may be made in the prescribed wording; or, of an altogether different nature, one of the prospective partners may already be legally married. All of these false starts and flaws Austin terms *infelicities*.

Enlarging on this idea, Searle (1969) has hypothesized that all illocutionary acts are rule-governed. Utterances are successful as speech acts only to the extent that certain conditions are met. These conditions are of three kinds:

---

[1] Nor is the perlocution necessarily intentional, according to Austin. I may frighten someone by, say, stating something, without intending to do so.

a) *Preparatory conditions.* These describe the state of affairs which the speaker presupposes to exist at the time of the utterance. In order to promise felicitously, for instance, a speaker must believe that the hearer wants what is promised done and the hearer must indeed want it done. Furthermore, it must be obvious to both speaker and hearer that what is promised will not get done anyway.

b) *Sincerity conditions.* These describe the psychological state related to the proposition which the speaker expresses in performing an illocutionary act. For instance, in promising, the speaker expresses his/her intention to do the thing promised. If the speaker does not intend to do the thing promised, the promise is insincere.

c) *Essential conditions.* These distinguish a given illocutionary act from every other one and thus *constitute* the act rather than regulate it. With respect to promising, for instance, the essential condition is that the speaker undertakes an obligation to do the thing promised.

In abbreviated form the rules for a felicitous promise might look something like this (A = act, S = speaker, H = hearer):

*Promise*

| | |
|---|---|
| Proposition: | Future act A of S |
| Preparatory conditions: | 1. H would prefer S's doing A to his not doing A, and S believes H would prefer his doing A to his not doing A. |
| | 2. It is not obvious to both S and H that S will do A in the normal course of events. |
| Sincerity condition: | S intends to do A |
| Essential condition: | Counts as the undertaking of an obligation by S to perform A. |

(1969:63)

## 1.2 The classification of illocutionary acts

Austin himself reckoned there to be well over a thousand different illocutions, based on the number of so-called performative verbs. But this assumed that every illocutionary act has a corresponding performative verb. In fact, innumerable exceptions come to mind: *\*I. hereby insinuate...*, *\*I hereby imply...*, *\*I hereby contradict you*, etc. Austin's preliminary classification of speech acts into five categories[2] has been criticized for this reason, and for making the (unwarranted) assumption that for every verb which can be used performatively, there is a corresponding illocutionary act. Actually the set of verbs which can be used performatively is much smaller than the set of illocutions, since for some speech acts there is no associated performative. Furthermore, the set of so-called illocutionary verbs, those which designate speech acts, should actually be kept separate from the set of speech acts themselves. As Searle

---

[2] These include: Verdictives (giving a verdict), Exercitives (exercising powers, rights or influence), Commissives (promising or otherwise undertaking), Behabitives (demonstrating attitudes and/or social behaviour), and Expositives (fitting utterances into the course of an argument or conversation) (1962:150f.).

has pointed out, illocutionary acts belong to language, performative and illocutionary verbs to specific languages (1975a:1).

Based on the ways illocutions differ from one another, Searle establishes a taxonomy of speech acts according to three major principles:

a) *Illocutionary point*. This is the purpose to which an utterance is put. In Searle's words:

> ... there are a rather limited number of basic things we do with language: we tell people how things are, we try to get them to do things, we commit ourselves to doing things, we express our feelings and attitudes and we bring about changes through our utterances. (1975a:19)

b) *Direction of fit*. This involves a distinction between whether the words (i.e. the propositional content) are intended to 'match the world', or whether the world is intended to be manipulated so as to 'match the words'. Statements and descriptions, assertions, etc. do the former, because they refer to the way things are; promises, threats, commands do the latter, because they refer to the way things could, should, might be, etc.

c) *Psychological state*. In performing an illocutionary act, the speaker always expresses "a belief, desire, intention, regret or pleasure in the performance of the speech act" (1975a:3).

According to how illocutions rate with respect to these principles, five major classes can be established:

Fig. IX/1   A classification of speech acts (based on Searle 1975a)

| | Illocutionary point | Direction of fit | Psychological state | Examples |
|---|---|---|---|---|
| I.   Representatives | Commit speaker to truth of expressed proposition | Words→ world | Belief | Asserting, describing, hypothesizing, stating, boasting, complaining, concluding, deducing |
| II.  Directives | Attempts by speaker to get hearer to do something | World→ words | Desire | Requesting, ordering, commanding, asking, praying, pleading, begging, entreating |
| III. Commissives | Commit speaker to some future course of action | World→ words | Intention | Promising, vowing, threatening, pledging |
| IV.  Expressives | Express psychological state in sincerity condition about state of affairs in $p$ | ø | (Feeling/ attitude) pleasure, regret, sympathy, etc. | Congratulating, welcoming, thanking, apologizing, condoling |
| V.   Declaratives | Successful performance brings about correspondence between $p$ and reality | Words→ world | ø | Resigning, firing s.o., excommunicating s.o., appointing s.o. chairman, declaring war [in performative sense] |

Within each class further subdivisions are possible with respect to subsidiary principles such as (a) degree of force or strength of illocutionary force [e.g. under (I), hypothesizing vs. flatly stating]; (b) relative status of speaker and hearer [e.g. under (II), commanding vs. requesting]; (c) relation to interest of speaker and hearer [e.g. under (I), boasting vs. complaining]; (d) relation to rest of discourse [e.g. under (I), concluding vs. deducing], etc. (1975a:3ff.).[3]

## 1.3 Illocutionary vs. grammatical category

Both Austin and Searle agree that illocutionary force is often marked in the syntax and/or lexis of the utterance. On the other hand, it need not be. Thus it happens that one and the same grammatical construct may be used with a number of different intentions:

> An 'imperative' may be an order, a permission, a demand, a request, an entreaty, a suggestion, a recommendation, a warning ('go and you will see'), or may express a condition or concession or a definition ('Let it ...'), etc. (Austin 1962:76f.)

It is for precisely this reason that some linguists have found it useful to introduce categories which combine grammatical form and illocutionary force. Sadock (1974), for instance, distinguishes for the *interrogative* form:

a) *Whimperatives*, a subcategory of the larger class of 'impositives', by which the speaker indicates that he wishes to impose his will on the addressee (orders, demands, requests, pleas, suggestions, offers, wishes, etc.):[4]

> Will you please close the door?

These are usually formed with modal verbs and may have an (optional) negative particle. We may also distinguish *why (not), shouldn't* and *how about/what do you say* impositives:

> Why don't you put a record on?
> Shouldn't you drive slower?
> How about treating ourselves to a malt?
> What do you say you take out the garbage?     (Sadock 1974:114–8)

b) *Requestions*, queries asked without personal interest in the answer; the utterer only wants to *hear* the answer, not *know* it:

> (Teacher) Johnny, who discovered the Bronx please?
>
> (Census-taker) How many children do you have please?     (Sadock 1974:120f.)

The fact that *please* can be attached to these questions proves that they are requests.

c) *Queclaratives*, questions by which the utterer commits himself to the opposite view from what the question appears to imply:

---

[3] Cf. Wunderlich (1980:297) for a critique of this classification.

[4] The term 'impositive' comes from Green (1973).

Who did Bill ever loan money to?     (Sadock 1974:125)

(implied: Bill loaned money to someone)
(meant: Bill never loans money to anyone)

I don't know anything about income tax law. But then who does?

(implied: Somebody knows something about income tax law)
(meant: Nobody knows anything about income tax law)

## 1.4   Indirect speech acts

The above categories are actually illustrations of what Searle has called *indirect speech acts* (1975b:59f.), utterances which are issued with one literal meaning or illocution but at the same time indirectly perform another illocutionary act. Indirect speech acts are used regularly in our society to make polite requests:

Have you got change for a dollar?
Hadn't you better go now?
I would appreciate your making a little less noise.

Other indirect speech acts are less formulaic but perfectly clear in context:

(i)   A:  Wouldn't you like a bite to eat?
      B:  I'm on a diet.

(ii)  Child:   May I have a piece of candy?
      Parent:  I don't think it's a good idea to eat sweets before dinner.

(iii) EP:  I suppose that's the BBC syndrome in uh uhm Sir Huw Wheldon's case.
           However uhm ...
      HW:  Now then just a minute. I haven't quite followed that.
      EP:  I thought you detected a kind of resemblance between British Airways and uh
           the BBC. (E1/EP$_2$ – HW$_3$)

Both (i) and (ii) contain literal statements of fact by the second speaker but the primary speech act performed is to refuse a suggestion or request by the first speaker. In (iii) the second speaker's statement of fact is at the same time a request for the first speaker to elaborate.

## 2.   Illocution and intonation

Language philosophers and linguists have continually pointed to the role of intonation as a marker of illocutionary force.[5] To date, however, only few studies have dealt with the question of how the two are linked specifically.

---

[5] This was also what Gunter (1972) meant by saying that the role of intonation is the marking of (contextual) "relevance" (1972:214).

## 2.1  The one-to-one hypothesis

There are a number of different ways intonation and illocution could be related, hypothetically speaking. For instance, there could be a one-to-one relationship between the two such that for every distinct illocution there is a distinct intonational marking (either in the form of a holistic contour or a complex of intonational features). A strong version of this hypothesis would claim that a given intonational marking *always* occurs when a particular illocution is present and *never* occurs with any other illocution. A weaker version of the same hypothesis would claim only that a given intonational marking is *possible* when a particular illocution is present, no matter whether it occurs elsewhere or not.

The one-to-one hypothesis has been advanced by Liberman/Sag (1974) with respect to the illocutionary act of *contradiction*. For instance:

Fig. IX/2
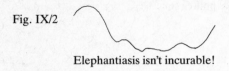

Elephantiasis isn't incurable!

The contour illustrated here is characterized by an initial rise on the first syllables, followed by a rapid fall to mid range or below, with a final rise usually on the last syllable. The body of the contour is flattened. Liberman/Sag identify this shape as the 'contradiction' contour. No matter what the lexical content, they claim, this contour is always appropriate when the utterance contradicts what another speaker (or the same speaker) has said, implied or assumed. Even when it is used with, say, an apology, the resultant meaning is still contradiction:

A:  You're sitting in my seat

B:  I beg your pardon      (Glenn 1977:48)

However, as appealing as this hypothesis may sound, a certain amount of counterevidence has emerged. Cutler (1977), for instance, demonstrates that the same contour may appear although no element of contradiction can be detected:

Fig. IX/3    Father (to son who has been ignoring a friend's
              attempt to attract attention from outside the window):

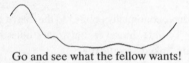

Go and see what the fellow wants!

Here we have an element of disapproval rather than of contradiction, as the contour would lead us to expect. Thus − if the one-to-one hypothesis holds at all − only a weaker version can be maintained: viz., if the illocutionary act of contradiction is present, the 'contradiction' contour will always be at least *possible*.

However, even this weaker version does not hold in the case of illocutions marked performatively. If we attempt, say, to elicit information from someone by using the verb *ask* performatively, *I (hereby) ask you whether you saw the murderer*, a questioning intonation contour (cf. Fig. IX/5b) is wholly out of place. In fact, utterances with performative marking – regardless of illocutionary force – do not appear to differ systematically in terms of intonational shape:

Fig. IX/4

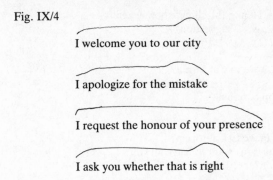

Consequently, it appears that any distinctive intonational marking which may exist for a given illocution is neutralized in the case of explicit performatives. For this reason a strict one-to-one hypothesis is virtually impossible to maintain (Glenn 1977:49f.).

## 2.2   The disambiguation hypothesis

Another conceivable hypothesis is that intonation distinguishes illocutionary force only when there are no explicit performatives. This would not only explain why intonation is not distinctive in the case of utterances with explicit performatives, but would also offer a plausible explanation for how a speaker may say one thing but mean another. In fact, Searle himself has observed that locutions functioning as indirect speech acts have a different intonation from that appropriate if they are used 'literally'. Compare, for instance:

Fig. IX/5    a)  (To a child who has been talking too much)

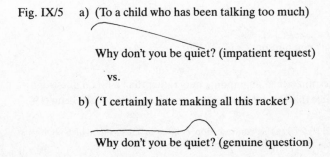

According to Searle, the intonation of these sentences uttered as indirect requests is different from their intonation when uttered literally. Furthermore, the indirect request intonation is similar to that of literal directives (1975b:69).

Following up on this observation, Sag/Liberman (1975) investigate the intonation of indirect speech acts involving interrogatives. They establish that at least two different contours are feasible for *wh*-questions:

Fig. IX/6   a)  Max: You know, Henry, the climate here is really
                    bad for you. I've got a suggestion –

Why don't you move to California?

b)  Max: Henry, I'm curious –

Why don't you move to California?
Is it because you don't want to leave all your
friends in Boston?   (1975:488, 494)

The contour in (a) – used here for the utterance with the indirect illocutionary force of a suggestion – is characterized by initial low pitch in conjunction with a stressed syllable, followed by high pitch on the last major stress and an abrupt fall. The contour in (b) – used for the same utterance as a literal question – is characterized by high pitch on the *wh*-word, followed by a fall to low pitch on the next stressed syllable, and a rise in pitch on the last syllable. [Because of its characteristic shape, it is called a 'tilde'.[6]]

Sag/Liberman's investigation suggests that, whereas the contour in (a) [which we shall dub the 'modified hat'] may be associated with either a literal question or a suggestion, the 'tilde' contour is used only for literal *wh*-questions. Their conclusion is that "some intonation contours can 'freeze' an utterance pragmatically, i.e. require a literal interpretation, but no intonation can force an indirect interpretation" (1975:496).

However, this claim too has come under attack. Cutler (1977), for instance, demonstrates that the 'tilde' contour does not always force a literal interpretation of *wh*-questions. Consider, for instance:

Fig. IX/7

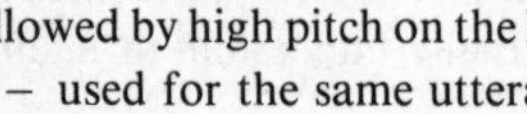

Why don't you butt out?   (1977:109)

This is surely a suggestion (albeit an impolite one) rather than a literal question. [It is of course conceivable that the contour is being used ironically.] And Glenn (1977)

---

[6] The 'tilde' contour differs from the 'contradiction' contour in that its initial high pitch *must* come on the *wh*-item and not simply on the first syllable(s).

in fact maintains that just the opposite of what Sag/Liberman claim is true, namely that intonation *can* force an indirect interpretation. For example, the following sentence, she claims, could only be understood as a request:

Fig. IX/8

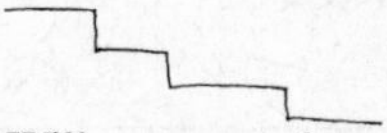

Will you come here    (1977:52)

just as Searle's (1975b) example *Why don't you be quiet?* can only be meant as a request with the stepping intonation contour above.

However, if intonation can force an indirect interpretation, it nevertheless does not appear to be the case that a different intonation contour will unambiguously signal a different illocution for one and the same utterance. Thus:

Fig. IX/9

Will you come here?    (1977:51)

is still a request (as evidenced by the fact that *please* can be added without changing its meaning), although this intonation contour is quite different from the stepping one above. For this reason, the disambiguation hypothesis also appears untenable.

## 2.3   The altered felicity condition hypothesis

Glenn (1977) proposes yet a third variant of the relationship between intonation and illocution. She argues for a general class of, say, *impositives*, with felicity conditions such that 'S wants H to do some future act A'. For this generic class there is, she claims, an (unmarked) intonation contour which is always appropriate. However, marked intonation contours may be used to signal that the felicity conditions have been altered or modified in certain ways, thus creating subclasses of impositives such as those outlined in Fig. IX/10.

Glenn's analysis is appealing because it represents an attempt to establish 'natural classes' of illocutionary acts based on distinctive features (or conditions) held in common. The intonation contour, it is claimed, serves as a reflex of these illocutionary subclasses.

A number of comments, however, are in order. For one, the subclasses proposed are not mutually exclusive, as evidenced by the fact that Orders appear under (1) and (5), and Demands under (3) and (5). Is the distinction between Orders (1) and Demands (3) then neutralized when they have contour (5)? [The distinguishing feature under (5), namely redundancy, is arguably an optional one which may occur in conjunction with other features, but this would put category (5) on a different level from categories (1)–(4).]

Second, the status of at least one of the subcategories, namely (2), is dubious, as evidenced by the fact that the distinguishing feature – annoyance – is not a felicity

167

Fig. IX/10   The intonation of impositives (orders, demands, requests, pleas, suggestions, offers, wishes) [based on Glenn 1977]

| Illocutionary act \ Felicity conditions | Propositional content | Preparatory conditions | Sincerity conditions | Essential condition | Intonation contour |
|---|---|---|---|---|---|
| I. Impositives | Future act A of hearer H | 1. H is able to do A. S believes H is able to do A<br><br>2. It is not obvious to both S and H that H will do A in the normal course of events of his own accord | S wants H to do A. | Counts as an attempt to get H to do A | Stop picking the flowers |
| 1. Orders Comments Acts of forbidding and prohibition | | 3. S is in a position of authority over H | | … in virtue of the authority of S over H |  Stop picking the flowers |
| 2. ?? | | | S is annoyed | … in virtue of S's annoyance that H is not doing A | 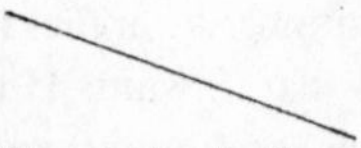 Stop picking the flowers |
| 3. Demands Warnings | | | S wishes to impose his will on H | … in virtue of S's wish to impose his will … | 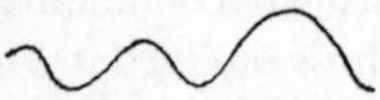 Stop picking the flowers |
| 4. Requests Suggestions Invitations | | | S does not want (to appear) to impose his will on H | … in virtue of S's not wanting to impose his will … |  Stop picking the flowers |
| 5. Orders Demands Appeals Pleas Acts of imploring, insisting, forbidding | | | S believes H already knows p [redundant] | … in virtue of S's believing H already knows … |  Stop picking the flowers |

condition for any independently established speech act. Glenn rightly points out that attitudes and emotions are not lacking from felicity conditions for speech acts: in order to boast a speaker must feel proud, in order to confess a speaker must feel guilt, in order to congratulate a speaker must be pleased, etc. However, one would hope that such attitudes could be independently established and constrained by the system, rather than being introduced ad hoc as in the case of annoyance. The more basic problem may be that illocutionary contrasts shade into attitudinal contrasts and it is difficult to know where to draw the line.

Similar results have emerged from the work of Gibbon (1976a), who explores the possibility of a direct relation between the so-called 'call' contour and illocutionary force. The 'call' contour is described as a chanted or sing-song intonation pattern which steps down from one level pitch to another with an interval of approximately a minor third: ⁻*John___ny*. Gibbon comes to the conclusion that no one illocution can be linked to the 'call' contour. The common denominator of those associated with it, he hypothesizes, is physical *distance* between the interlocutors, the final long level tone having the effect of enabling the speaker to maintain volume and thus 'secure uptake' from the hearer.[7] The 'call' contour thus serves to mark the fact that one of the basic felicity conditions for successful speech acts has not been fulfilled, viz. that "normal input and output conditions obtain" (Searle 1969:61). Gibbon concludes that "intonational patterning marks an independent cross-classification of illocutions rather than illocutions themselves" (1976a:285).

## 3.   Intonation and questioning

The one area of language structure in which the role of intonation has long been undisputed is that of questions. And yet considered from a speech-act point of view, the category 'question' seems dubious indeed. As one linguist/sociologist has put it: "... the question form can be used for actions other than questioning, and questioning can be accomplished by linguistic forms other than questions" (Schegloff 1978:86). Nevertheless, questioning *is* something we normally do with words and if only on intuitive grounds, it would seem to qualify as a speech act. But how can questioning be defined without restricting it to the interrogative form? Note that the definition must encompass not only:

(i)   A: *How old are you?*
      B: Three.

(ii)  A: *Do you see that house over there?*
      B: Yes

but also:

---

[7] According to Ladd, however, the function of these 'stylized' tones is "to signal an element of predictability or stereotype in the message" (1978:248).

(iii) A: Why don't you come over and see me tomorrow?

   B: *I'm not sure I know where you live.*

   A: It's 314 Maple Street.

   B: Okay.

(iv) A: *I take it you're finished.*

   B: No, I'm not actually.


## 3.1   On defining the speech act 'Question'

According to Searle, the following conditions govern the act of 'asking a question':

*Question*

| | |
|---|---|
| Propositional content: | Any proposition or propositional function |
| Preparatory conditions: | 1. S does not know 'the answer', i.e. does not know if the proposition is true, or, in the case of the propositional function, does not know the information needed to complete the proposition truly. |
| | 2. It is not obvious to both S and H that H will provide the information at that time without being asked. |
| Sincerity conditions: | S wants this information. |
| Essential condition: | Counts as an attempt to elicit this information from H |

(1969:66f.)

Accordingly, a question would be an attempt by the speaker to elicit information which s/he does not have from the hearer. The problem with this definition, however, is that the condition 'S does not know the answer' holds with varying degrees of certainty. If a speaker on entering an unfamiliar grocery store asks *Do you stock Heinz baby foods?*, it is indeed probable that s/he does not know the answer. But if a speaker says to a friend *Did your children really go to school today?*, s/he may suspect that the children didn't and want the hearer to consider this possibility too. Or if a speaker says upon seeing a familiar figure enter the room *Oh are you back already?* s/he is of course quite certain that the person is back but may want the hearer to know that s/he knows (examples from Hudson 1975:16f.). The latter two sorts of question – in which the speaker suspects what the answer is or even already knows it – are referred to as *conducive* questions. They make one possible answer (*yes* or *no*) more likely than the other.

In order to handle conducive as well as straightforward *yes–no* questions, Hudson has proposed an additional felicity condition to the effect that "… the speaker believes that the hearer knows at least as well as he himself does whether the proposition is true or false" (1975:12). This condition would motivate both straightforward and conducive questioning as follows: the speaker either wants to learn whether the proposition is true or false him/herself, or wants to be agreed with in the opinion that the proposition is true or false.[8] It would, however, still be necessary to

---

[8] The same condition with minor alterations would presumably also apply to *wh*-questions.

formulate another felicity condition for the extreme case of the classroom question, where the teacher already knows the answer him/herself and does not necessarily have grounds to believe the pupil knows the answer as well or better, but wants to *find out* whether the pupil does.

## 3.2   Intonational correlates of 'Question'

There are still a number of unsolved problems in defining the illocutionary act of 'posing a question'. But assuming for the moment that a satisfactory definition can be worked out, several syntactic subtypes can be distinguished. These include: polar or *yes—no* questions, *wh*-questions, echo questions, declarative questions ["a type of question identical in form to a statement",[9] Quirk et al 1972:392], etc. However, as constructed examples and empirical data show, there appear to be no recognizable intonational correlates of the 'question' illocution nor of any syntactic subcategories of the 'question' illocution (Ch. VIII §3.3.2).

On the other hand, there is some evidence that intonation may correlate with *conduciveness*. Brown/Kenworthy/Currie (1980) report that based on investigations with Scottish English, the choice of one of three possible terminal tones (A) rise-to-high, (B) fall-to-mid and (C) fall-to-low appears to depend crucially on whether the question is conducive or not:

> Where the questions appear to be non-conducive, as in some polar questions, all WH-questions and some echo-questions, the terminal is either A or B. (...) Conducive questions, [i.e.] all declarative questions and some polar questions, are regularly asked on a fall-to-low, C.[10] (1980:187)

If these conclusions are applicable to standard British English as well [there is already some indication of their validity for American English; cf. Bolinger 1958d], then it would appear that intonation correlates with a modification of one of the felicity conditions operating on the speech act 'Question' – a conclusion which sounds surprisingly similar to the one Glenn (1977) reached for a different category of illocutionary act.

However, there is ample counter-evidence. Declarative polar questions [i.e. those answerable with *yes* or *no*] – which are generally conducive – may also occur with rising intonation: *you've got the exPLOsive?* (Quirk et al 1972:392). And declarative *wh*-questions [i.e. those answerable with information other than *yes* or *no*] such as *I wonder what time it is* or *I don't suppose you know how much money was stolen* [also example (iii) in §3 above] are generally non-conducive, yet they tend to have

---

[9] Note, however, that declarative questions need not necessarily be polar (answerable with *yes—no*): statements with embedded *wh*-words are also used to elicit information, e.g. *I wonder what time it is; No one can tell me what this is called, I presume; I don't suppose you know how much money was stolen*, etc.

[10] Brown et al may be somewhat overhasty in equating all declarative questions with conduciveness (as do Quirk et al). If a declarative *wh*-question is also recognized, then clearly not all utterances with statement form but questioning illocution are conducive; see examples in Note 9.

falling intonation, not infrequently fall-to-low. Furthermore, constant-polarity tag questions of the sort *caterpillars have legs, do they?* are conducive but tend to have rising intonation (Hudson 1975:27, Bald 1980:270). So although we may have come a step closer to establishing how intonation and the 'question' illocution are related, we do not fully understand the matter yet. And this is only one of a large number of attested speech acts whose interaction with intonation has yet to be investigated.

If the results obtained so far are any indication, however, it will not be possible to establish a direct link between illocution and intonation. If at all, only an indirect one is likely: a particular intonation contour signals that one of the felicity conditions for an illocutionary act has been altered. But to the extent that these felicity conditions relate to the psychological state of the speaker, the illocutionary function of intonation becomes an attitudinal one instead.

## References

Abe 1962
Austin 1962
Bald 1980
Bolinger 1958d
Brown/Currie/Kenworthy 1980
Bublitz 1970
*Cutler 1977
Gibbon 1976b
Glenn 1977
Goody 1978
Green 1973
Grice 1975
Gunter 1972
Hudson 1975
Kenworthy 1978
Kohler 1973

Ladd 1978
*Liberman/Sag 1974
Quirk/Greenbaum/Leech/Svartvik 1972
Sadock 1974
*Sag/Liberman 1975
Schegloff 1978
Searle 1969
Searle 1971
Searle 1975a
Searle 1975b
Searle 1976
Searle/Kiefer/Bierwisch 1980
Wunderlich 1976
Wunderlich 1980
Yorio 1973

Chapter X
# Intonation and attitude

It is an undisputed fact that intonation has an important role to play in the expression of emotions and attitudes.[1] The linguist's task therefore is not so much to determine *whether* intonation expresses a speaker's inner states or not but rather *how much* of this expression is indeed linguistic in the sense outlined in Ch. VI.

## 1. Separating the linguistic from the non-linguistic

The crux of the matter, as one scholar has said, is: "An angry person does not raise his voice in English or in German but simply in anger".[2] Emotion, it appears, has a language of its own. If it is true that we all express emotional states the same way, then, so the argument goes, this is because the expression of emotion originates in universal physiological reactions which preclude the use of culturally determined, language-specific patterns.[3] The conclusion which many linguists have drawn is that intonation is "on the edge of language", as Bolinger (1972a) has put it, or worse yet, that intonation is wholly outside the realm of linguistics proper and is external to that central object of linguistic endeavor, the 'grammar':

> If uses of pitch which change only the emotional overtones of the message are included in the grammar, then why not include other equally effective message modifiers such as gestures and facial expressions? (Frank 1974:100)

On the other hand, there have been a few objections. For instance, Stankiewicz has pointed out that there is often a confusion between "the instinctive nature of 'sound-gestures' [and] what can properly be considered as the linguistic dimension of 'expressiveness' or of the emotive function" (1964:239):

---

[1] Whether intonation has an *exclusive* role to play in the expression of emotion and attitude is, however, another question. Stankiewicz (1964) argues convincingly that languages have many ways of expressing emotive meaning, including the metaphorical use of lexical items, the substitution of grammatical forms and constructions, certain types of derivation, code-switching, etc.

[2] "Wer wütend die Stimme hebt, tut dies weder auf Englisch noch auf Deutsch, sondern eben nur wütend" (Lieb 1980:34).

[3] Scherer (1979), for instance, points out that arousal of the sympathetic nervous system, which characterizes emotional states, (a) increases muscle tonus [which in general tends to mean an increase in fundamental frequency]; and (b) affects the coordination and the rhythms of reciprocal inhibition and excitation of muscle groups. "It is to be expected that disruption of neuro-muscular coordination will affect pitch and loudness variability, stress patterns and intonation contours, speech rate (in terms of length of phonemes as well as number and length of pauses), the onset and decay of phonations, the precision of articulation, rhythms of speech, and many other speech parameters" (1979:501f.).

The symbolic aspect of emotive language can be identified only if we acknowledge (...) a distinction between an "emotional" plane, which reveals itself in a variety of articulated or non-articulated "forms" of a symptomatic nature, that is, through signals which are inextricably bound to the situation which evokes them and which they evoke, and the "emotive" plane, which is rendered through situationally independent, arbitrary symbols. (1964:240)

If this distinction is granted, it would be on the 'emotive' plane that linguistic means of expression are to be sought.

The most convincing arguments for the linguistic nature of affective expression come from psychologists and social psychologists who distinguish between "expression as a physiologically mediated externalization mechanism" and "expression as strategically used, communicative behavior in social interaction" (Scherer 1979:524). The former is to be found, both ontogenetically and phylogenetically, in the *autistic* expression of affect, in vocalizations which are mere externalizations of inner states. This stage in development, however, is normally replaced by the *communicative* expression of affect, in which vocalizations are made and used in order to have some effect on the external environment.[4] It is here that we find culturally determined *display rules*, conventions which regulate the control of emotional expression, as well as individually determined *coping strategies*, "centrally initiated regulation attempts to make one's vocal behavior conform to cultural or situational norms or to adopt a 'stance' that is deemed advantageous in covering up or externalizing stress, depending on the individual's strategic decisions in the interaction" (Scherer 1979:507f.).

As linguists dealing primarily with the language of the speech community, individual coping strategies need not concern us. However, the existence of so-called display rules offers clear proof that there is room for convention and ritual in the expression of (physiologically anchored) emotion and attitude. This view is echoed by Faure (1970), who points out that inner states need not be restricted exclusively to emotions which escape from the speaker uncontrollably, but that they may also be subject to will, reflection and various different motivations without necessarily involving emotive agitation (1970:98).

In sum, we must distinguish an unmonitored, purely physiologically determined externalization of emotional state, presumably universal across linguistic communities, from a 'cognitively' monitored expression of attitude, conventionalized and communicative in purpose. [In order to distinguish the two, we shall restrict the term *emotion* to the former and *attitude* to the latter.]

The question which now arises is what the linguistic means of attitudinal expression

---

[4] The transition from autism to communication is depicted by Fónagy (1971) as follows: "... the narcissistic babbling of the infant or the angry cries by which he tries directly to reduce internal tension will be interpreted as signals by those around him. Realizing this, the child will reproduce the same vocal gestures to obtain the same results, thus resolving the tension by a real gratification of his desires. The expressive phonational gestures – pulmonary, glottal, or buccal – seem thus to recall narcissistic phonational play. These movements had originally the sole aim of reducing tension in an immediate way: they were literally *ex-pressive* – but then became *expressive* in the transferred sense of the term. As expressive gestures, they are half-way between real actions and the arbitrary signs with which they are integrated" (1971:170).

are and whether intonation is one of them. According to Fónagy/Bérard (1972), intonation is indeed used in a language-dependent, i.e. linguistic, way to express attitude. Comparing French and Hungarian, they remark that whereas there are apparently only vague guidelines for the intonational configuration of 'indignant justification' in French, in Hungarian the intonation is well-defined and associated by convention with a specific pattern. They conclude:

> This case, like many others, shows that the melodic expression of attitudes may be more or less perfectly integrated into the linguistic code, and that consequently the decoding process may cause members of the linguistic group greater or lesser difficulty. Perfect integration reduces the ambiguity of the gestural expression to zero – but at the same time constitutes a source of error for those who speak the language in question as a foreign language.[5] (1972:173)

As for English, a certain amount of anecdotal evidence implies that intonation has a similar linguistic function. O'Connor/Arnold, for instance, cite the following example:

> ... the phrase *Thank you* may be said with one tune which makes it sound genuinely grateful, and with a different tune which makes it sound rather casual. Now if the foreign learner unintentionally uses the casual form when an English listener feels entitled to the other one, then the listener may get a very bad impression, since he will probably assume that the casual effect given by the tune was the one which the speaker deliberately set out to give. ([2]1973:2)

Thus it appears that there are also specific intonational patterns in English associated with the expression of attitude. Which attitudes and what patterns, however, is still a subject of discussion.

## 2.  Investigations of intonation and attitude

At least three different approaches have been employed in the study of intonation and attitude, each of which reveals a different set of assumptions concerning the way the two relate. In the following we shall review a representative example of each, demonstrating inherent strengths and weaknesses.

### 2.1  Acoustic parameters and attitude

In one typical approach to the study of intonation and attitude, the working hypothesis is that the acoustic parameters of intonation relate directly to certain intuitively determined 'attitudes'. Lieberman/Michaels (1962), for instance, obtained naturalistic recordings of a set of neutral statements (e.g. *The lamp stood on the desk*; *They have bought a new car*) spoken in eight different 'emotional modes':

---

[5] "Ce cas, comme beaucoup d'autres, montre que l'expression mélodique des attitudes peut être plus ou moins parfaitement intégrée au code linguistique, et, que par conséquent leur décodage peut causer plus ou moins de difficulté aux membres du group linguistique. Une intégration parfaite réduit à zéro l'ambiguité de l'expression gestuelle – ceci, en même temps – constitue une source d'erreur pour ceux qui parlent la langue en question comme langue étrangère."

1. a bored statement
2. a confidential communication
3. a question expressing disbelief or doubt
4. a message expressing fear
5. a message expressing happiness
6. an objective question
7. an objective statement
8. a pompous statement

These recordings were then manipulated instrumentally in order to isolate single acoustic parameters such as pure pitch, amplitude, smoothed pitch, and combinations thereof. Listeners were asked to identify the emotional modes of the manipulated tapes. The percentage of correct recognition, correlated with the type of acoustic manipulation, it was thought, would provide information on the relative importance of each acoustic feature in the transmission of emotional content.

With a little reflection, however, it becomes apparent that Lieberman/Michaels' experiment — and others like it — suffers from several weaknesses:

(i) Lack of a theory of intonation. The relation between acoustic parameters and intonational meaning is assumed to be a direct one. Yet Lieberman/Michaels themselves note that speakers may favour different acoustic parameters in *transmitting* emotions; and of course listeners may also rely on different acoustic parameters in *identifying* emotions. Acoustic experiments alone are of little help in revealing what use listeners make of acoustic signals, since these are "processed through the filter of linguistic categories on their way to being interpreted" (Ladd 1978:196). One of the problems with this type of approach then is that the relation between acoustic parameters and meaning is not direct but mediated by the existence of intonational features and categories which presumably a theory of intonation must provide.

(ii) Unmotivated choice of 'emotional modes'. Whereas 'bored', 'confidential', 'disbelief', 'fear', 'happiness' and 'pompous' may perhaps pass as descriptors of affective states (cf., however, §3.4), the same can hardly be said of 'objective question' or 'objective statement'. The terms *statement* and *question* refer to what are typically thought of as grammatical or illocutionary categories. In short, what is lacking here is a theoretical framework which would delimit the concepts and specify the categories of emotion and attitude.

## 2.2 Contours and attitude

A second type of approach is characterized by the attempt to match a motivated choice of attitudes with over-all intonational contour. Uldall, for instance, adopts Osgood/ Suci/Tannenbaum's (1957) theory that there are three main kinds of affective 'meaning' transmitted in speech: (1) amount or strength of feeling or interest [*activity*], (2) pleasantness or unpleasantness of personal relations [*evaluation*], (3) the 'power' relationship between speaker and listener [*potency*] (Uldall 1960:227). The technique for measuring this kind of 'meaning', known as the *semantic differential*, involves asking listeners to rate concepts in terms of polar adjectives expressive of these dimensions.

In order to measure the affective meaning of intonational patterns, Uldall (1960, 1964) took four neutral sentences representing different grammatical categories [statement, *yes−no* question, *wh*-question and command] and imposed sixteen different intonational contours upon them synthetically. The contours chosen were as follows:

Fig. X/1                                                                 (1964, 1972:252)

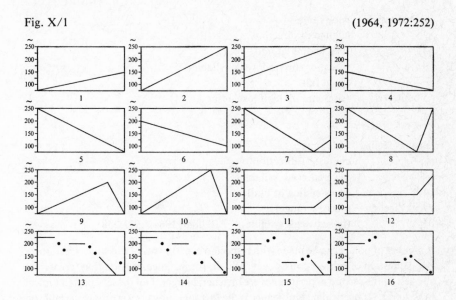

Each sentence with each contour was played to a group of native speakers, who were asked to rate judgments of speaker emotion based on the following adjective pairs:

    bored − interested
    polite − rude
    timid − confident
    sincere − insincere
    tense − relaxed
    disapproving − approving
    deferential − arrogant
    impatient − patient
    emphatic − unemphatic
    agreeable − disagreeable

[In the second experiment *authoritative/submissive*, *unpleasant/pleasant*, *genuine/ pretended* (feeling) and *weak/strong* (feeling) were added.]

The results of the (second) experiment can be summarized as follows with respect to Osgood's types of 'meaning' (parameters in parentheses are less consistently linked with a given attitude):

*Pleasantness*

| | |
|---|---|
| 'pleasant' | rises ending high |
| | change of direction [excluding no. 7] |
| 'unpleasant' | raised weak syllables |
| | (lowered weak syllables) |
| | (narrow range) |

*Power*

| | |
|---|---|
| 'authoritative' | wide range |
| | change of direction |
| | rises ending at mid |
| | raised or lowered weak syllables |
| | (final fall) |
| 'submissive' | (rises ending high [excluding no. 8]) |

*Interest*

| | |
|---|---|
| 'strong' feeling | wide range |
| | change of direction |
| | lowered weak syllables |
| | (rises ending at mid) |
| 'weak' feeling | (narrow range) |
| | (raised weak syllables)      (Uldall 1964, 1972:258) |

A number of points can be made with respect to experiments of this kind. First, there is the question of subject consistency. Uldall, for instance, reports that 'errors' on a re-test in the second experiment were in general larger than those reported typical by Osgood. Of particular significance is the fact that subjects were more variable on test-retest with respect to their judgments of speaker intention (strong–weak) than with respect to their own reactions (pleasant–unpleasant) (1964:274f.). We shall return to this point shortly (§3.4).

Second, no indication is given of the extent to which sentences with imposed intonation were felt to be natural utterances. [Presumably, phonetic content was not removed, although no explicit statement is made to this effect.] Both experiments were forced-choice, i.e. each sentence-plus-intonation had to be rated for each parameter (although subjects did have the possibility of marking 'neither'). Nevertheless, it was not possible to add, delete or alter attitudinal descriptors of the utterances produced. To this extent, the results do not tell us a great deal about intonation in its natural environment nor about spontaneous (i.e. non pre-determined) reactions to specific contours.[6]

Finally, this sort of experimental design implies that both the intonational and the attitudinal categories chosen are indeed the pertinent ones. Yet as Uldall's own results demonstrate, some of the attitudes selected are apparently rarely expressed

---

[6] This is obviously a methodological problem: allowing for spontaneity makes systematization less probable, but providing systematized labels precludes spontaneity.

by intonation. [The adjective pair 'genuine/pretended', for instance, was a total failure.] Thus there is reason to suspect that Osgood's theory of affective 'meaning' may not be fully significant for intonation. Furthermore, the choice of intonational contour, at least in Uldall's case, does not appear to be motivated by any systematic approach to intonation. For instance, whereas contours /1/ and /2/ presumably incorporate the difference between narrow and wide rise, it is unclear to what feature contour /3/ corresponds. Moreover, the relative position of unstressed syllables appears on a par with steep vs. flat falls, rises, fall−rises and rise−falls; yet this feature is quite secondary in most systematic approaches to intonation. Uldall's contours, in fact, seem to be based on ad hoc speculation as to what features might be significant in the expression of attitude (Ladd 1978:190).

## 2.3   Tune, sentence type and attitude

The third type of approach, as illustrated by Schubiger (1958) and O'Connor/Arnold ([2]1973), differs significantly from the other two in that it employs neither instrumental techniques nor controlled laboratory experimentation. Intended primarily for didactic use, studies of this sort are above all concerned to present as wide a coverage as possible of the attitudinal connotations which intonation can have in speech. In contrast to Lieberman/Michaels and Uldall, however, they start with a clear hypothesis as to what the system of English intonation is. O'Connor/Arnold, for instance, attempt to determine empirically the attitudes conveyed by each of the ten basic 'tone groups' (Ch.IV §2.3.3) when used with five different sentence types [statement, *wh*-questions, *yes−no* questions, commands, interjections]. Tone Group 5 (basically a falling−rising tune with optional low pre-head and tail), for instance, is said to convey the following attitudes in conjunction with *statements*: "grudgingly admitting, reluctantly or defensively dissenting, concerned, reproachful, hurt, reserved, tentatively suggesting; (in echoes) greatly astonished". For example:

'I thought they all took one.'     Ănn 'did. (But the others didn't.)

([2]1973:170)

In conjunction with *questions*, the same tone group signals: "(in echoes) greatly astonished; otherwise, interested and concerned as well as surprised". For example:

'Peter paid for the beer.'     Whŏ 'paid? (Surely not Peter?)

([2]1973:172)

In conjunction with *commands*: "urgently warning with a note of reproach or concern":

'I'll dump the suitcases here.'     Gĕntly. (They're not made of iron.)

([2]1973:173)

And in conjunction with *interjections*: "scornful":

'Going for a swim today?'     Not mĕ! (It's freezing.)

([2]1973:190)

Since each of the ten different tone groups is glossed with attitudinal descriptors for four to five main sentence-types, from forty to fifty different categories (and many more descriptors) are produced.

The main problem with such an approach, however, is the lack of a theory of attitude to constrain the categories and labels introduced. This makes the results vulnerable on two accounts:

(i) The attitude identified is often suspiciously similar to the lexical content of the sentence. Consider, for instance, two of the 'attitudes' associated by O'Connor/Arnold with the falling−rising tune: "grudgingly admitting" and "reluctantly dissenting". How do we know these are two different attitudes? Is it not possible to change an admitting statement like *Ann did* into a dissenting statement by the simple addition of a negator: *Ann didn't?* If so, the 'attitude' in question is a function of the words and not of the intonation. Once abstraction has been made of lexical content, what remains is the notion of "grudging" or "reluctant" − but even this 'attitude' should be motivated within a broader framework of affective meaning.

(ii) The choice of descriptors is virtually unlimited. Crystal (1969) has estimated that between the two studies by O'Connor/Arnold and Schubiger, nearly 300 different labels are employed to describe the affective meaning of intonation, e.g. "abrupt, accusing, affable, affected, affectionate, aggressive, agreeable, airy, amused, angry, animated, annoyed, antagonistic, apologetic, appealing, appreciative, apprehensive, approving, argumentative, arrogant, authoritative, awed, bantering, bluff, blunt, booming, bored, bright, brisk, brusque, businesslike..." (Crystal 1969:295), to name only a few. Clearly the only bounds imposed here are those of the English lexicon. It should be obvious that in the face of such a multitude of labels and 'attitudes', some kind of systematization is indispensable.

## 2.4 A survey of intonational cues to attitude

As the foregoing discussion suggests, virtually all past studies of intonation and attitude have been unsatisfactory in one way or another. It is hardly an exaggeration to say that more work remains to be done here than in any other area of sentence intonation. The heterogeneity and the inadequacy of past experiments make a comparison, indeed even a compilation of results extremely difficult. Nevertheless, provided due caution is exercised in drawing conclusions, the value of such an overview may outweigh its drawbacks. The following table presents a survey of attitudes which have been linked with specific prosodic features of English in recent experimental studies (as of 1960). [The respective reference is indicated in parentheses.]

Although the studies evaluated differ widely in experimental technique and set-up, there is a certain amount of apparent agreement. Note, however, that some results do conflict. The pitch level of 'anger', for instance, is established as high in some studies, as low in others. 'Fear' is said to have extremely narrow pitch range by some, but to have occasional high peaks by others. Discrepancies of this sort may be of varying origin. For one, the attitude itself is often poorly defined. 'Fear', for instance,

Fig. X/2  Reported prosodic correlates of selected emotions and attitudes

| Attitude or emotion \ Prosodic feature | Pitch level (average) | Pitch range | | Tone | Loudness | Tempo | Other |
|---|---|---|---|---|---|---|---|
| | | Intervals between tones | Width of glides | | | | |
| Anger | high (D,W/S) low (C,H) | greater than neutral (W/S) <br> steps down (C) | | simple falling (C) | loud (C) | fast (C) | strong stress (C) high unstressed syllables (C) |
| Amusement | | | | rise–falls (C) | | | |
| Boredom | low (D,H) | | | level (C) | soft (H) | slow (H) | |
| Complaint | | | | semi-tone rises (F/M) | | | smooth melody rhythmically interrupted (F/M) |
| Confidence | high (S/L/W) | | | | loud (H,S/L) | fast (H,S/L) | |
| Coquetry | | | | | suppressed (F/M) | | soft tertial up-glide on last stressed syllable (F/M) |
| Excitement | | high step-ups (C) | wide (C) | falling and rise–fall type (C) | loud (C) | fast (C) | |
| Fear | lower than for anger (W/S) mid (F/M) | extremely narrow (F/M) occasional high peaks (W/S) | | | | duration longer than for anger (W/S) | rigid melodic line (F/M) |
| Happiness (= joy) | high (D,H, F/M) | increased (F/M) | | frequently ascending at irregular intervals (F/M) | loud (D,H) | fast (D) lively (F/M) | irregular stress distribution (F/M) |
| Longing | | narrowed (F/M) | | slightly rising, descending, gently ascending finally | | restrained (F/M) | |
| Pleasure | high (H) | | | | | | |
| Puzzlement | high (C) | high step-ups (C) | wide (C) | rising type (C) | piano (C) | lento (C) | |
| Sadness (= sorrow, grief) | low (D,H) lower than neutral (W/S) | narrow (W/S) | | | soft (H) | slow (W/S) | |
| Surprise | | increased (F/M) | | sudden fall (F/M) | | | |
| Tenderness | high (F/M) | narrow (F/M) | | | restrained (F/M) | | audible off-glide in long stressed syllables (F/M) |
| Timidity | | | | | soft (H) | slow (H) | |

C = Crystal 1969, D = Davitz 1964, F/M = Fónagy/Magdics 1963, H = Huttar 1968b, S/L/W = Scherer/London/Wolf (1973), W/S = Williams/Stevens 1972

could well be associated with any of the situations in which the following utterances would be appropriate:

a) Shh, I think I hear footsteps coming towards us
b) Good grief! You've got a snake crawling up your leg!
c) It's almost eight o'clock and Johnny hasn't come home from school yet

Yet these utterances may have quite different expressive prosody.

Furthermore, even a relatively clearly defined attitude or emotion may be subject to display rules which prescribe the extent to which a feeling should be shown in a given situation. In an explosive argument, for instance, it might be acceptable to express anger freely — but in another situation where direct display is prohibited, anger could very well be repressed, resulting in quite different prosodic features.

In addition, discrepancies may arise because different standards of comparison have been employed. Thus, Williams/Stevens (1972) compare the prosodic features associated with four attitudes among themselves and determine, for instance, that 'fear' generally has a lower average pitch level than 'anger'. But does this mean that its pitch level is therefore low? If the pitch level of 'anger' is high, could it not also be mid? Needless to say, there is a plethora of hidden problems of this sort in the above compilation, so that any apparent agreement or disagreement is as likely to be an artefact of the comparison as a reflection of linguistic truth.

## 3.   Resolved and unresolved problems

A number of pitfalls face all studies of intonation and attitude. It is to these that we turn our attention now.

### 3.1   Attitude vs. grammar

Traditionally, intonation has been thought to function attitudinally only in cases where some contour other than the 'neutral' one is used with a given sentence-type (Ch. VIII §3.3.1). The difficulty with such a view, as will have become obvious above, is drawing a clear line between grammatical and attitudinal meaning. The effect of using a rising intonation on, say, *You're coming* rather than a falling one can be just as easily called attitudinal (surprise vs. non-surprise) as grammatical (question vs. statement) (Cruttenden 1970:188). And the so-called grammatical distinction between command and request, e.g. *Shut the door* on a falling as opposed to a rising intonation, can also be accounted for in terms of attitude (definiteness vs. tentativeness).

The fundamental mistake is the belief that grammatical and attitudinal functions are discrete and non-overlapping. To consider the intonation of an utterance either purely grammatical, i.e. carrying no attitudinal meaning [often described as 'matter-of-fact'], or purely attitudinal, i.e. pleased, angry, reserved, gleeful, etc., is a gross oversimplification. Attitudinally marked utterances are still grammatical configurations, and even 'matter-of-fact' statements carry attitudinal information. In Crystal's words, "we communicate our attitude towards all utterance, even if this is to indicate as far as possible that we have no attitude" (1969:289).[7] It is only reasonable to conclude that both grammatical and attitudinal factors are present in every utterance.

---

[7] Cf. also Fónagy (1971), who views the expressive aspect of speech as resulting from a 'distorter' component through which all phonemes pass during the encoding process: "Non-distorting is not necessarily less expressive than distorting — it simply expresses something else" (1971:162).

However, this is not to say that utterances may not be marked or unmarked prosodically with respect to affective meaning. Crystal's (1969) investigation of the prosodic correlates of attitude indicates that of the attitudes examined, 'matter-of-fact' was accompanied by the fewest number of marked polysyllabic contrasts.[8] He concludes that it "may well approximate to an 'unmarked' norm of utterance for statements", without however being devoid of attitude (1969:303).

## 3.2   Attitude vs. lexis

There are two extremes with respect to this issue. At one extreme, the initial expectation is that intonation contours play discrete, unique roles in the communication of attitude – for instance, that a boosted falling pattern indicates pleased surprise, as in *You did!*. However, such a theory falls flat when counter-examples like *Don't!* are produced which have the same contour but convey a totally different attitude (e.g. insistence). The culprit appears to be lexis.

At the other extreme, all hope of finding unique attitudes for specific melodies is renounced and basic tune types are assigned very broad 'meanings' which take on different colourings according to lexical content. Cruttenden, for instance, describes all rising movement as tentative and all falling movement as definite (1970:187). Likewise, Halliday states that the general meaning of rising contours is uncertainty, that of falling contours, certainty (1970a:23). This rather appealing approach is, however, ultimately self-defeating: it places the burden of explanation on lexis and reduces the attitudinal function of intonation to a simple binary opposition.

The fact is that, laboratory experiments aside, intonation always occurs concurrently with lexis in actual speech. Rather than suppose that one component is responsible for affective meaning to the exclusion of the other, it is more reasonable to hypothesize that the two interact. Concretely this might look as follows: where words and attitude do not match, intonation may carry the affective meaning. For example, *Thank you* said in a flippant tone of voice, or *John's a great football player* said ironically, etc. But similarly, where attitude and intonation do not match, words may carry the affective meaning: e.g., Ladd's example of the stewardess who says *Put that goddam pipe away* to an airline passenger smoking against the rules (Ch. VI §2.3). The conclusion to be drawn is that lexis and intonation may be used by speakers both *singly* and/or *in conjunction* to express attitude.

But to speak solely of lexis here is somewhat misleading. Indeed we must not overlook the fact that the same words – say, *Put that goddam pipe away* – could be uttered with exactly the same intonation but by an interlocutor in a different situation [say, an intimate friend in the bedroom rather than a stewardess in an airplane]; if so, the attitude communicated would be wholly different. Just as we have seen that the pragmatic role of intonation relies to a certain extent on attitudinal information (Ch. IX), so it appears that the attitudinal role of intonation depends

---

[8] This is not surprising given the fact that his notation system relies heavily on the concept of norm, e.g. in dealing with simple pitch-range, onset, complex pitch-range, loudness, tempo, etc.

on pragmatic information. In other words, we are dealing not merely with a two-way interaction between intonation and lexis, but with a three-way interaction between intonation, lexis and context. It is in the interplay of these three factors that the cues to affective meaning must be sought.

## 3.3   Intonation vs. paralinguistic features

Intonation has often been overrated as the primary means of conveying expressive meaning − usually at the expense of other, equally important non-verbal phenomena. For one, the importance of kinesic information − e.g. a raised eyebrow, a wrinkled forehead − is frequently neglected. But even if the domain of inquiry is restricted to auditory effects alone, *paralinguistic* cues such as voice qualifiers (whisper, breathy voice, etc.) or voice qualifications (giggle, sob, etc.) are often not given their due: either they are subsumed under the heading *intonation* or *prosody* or they are ignored altogether.

Indeed studies of intonation and attitude have frequently made no sharp distinction between linguistic and paralinguistic features. This is most immediately apparent in the terminology, when phrases such as 'prosodic variables', 'paralinguistic cues', 'tone-of-voice' and 'voice quality' are used interchangeably with reference to one and the same thing. Studies which do distinguish carefully between linguistic and paralinguistic aspects, however, emphasize that both types of non-verbal effect may be important in the identification of attitude. According to one recent experimental study, certain attitudes are distinguishable on the basis of paralinguistic cues, but indistinguishable on the basis of intonation (Silverman et al 1983).[9] In fact, it is hard to escape the suspicion that auditory judges of attitude in the past may have been unknowingly relying on paralinguistic, rather than on intonation cues.

Separating the prosodic from the paralinguistic may prove very difficult in auditory discrimination. But the distinction is a crucial one if the precise linguistic role of intonation in communicating attitude is to be properly assessed. It may be the case that not all attitudes have specific prosodic marking − some may be conveyed wholly by paralinguistic means. If such a distinction could be shown to relate to specific subclasses of emotion and attitude, then we would be well on our way to pinning down the linguistic role of intonation as a conveyor of affective meaning.[10]

---

[9] Recordings of utterances with clear non-verbal attitudinal messages were manipulated such that (a) only paralinguistic and 'voice quality' cues remained; and (b) only intonation contours remained. Subjects were then asked to identify attitudes with the manipulated tapes. Attitudes which could be identified as well with (a) as with the original recordings included: *polite, relaxed, friendly, understanding, reproachful, aggressive, impatient*. However, only *polite* could be identified as well with (b) as with the originals.

[10] Silverman et al (1983) indeed suggest that only 'cognitive' or 'interpersonal' attitudes such as *reproachful* or *understanding* are conveyed by linguistic choices, whereas 'arousal-related attitudes' such as *relaxed* or *impatient* are communicated via paralinguistic and/or 'voice quality' features.

## 3.4 Towards a theory of emotion and attitude

The major unresolved problem at the moment is lack of systematization in the field of emotion and attitude. Nor will just any theory of emotion do. For example, Osgood's widely acclaimed tri-partite classification of affective meaning into activation [activity], evaluation [valence] and potency [strength] has not proved fully applicable with respect to intonation choice (§2.2). Uldall (1964), for instance, found that certain attitudes − in particular in the category 'evaluation' − were not expressed by intonation at all. Davitz (1964) likewise finds little or no correlation between the dimensions of valence and strength and the auditory cues of over-all loudness, pitch-range, timbre and rate. He concludes that only the activity dimension is reliably conveyed by such features (1964:108). There is thus an additional stipulation to be placed on a theory of emotion and attitude: in addition to being psychologically valid, it must also embody categories which are meaningful with respect to intonational choice.

In the past, as the abundance of labels indicates, the tendency has been to include virtually any adjective or noun remotely expressive of affect. This has given the false impression that there is agreement on what qualifies as an emotion or attitude, and at the same time has obscured important semantic distinctions between types of affect. As an example of some of the confusion, take the pilot study of prosodic/para-linguistic features and selected attitudes reported by Crystal (1969). Subjects were asked to read a number of neutral sentences "in a ... tone of voice". Among the attitudes they were asked to produce was "bored" (1969:297) − an adjective which describes a feeling which a *speaker* has. Yet later, the same attitude is referred to as "boring" (1969:307) − an adjective which, however, describes a reaction evoked in the *listener* by the behaviour of the speaker. Needless to say, the (perceived) feeling of a speaker and the reaction in the listener to the speaker are two very different things.[11]

To clarify the matter, let us picture what happens in a simple communicative act: a speaker encodes his propositional/illocutionary message in its phonological form, which, according to one theory, then passes through a 'distorter' component for affective meaning before being transmitted to the hearer. Subsequently the hearer decodes the message with both its propositional/illocutionary and expressive components, whereupon s/he is in a position to make the following types of judgment: (i) what the propositional and illocutionary content of the speaker's utterance is (perceived to be); (ii) what the speaker's inner state or feeling is (perceived to be); (iii) how the speaker is (perceived to be) acting in making the utterance; (iv) the effect the speaker's utterance and/or behaviour has on the hearer. That is, there are three different kinds of affective judgment which the hearer can make as a result of the communicative act: (ii), (iii), (iv). However, only (ii) and (iii) are directly relevant to the question of what affective meaning the intonational shape of the speaker's

---

[11] Uldall unknowingly confirms this when she finds that subjects differed in reliability depending on whether they were judging their own reactions or judging speaker intention (1964:254) [also §2.2].

utterance conveys: speaker encoding is not involved in (iv) at all. Thus the use of affective adjectives such as *boring, amusing, appealing, irritating, frightening* – and even *pleasant, unpleasant* to the extent that they are interpreted as hearers' "own reactions to the contours" (Uldall 1964:254) – must be excluded on the grounds that they do not describe attitudinal meaning which is purposively conveyed from speaker to hearer.

As for affective judgments of type (ii) and (iii), these appear to embody precisely the distinction made earlier between *emotion* and *attitude*. In the former, it is the speaker's inner state which is evaluated, whereas in (iii) it is some characteristic of the speaker's behaviour which is being judged. Expressed somewhat differently, we can say "$x$ is __ (in uttering $p$)" for adjectives under (ii), whereas for adjectives under (iii) it is more meaningful to say "$x$ is being __ (in uttering $p$)".[12] Thus compare:

| (ii) $x$ is __ | (iii) $x$ is being __ |
|---|---|
| amused | affectionate |
| angry | arrogant |
| anxious | coquettish |
| bored | critical |
| frightened | deferential |
| grieved | friendly |
| happy | haughty |
| impatient | matter-of-fact |
| relaxed | pleasant |
| sad | polite |
| surprised | precise |
| | sexy |
| (cf.: *$x$ is being __) | understanding |

It is possible that these two categories overlap with the activity, and the valence/strength dimensions of the Semantic Differential [Osgood/Suci/Tannenbaum; cf. §2.2 above], respectively: the emotions under (ii) all seem to involve different levels of activity or physiological arousal, whereas those under (iii) do not necessarily. Arousal-related emotions are often thought of as unlearned, spontaneous reactions to a given situation, while attitudes such as those under (iii) are more apt to be learned, conventionalized patterns of behaviour. But if this is the case, it is surprising that research up to now has been able to establish clear links only between the *activity* dimension of affective meaning and the prosodic cues of over-all pitch level, pitch-range, loudness and tempo. Since activity is so closely related to arousal level, this would imply that these features are of little *linguistic* value in conveying affective meaning. On the other hand, culturally determined norms affecting the exteriorization of arousal-related emotions (i.e. display rules, cf. §1 above) do make conventionalized prosodic correlates even here at least theoretically possible. It is conceivable that these, as well as learned attitudes such as those under (iii), are distinguished by more complex

---

[12] Some adjectives can be interpreted either way, e.g. '$x$ is aggressive' or '$x$ is being aggressive', depending on whether the speaker's state or the speaker's behaviour is more in the foreground.

features such as off-glides, rhythmic/arhythmic patterns, and local (rather than global) pitch configurations. It is along these lines that future research must proceed in the search for specifically linguistic links between intonation and attitude.

## References

Abe 1980
Barry 1981a
Chiţoran 1981
Costanzo/Markel/Costanzo 1969
Cruttenden 1970
*Crystal 1969 (Ch. VII)
Davitz 1964
Davitz 1969
Darwin 1873
Faure 1970
Fónagy 1971
Fónagy 1978
*Fónagy/Bérard 1972
Fónagy/Magdics 1963
Fourquet 1976
Frank 1974
Halliday 1970a
Huttar 1968a
Huttar 1968b
Jakobson 1960
Labov/Fanshel 1977
*Ladd 1978 (Ch. VI)

*Ladd/Scherer/Silverman 1984
Léon 1970
Léon 1979
Lieb 1980
Lieberman/Michaels 1962
Malmberg 1966
Markel/Bein/Phillis 1973
O'Connor/Arnold [2]1973
Osgood/Suci/Tannenbaum 1957
Rigault 1964
Scherer 1979
Scherer/London/Wolf 1973
Schubiger 1958
*Silverman/Scherer/Ladd 1983
Stankiewicz 1964
Trojan 1957
Uldall 1960
Uldall 1964
Williams/Stevens 1972
Wodarz 1962
Zillig 1982

Chapter XI
# Intonation and text/discourse

The textual/discourse role of intonation presupposes a consideration of stretches of speech larger than one utterance. Intonationally speaking, since chains of utterances generally comprise more than one tone-unit, we shall be concerned primarily with sequences of tone-units.

## 1. On the notions of text and discourse

To some it may appear that two very different aspects of speech have been forced together under one heading. Indeed it has been proposed that *text* be distinguished from *discourse* along the following lines:

> Discourse is linguistic communication seen as a transaction between speaker and hearer, as an interpersonal activity whose form is determined by its social purpose. Text is linguistic communication (either spoken or written) seen simply as a message in its auditory or visual medium. (Leech/Short 1981:209)

Under this view discourse is a dynamic process, whereas text is static, disembodied from the social context in which it occurs. Because of the explicitly interactive nature of discourse, it is naturally associated with dialogue; conversely, monologue is typically treated as text.

Yet it can be argued that the borderline between monologue and dialogue − and by extension between text and discourse − is by no means clear. It is not unusual to find monologue passages within a section of dialogue. Nor is it unthinkable that one might find dialogue passages within a monologue. Since in both instances we are dealing with the chaining together of utterances, or textually speaking with the development of a 'topic' (by one or several speakers), there are grounds for treating monologue and dialogue as related in very basic ways. Similarly, a text in the above definition can hardly be severed from the (discourse) context in which it occurs: linguistic encoding does not take place in a vacuum. In fact, since language is by definition interactional, all texts are embedded in discourse and all discourse consists of texts. It is for these reasons that we propose to treat both here. Specifically, we shall examine (a) the role of intonation in texts by considering sequences of utterances *within the speech turn of one speaker* and (b) the role of intonation in discourse by considering sequences of utterances *across speaker boundaries*.

## 2.    The role of intonation in texts

The extent to which a textual role can be attributed to intonation depends greatly on our understanding of what a text is. This question has preoccupied linguists for some time. If text is viewed merely as any random passage of uninterrupted speech (by one speaker), then the textual role of intonation is restricted to the recurrence of recognizable patterns in tone-unit sequences. It is difficult, however, to establish any kind of motivation for this sequencing other than chance.[1]

On the other hand, one can adopt a more stringent view of *text*, as for instance Halliday/Hasan (1976) have done. For them a text is "any passage, spoken or written, of whatever length that (...) form[s] a unified whole" (1976:1). In this sense, a text is a gestalt, an organized whole.[2] If this is the case, then texts will be likely to have characteristics which are common to all organized wholes, i.e. they will be clearly segmentable into hierarchically organized parts, internally cohesive within these parts, and will have a center of focus (de Groot [2]1968:540f.). Given this view of text, it can be shown that intonation has an important contribution to make in the organization and structuring of text.

### 2.1    Textual sub-units

Much of the research into textual organization focuses on the notion of paragraph. The paragraph − as a conceptual, not an orthographic unit[3] − is considered one of the most important building blocks of texts. The conceptual paragraph has been defined as "a unit in speech or writing which maintains a uniform orientation" (Hinds 1979:136). Texts can be seen as consisting of an unspecified number of these sub-units which are organized around *topics*, to use a related term.[4]

#### 2.1.1 Major paratones

The intonational equivalent of the conceptual paragraph, it has been suggested, is the so-called 'paratone', or rather − since greater precision will be necessary shortly

---

[1]  Crystal explores this possibility briefly but concludes: "Phonological analysis of tone-sequences of any length is clearly of limited application, without a grammatical frame of reference of some kind" (1969:243).

[2]  A more modern term might be *global structure* (van Dijk 1980:3): "we take global structures to be a kind of (w)*holistic* structure, and we say that the parts, members, etc., 'make up', 'constitute', 'form', or 'compose' them. The intuitive 'unity' of a whole then will be determined in terms of spatiotemporal continuity and its cognitive correlates (e.g., coherence) and externally by its distinction from and substitutivity with respect to other (whole) objects". Cf. also van Dijk (1980:202f.).

[3]  The orthographic paragraph is signalled initially by an indented graphical/typographical line and finally by an incomplete graphical/typographical line. [The latter feature may be absent if the end of the paragraph text coincides with the end of a graphical/typographical line.] Of course the orthographic paragraph may overlap with the conceptual paragraph − but it need not do so.

[4]  Not to be confused with the *topic* of topic-comment, or given-new (Ch. VII).

– the *major paratone* (Yule 1980b). A major paratone, according to Yule, is characterized at its beginning by the presence of high onset or in Brazil's terms, high key. The end of a major paratone is signalled by very low pitch and the presence of a noticeable pause.[5] However, whereas the initial marking of a major paratone is obligatory, the final marking – in particular, the pause – may be lacking. Nonetheless the final boundary may be established in retrospect by the presence of a following initial boundary.

The claim is then that phonological units larger than a single tone-unit can be identified in speech on the basis of intonational cues alone, and that these correspond to conceptual paragraphs. Obviously a great deal more research must be done before such claims can be fully substantiated. However, their validity for the material on the accompanying cassette can be demonstrated as follows [only onset and nucleus notated in each tone-unit]:

Fig. XI/1

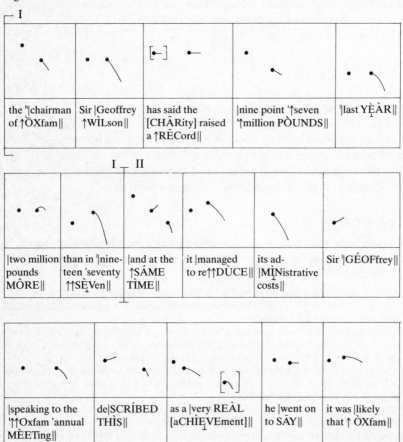

| the ⁿ|chairman of ↑O̲Xfam‖ | Sir |Geoffrey ↑WI̲Lson‖ | has said the [CHĀRity] raised a ↑RĒCord‖ | |nine point '↑seven '↑million PÒUNDS‖ | ‖last YE̲ÀR‖ |

| |two million pounds MÔRE‖ | than in ⁿ|nine-teen 'seventy ↑↑SE̲Ven‖ | |and at the ↑SÁME TÌME‖ | it |managed to re↑↑DÙCE‖ | its ad- |MI̲Nistrative costs‖ | Sir ‖GÉOFfrey‖ |

| |speaking to the ↑↑Oxfam 'annual MÈETing‖ | de|SCRÍBED THÌS‖ | as a |very REÀL [aCHIE̲VEment]‖ | he |went on to SĀY‖ | it was |likely that ↑ ÒXfam‖ |

[5] In the data referred to by Yule, the pause is frequently one second or more (1980).

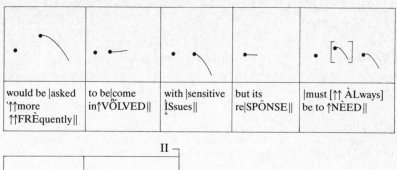

| would be \|asked '↑↑more ↑↑FREquently\|\| | to be\|come in↑VŎLVED\|\| | with \|sensitive ÌSsues\|\| | but its re\|SPŌNSE\|\| | \|must [↑↑ ÀLways] be to ↑NĚED\|\| |
|---|---|---|---|---|

II

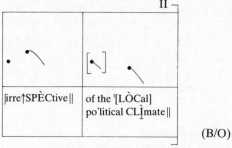

| \|irre↑SPÈCtive\|\| | of the '[LÒCal] po'litical CLĮmate\|\| |
|---|---|

(B/O)

The beginning of the first paratone is signalled by the use of extra high onset on *Chairman* [compare this to the onset on *Geoffrey*]. No subsequent onsets are higher than this one until that on *and*) which signals the beginning of the next major paratone. The end of the paratone is likewise signalled here by extra low pitch (in particular, a fall to bottom or near-bottom on *seven* and *climate*) and by a noticeable pause after *climate*. These phonologically determined major paratones coincide, furthermore, with a single news item. The subsequent news item begins with another high onset on *employment*.

The passage in Fig. XI/2 contains two major paratones according to the criteria set forth above. The beginning of the first paratone is signalled by extra high onset on *abortion*. [Notice that the end of the preceding paratone is signalled, inter alia, by a *filled* pause /ɜːm/.] Subsequent onsets are all lower than this one until *I*, which again has extra high pitch and signals the beginning of a second major paratone. The final boundary of the first paratone is marked by a low fall to near-bottom on *move* and followed by a filled pause /ɜː/. The final boundary of the second major paratone is not unequivocally marked. There is a wide fall to near-bottom on *request*, but we do not know whether the speaker might not have continued this major paratone if EP had not interjected *Why not?*. We can thus consider this either as the unmarked end of a complete paratone or as an incomplete paratone. Subsequent to this interruption, BD starts a new paratone signalled by an extra high onset on *fully*.

### 2.1.2 Minor paratones

In addition to major paratones, whose existence is relatively widely acknowledged (Crystal 1969:144, Lehiste 1975, Rees/Urquhart 1976, Enkvist/Nordström 1978, etc.), it has recently been suggested that another level of tonal organization may exist

191

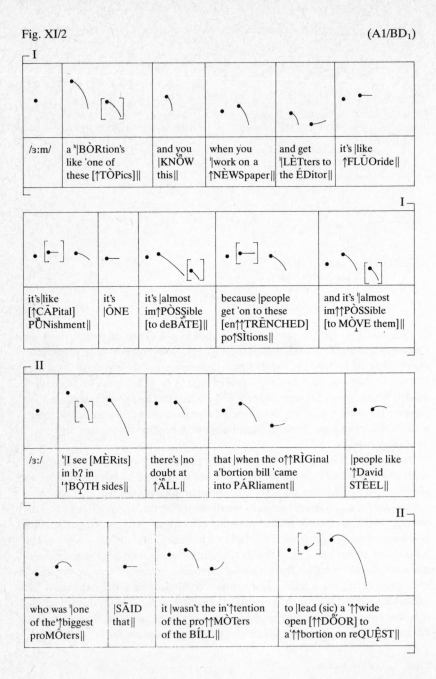

**I**

| /ɜːm/ | a ʰ|BÒRtion's like 'one of these [↑TÒPics]‖ | and you |KNŎW this‖ | when you 'work on a ↑NÈWSpaper‖ | and get ʰ|LÈTters to the ÉDitor‖ | it's |like ↑FLŪOride‖ |

**I**

| it's|like [↑CĀPital] PŬNishment‖ | it's |ŌNE | it's |almost im↑PÒSSible [to deBĀTE]‖ | because |people get 'on to these [en↑↑TRĒNCHED] po↑SĪtions‖ | and it's '|almost im↑↑PÒSSible [to MÒVE them]‖ |

**II**

| /ɜː/ | ʰ|I see [MÈRits] in b? in '↑BŎTH sides‖ | there's |no doubt at ↑ĂLL‖ | that |when the o↑↑RÌGinal a'bortion bill 'came into PÁRliament‖ | |people like '↑David STÊEL‖ |

**II**

| who was '|one of the'↑biggest proMŌTers‖ | |SĀID that‖ | it |wasn't the in'↑tention of the pro↑↑MŎTers of the BÍLL‖ | to |lead (sic) a '↑↑wide open [↑↑DŎOR] to a'↑↑bortion on reQUÊST‖ |

between these and single tone-units. The unit postulated at this level is called the *minor paratone* (Yule 1980, Couper-Kuhlen 1983). As its name indicates, the minor paratone tends to be smaller in size than the major paratone, i.e. it typically comprises fewer tone-units – although this is by no means a *sine qua non*. The minor paratone comes closest to what Brazil/Coulthard/Johns (1980) call a *pitch sequence* (Ch. V §3.1).

In contrast to a major paratone, which is characterized by high onset at its beginning, a minor paratone has unspecified pitch height at its beginning, i.e. it may have any initial onset choice: high, mid or low. Its final boundary, on the other hand, is specific and obligatory: the nuclear tone must end low, generally with a fall to bottom or near-bottom of the speaker's voice range. [In the notation adopted here this would be / `_ or ʌ/.] The closest equivalent in Brazil's system would be *low termination* (cf. Ch. V §3.1).[6]

By virtue of the fact that minor paratones can begin in at least three different ways, the following sub-classes are formed:

a) minor paratones which begin with high onset
b) minor paratones which begin with mid onset
c) minor paratones which begin with low onset

Each of these sub-groups can be shown to fulfil a particular function in the organization of the text:

a) Minor paratones which begin high initiate major paratones, i.e. signal a *new* topical orientation.

b) Minor paratones which begin mid represent paratactic *additions to* or extensions of what precedes.

c) Minor paratones which begin low represent hypotactic *subordinations to* or inclusions in what precedes.[7]

For example, consider the following news item:

Fig. XI/3

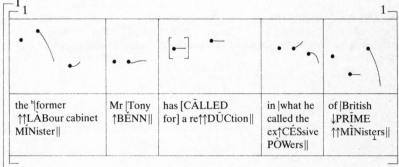

| the ʰ|former ↑↑LÁBour cabinet MÍNister‖ | Mr \|Tony ↑BĔNN‖ | has [CĂLLED for] a re↑↑DŬCtion‖ | in \|what he called the ex↑CÉSsive PÓWers‖ | of \|British ↓PRĪME ↑↑MÌNistęrs‖ |

---

[6] Note, however, that Brazil's 'low termination' requires a low *beginning-point* rather than a low ending-point. But if this criterion is used, it is necessary to discount a number of clear phonological 'breaks' in the intonational configuration of texts, e.g. that after *Ministers* in Fig. XI/3, where the nucleus has a high beginning-point but a low ending-point.

[7] At times, however, subordination is indicated by a shift from low to mid onset (Couper-Kuhlen 1983).

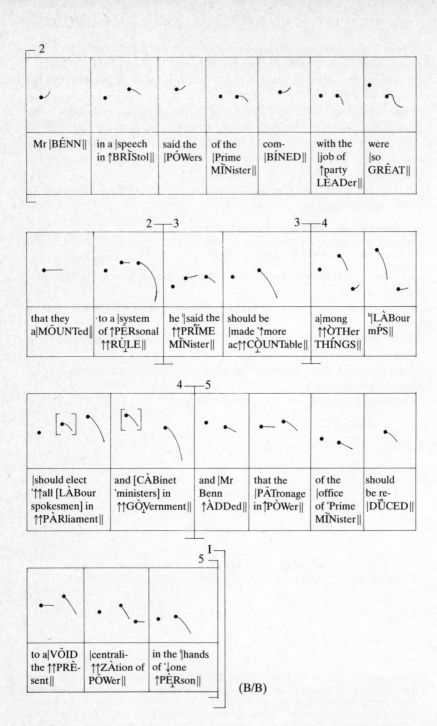

2

| Mr \|BÉNN\|\| | in a \|speech in ↑BRĬStol\|\| | said the \|PÓWers | of the \|Prime MĬNister\|\| | com-\|BÍNED\|\| | with the \|job of ↑party LEADer\|\| | were \|so GRÊAT\|\| |

2—3　　　3—4

| that they a\|MŌUNTed\|\| | ·to a \|system of ↑PÉRsonal ↑↑RÙLE\|\| | he ʺ\|said the ↑↑PRĬME MĬNister\|\| | should be \|made '↑more ac↑↑CÒUNTable\|\| | a\|mong ↑↑ÒTHer THÍNGS\|\| | ʰ\|LÀBour mPS\|\| |

4——5

| \|should elect '↑↑all [LÀBour spokesmen] in ↑↑PÀRliament\|\| | and [CÀBinet 'ministers] in ↑↑GÒVernment\|\| | and \|Mr Benn ↑ÀDDed\|\| | that the \|PÁTronage in↑PÒWer\|\| | of the \|office of 'Prime MĬNister\|\| | should be re-\|DŬCED\|\| |

5——I

| to a\|VŌID the ↑↑PRÈ-sent\|\| | \|centrali-↑↑ZÀtion of POWer\|\| | in the ʰ\|hands of '↓one ↑PÈRson\|\| | | | |

(B/B)

194

This item consists of one major paratone. However, a number of phonological sub-units or minor paratones can be identified according to the criteria set forth above. An extra high onset on *former* begins the major paratone and simultaneously the first minor paratone, which consequently exemplifies type (a) above. *Ministers* has a fall to low and constitutes the end of the first minor paratone. The following onset is mid, placing the second minor paratone in category (b) above. There are no further falls to low until *rule*, which constitutes the end of the second minor paratone. The next onset is low [with respect to the preceding one]; the third minor paratone consequently belongs to type (c) above. The fall to low on *accountable* signals another phonological boundary, with a fourth minor paratone beginning mid on *among* and ending in a fall to low on *Government*. The fifth minor paratone also begins mid (on *Mr*) and comes to an end with the fall to low on *person*. This final minor paratone boundary is likewise the end of the major paratone, since it is followed by extra high onset on *I believe*.

Textually the minor paratones in this passage fulfil different functions. Whereas minor paratone /2/ adds information to the proposition concerning excessive powers, minor paratone /3/ presents its content as hypotactic or subsidiary information. [This is reflected in the use of anaphoric *he* as well.[8]] Minor paratone /4/ is realized as a paratactic addition to the proposition concerning personal rule;[9] likewise minor paratone /5/ makes a paratactic addition (also reflected in the lexis *Mr Benn added*).

Based on this small sample, it appears that phonological units smaller than the major paratone but larger than a single tone-unit can be identified, and that they constitute phonological realizations of hierarchically ordered textual relations. The role of intonation in the segmentation and hierarchical organization of texts can thus be regarded as provisionally established.

## 2.2    Cohesion and cohesive devices

In a chain or sequence of tone-units, some units appear to 'stick together' more closely than others. In fact, this type of observation was what motivated the creation of *compound* tone-units (Ch. V §2.3), where the pre-head of the second tone-unit is incorporated into the tail of the first, and *subordinate* tone-units (Ch. V §3.3), in which the pitch range of one tone-unit is broadly encompassed in that of another. Trim (1959) likewise notes that some tone-units are integrated more closely than others and introduces the concept of 'major' tone-group[10] to account for "a unit in the intonational system composed of an integrated sequence of linked tone-groups" (1959, 1973:323), whose constituent parts are "integrated by some formal device or devices" (1959, 1973:321).

---

[8] As far as objective content goes, this proposition ('make Prime Ministers more accountable') could have been put on a par with that concerning personal rule and both made subsidiary to the proposition 'call for reduction in excessive powers'. However, this would have required different pronominal use and intonational configuration.

[9] Notice, however, that an indirect speech marker such as *Benn said* or *he said* is lacking.

[10] Not to be confused with major (vs. minor) paratones, nor with the major 'tone groups' of O'Connor/Arnold ([2]1973).

Little is known about the specific nature of these so-called 'consolidating devices'. However, analogizing from work done on the psychological nature of rhythmic units (Ch. III §1) – i.e. units in which rhythmic events or beats *cohere* – we can surmise that intonational cohesive devices will appeal to the same two principles of *alternation* and *succession*.

### 2.2.1 Alternating devices

A cohesive unit may be created by the alternation of two different events, one of which is subsidiary to the other. Restricting ourselves to nuclear pitch for the moment, we can observe this happening within a compound tone-unit where a rise alternates with a fall, and across tone-unit boundaries, as in:

(a) *Sir Geoffrey ... described this* (Fig. XI/1, lines 2–3).
(b) *to become involved with sensitive issues* (Fig. XI/1, line 4).
and in

Fig. XI/4   (c)

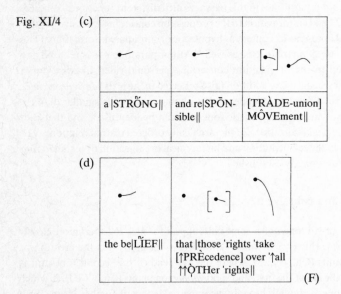

(F)

Because the rise has the subtle, quasi-musical effect of demanding a 'resolution', which however is 'postponed' until the next tone-unit, the two units are joined more closely than, say | ↘ | ↗ |. [In this case the fall would terminate one intonational sequence.[11]]

### 2.2.2 Successive devices

A cohesive unit may also be established by a succession of two or more identical or similar events. Once again with respect to nuclear pitch only, successive patterns may be found, for example, in:

---

[11] It is, however, conceivable that the first member of a cohesive pair might be a 'non-definitive', i.e. incomplete, fall or a level.

196

Fig. XI/5

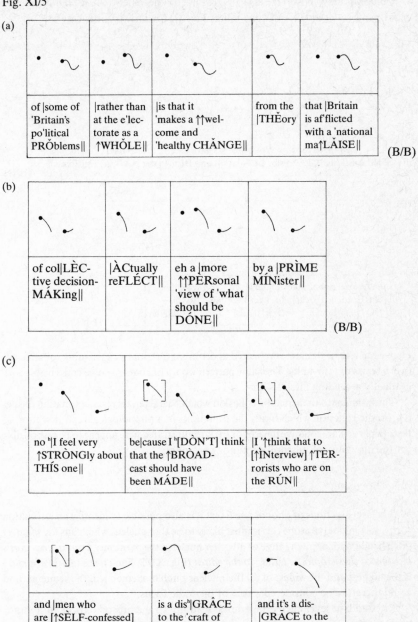

(a)

| of \|some of 'Britain's po'litical PRŎblems\|\| | \|rather than at the e'lectorate as a ↑WHŎLE\|\| | \|is that it 'makes a ↑↑welcome and 'healthy CHĂNGE\|\| | from the \|THĔory | that \|Britain is af'flicted with a 'national ma↑LĂISE\|\| |
|---|---|---|---|---|

(B/B)

(b)

| of col\|LÈCtive decision-MÁKing\|\| | \|ÀCtually reFLÉCT\|\| | eh a \|more ↑↑PERsonal 'view of 'what should be DÓNE\|\| | by a \|PRÌME MÍNister\|\| |
|---|---|---|---|

(B/B)

(c)

| no ʰ\|I feel very ↑STRÓNGly about THÍS one\|\| | be\|cause I ʰ[DÒN'T] think that the ↑BRÒADcast should have been MÁDE\|\| | \|I '↑think that to [↑ÌNterview] ↑TÈRrorists who are on the RÚN\|\| |
|---|---|---|

| and \|men who are [↑SÈLF-confessed] MÛRderers of 'people like Airy NÉEVE\|\| | is a disʰ\|GRÂCE to the 'craft of BRÓADcasting\|\| | and it's a dis-\|GRÂCE to the 'craft of JOURnalism\|\| |
|---|---|---|

(A2/ BD)

Such patterns are established by the reduplication of *identical* nuclear movements in two or more successive tone-units.

Cohesion may, however, also be created by the repetition of *similar* nuclear movements in a sequence of tone-units. This is, for instance, the case in:

Fig. XI/6

(a)

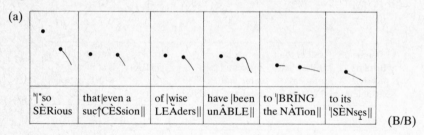

| ʰ\|ˮso SÈRious | that\|even a suc↑CÈSsion\|\| | of \|wise LEÂders\|\| | have \|been unÂBLE\|\| | to ˈ\|BRĪNG the NÀTion\|\| | to its ˈ\|SÈNsęs\|\| |
|---|---|---|---|---|---|

(B/B)

(b)

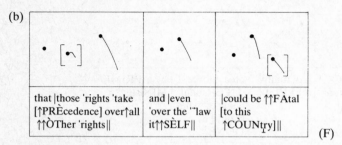

| that \|those 'rights 'take [↑PRÈcedence] over↑all ↑↑ÒTher 'rights\|\| | and \|even 'over the ˮlaw it↑↑SÈLF\|\| | \|could be ↑↑FÀtal [to this ↑CÒUNtry]\|\| |
|---|---|---|

(F)

Here a nuclear movement is repeated at different (gradually descending) pitch levels over a series of tone-units. The same pattern would of course also be conceivable with gradually ascending pitch levels.

Thus, similar to the semantic cohesion which characterizes texts, intonation creates a prosodic cohesion which binds the tone-units in a phonological text or section of text. In particular, cohesive devices of the sort illustrated here appear to be responsible for the intonational 'texture' of minor paratones.

## 2.3 Focusing

Within larger sections of phonological text it is also possible to identify an intonation *focus*. In a minor paratone this is most likely to be that nucleus which has the greatest pitch height and/or pitch range of all other nuclei in the paratone. Thus in *abortion's like one of these topics… letters to the editor* (Fig. XI/2, line 1), the fall on *abortion* is the highest and the widest of all the nuclear pitch movements in the sequence and could therefore be considered a sort of prosodic focus.

Rises and/or level nuclei sometimes 'lead up' to the prosodic focus of a minor paratone:

(a) *there's no doubt at all … request* (Fig. XI/2, lines 3–4). [The wide rise–fall on *request* is the prosodic focus.]

(b) *I feel very strongly … craft of journalism* (Fig. XI/5, example c). [The fall on *journalism* is the prosodic focus.]     and

198

Fig. XI/7  (c)

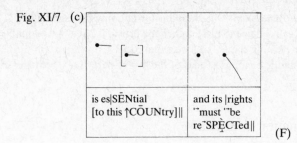

| is es\|SÉNtial [to this ↑CŌUNtry]\|\| | and its \|rights ˈˉmust ˈˉbe reˉSPÈ̱CTed\|\| |
|---|---|

(F)

Or arrested falls may build up tension by (gradually or suddenly) increasing pitch height and/or range:

Fig. XI/8

(a)

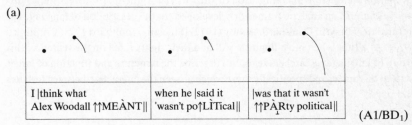

| I \|think what Alex Woodall ↑↑MEÀNT\|\| | when he \|said it 'wasn't po↑LĪTical\|\| | \|was that it wasn't ↑↑PÀ̱Rty political\|\| |
|---|---|---|

(A1/BD₁)

(b) *I see merits in both sides* (Fig. XI/2, line 3). [The wide fall on *both* is the prosodic focus.]

Both patterns produce the effect of a final climax. On the other hand, the prosodic focus may come first, so that what follows is anti-climax:

Fig. XI/9  (a)

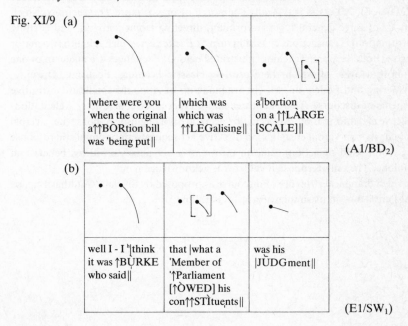

| \|where were you 'when the original a↑↑BÒRtion bill was 'being put\|\| | \|which was which was ↑↑LÈGalising\|\| | a'\|bortion on a ↑↑LÀRGE [SCÀLE]\|\| |
|---|---|---|

(A1/BD₂)

(b)

| well I - I ʰ\|think it was ↑BŬRKE who said\|\| | that \|what a 'Member of ↑↑Parliament [↑ÒWED] his con↑↑STĬtuents\|\| | was his \|JŬDGment\|\| |
|---|---|---|

(E1/SW₁)

199

In all of these cases, intonation appears to be responsible not only for establishing sections which are hierarchically related to one another and providing cohesion within these sections, but also for creating centers of (prosodic) focus. To what extent the latter coincide with the semantic or topical focus of the text or part of text remains to be investigated.

## 3. The role of intonation in discourse

The importance of intonation in the organization of conversation is just beginning to emerge. Most of what we know so far derives from the model of discourse intonation developed by Brazil and his co-workers in Birmingham. The term *discourse intonation* stems from an application of Brazil's (1975) theory of intonation to *discourse analysis*, an analytic framework developed for the description of language use by Sinclair/Forsyth/Coulthard/Ashby (1972) [Sinclair/Coulthard 1975; Coulthard 1977]. At a time when most linguists still had their sights fixed on the sentence, this group of language researchers set out to describe the structure and function of larger units of discourse, and specifically those which arise in the interaction between teachers and pupils.

### 3.1 A model of discourse analysis

Using taped recordings of actual lessons as data, Sinclair et al devised a descriptive system for classroom discourse comprising five units, the largest being *Lesson* (or Interaction). A Lesson is typically composed of one or more *Transactions*, which may be of three general types: informing, directing (some activity), and eliciting (information). Transactions consist in turn of *Exchanges*, which fall into two major classes, Boundary and Teaching (illustrated below). Exchanges are made up of one or more *Moves*, of which there are five classes: Framing, Focusing, Opening, Answering and Follow-up. Moves are made up of *Acts*, the smallest constitutive elements of discourse. There are three major types of discourse acts – elicitation, directive and information. An elicitation act requests a linguistic response (i.e. a verbal reply or its non-verbal correlate), a directive act requests a non-linguistic response (e.g. some kind of action), and an informative act passes on ideas, beliefs and opinions. The only response it calls for is acknowledgement.

The hierarchical structure of discourse as proposed by Sinclair/Coulthard can be diagrammed – in its simplest form – as follows:

Fig. XI/10   A model of discourse analysis (from Sinclair/Coulthard 1975)

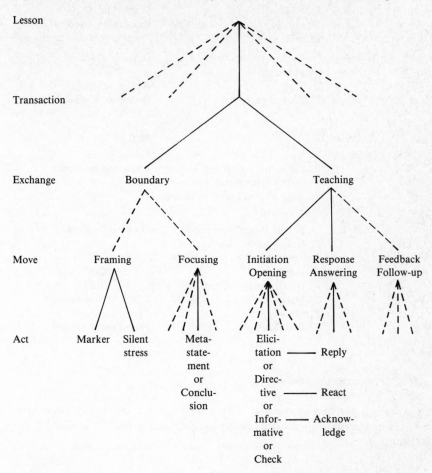

[Dotted lines indicate optional units; only acts which are obligatory constituents of moves figure in the diagram.]

The function of a Marker is to indicate a boundary in discourse; it is usually realized by a lexical item such as *well, good, right, okay*, etc., followed by silent stress (Ch. II §2.5). Metastatements and Conclusions are statements about the direction the discourse is going to take or has just taken.

This basic structure is illustrated in the following two excerpts from material analyzed by Sinclair et al:

| a) | EXCHANGE | | | MOVE : Act |
|---|---|---|---|---|
| | Boundary | T: | Now⌐ | Frame : Marker |
| | | | Let's just have a look at these things here | Focus : Metastatement |
| | Teaching | | Can you tell me, first of all, what's this? | Opening : Elicitation |
| | | P: | Paper | Answering : Reply |
| | | T: | Piece of paper yes | Follow-up : Evaluate[12] |

(1975:96)

| b) | EXCHANGE | | | MOVE : Act |
|---|---|---|---|---|
| | Boundary | T: | Now⌐ | Frame : Marker |
| | | | Let me test your brains let me see if you can think of the materials that I'm going to ask you about | Focus : Metastatement |
| | Teaching | | If your mummy was going to make a frock, what material would she use? | Opening : Elicitation |
| | | | Hands up | : Cue[12] |
| | | | NV (non-verbal action) | : Bid[12] |
| | | | Marie | : Nomination[12] |
| | | P: | Cloth | Answering: Reply |
| | | T: | Cloth good girl | Follow-up: Evaluate[12] |

(1975:104f.)

## 3.2 Discourse intonation

Given this model of discourse analysis, it is in particular at the level of the *exchange* that intonation has an important role to play, according to Brazil/Coulthard/Johns (1980).

### 3.2.1 Pitch concord

Successive moves within an exchange, they claim, display harmony of pitch level, or *pitch concord*, between "the termination choice of the final tone unit of one move and the initial key choice of the next move" (1980:75). This pattern can be found not only in teacher–pupil interaction, but also in doctor–patient exchanges and in other types of asymmetrical discourse. To illustrate, consider the following excerpts from a doctor–patient interview:[13]

---

[12] In an 'Evaluate' act the speaker presents a value judgment concerning the preceding response (e.g. *good, interesting, yes, no*). A 'Cue' (e.g. *Hands up, No shouting*) evokes a bid, a 'Bid' (*Miss, Sir*) indicates a desire to make a contribution to the discourse, and a 'Nomination' (*David, you*) selects or gives permission to someone to participate in the discourse.

[13] For ease of comparison, Brazil et al's notation has been translated into the system adopted here. The following equivalences are used: high key $^h|$, mid key $^m|$, low key $_|$; high termination ⇈, mid termination ↑ or →, low termination ↓ or $\phi$.

| (i) | *EXCHANGE* | | *MOVE* |
|---|---|---|---|

D: it's <sup>h</sup>|dry SKÎN ||  <sup>m</sup>|ÌSn't it ||   Opening
P: <sup>m</sup>|MM ||   Answering

| (ii) | *EXCHANGE* | | *MOVE* |
|---|---|---|---|

D: <sup>m</sup>|VERy ↑↑ÌRritating you say ||   Opening
P: <sup>h</sup>|VÈRy irritating ||   Answering

(Brazil/Coulthard/Johns 1980:75)

That is, if a non-final move in an exchange ends on *mid* termination, we find that the following move begins with mid key (i), whereas if a non-final move in an exchange ends with *high* termination, the following begins with high key (ii). On the other hand, if a (final or non-final) move in an exchange ends with *low* termination, i.e. coincides with the end of a pitch sequence, the next move may have any initial key choice whatsoever.

These patterns are not only present in the discourse analysed by Brazil and his co-workers: they are also claimed to be constraints which apply to the production of all (asymmetrical) discourse. Thus there is a 'pressure' towards pitch concord in the exchange with which discourse participants must comply or else be judged 'non-compliant' (1980:76). From the speaker's point of view, high termination indicates the expectation that the next speaker will begin high, and − because high key within the pitch sequence is viewed as having *contrastive* meaning (Ch. VII §2.2.2.2) − this is taken to mean that the second speaker is expected to *confirm* what has been said. Mid termination, on the other hand, indicates the expectation that the interlocutor will begin with mid key, i.e. (since mid key within the pitch sequence has *additive* meaning) that s/he will *agree* with what has been said. The theory thus provides a plausible explanation for why pupils in the classroom often use high termination in answering moves:

> We discover that very often the pupils are in fact *requesting* an evaluative, high key follow-up move by ending their answer with high termination. Only when the pupil is confident does he end with mid-termination requesting agreement; while low termination virtually never occurs and when it does is heard as 'cheeky' or 'sullen' because it suggests that the exchange has ended, evaluation or comment is superfluous and thus the pointlessness of the question. (Brazil/Coulthard/Johns 1980:78)

### 3.2.2 Pitch sequence and the exchange

More recently Brazil has illustrated how the pitch sequence (Ch. V §3.1) and the exchange relate to one another in discourse. The pitch sequence may be co-terminous with the exchange, as in:

| *EXCHANGE* | *MOVE* |
|---|---|

D: <sup>h</sup>|how ÒFten || do you <sup>m</sup>|GÈT these pains ||   Opening
P: <sup>m</sup>|every few→DÀYS doctor ||   Answering
D: <sup>m</sup>|every few ↓DÀYS ||   Follow-up

In this case, according to Brazil, the speaker reserves for himself the opportunity of initiating the next exchange, which might take one of the following forms:

| EXCHANGE | MOVE |
|---|---|
| (i) have you ^h\|had anything like this be⁻FÒRE \|\| | Opening |
| or | |
| (ii) and ^m\|how long do they ⁻LÀST \|\| | |
| or | |
| (iii) and you ^l\|get them as frequently as ⇈THÀT \|\| | |

Here the choice of key initiating the second pitch sequence (and the second exchange) indicates the relationship of the new exchange to the one which precedes it. *High* key (i) signals that the second exchange is unrelated to the first, *mid* key (ii) that the second exchange is an addition to or enlargement of the first, and *low* key (iii) that it "will result in a further presentation of the same information" (Brazil 1981:156).

The pitch sequence and the exchange need not overlap, however. Thus we may find that an exchange does not end with low termination:

| EXCHANGE₁ | MOVE |
|---|---|
| D: ^h\|how ÒFten \|\| do you ^m\|GÈT these pains \|\| | Opening |
| P: ^m\|every few ⁻DÀYS \|\| | Answering |

| EXCHANGE₂ | MOVE |
|---|---|
| D: and ^m\|how long do they ⁻LÀST \|\| | Opening |
| P: about a ^m\|half an ⁻HÒUR \|\| | Answering |
| D: ^m\|half an ↓HÒUR \|\| | Follow-up |

Since the end of the first exchange has mid termination, the pitch sequence continues into the second exchange. This is one way in which exchanges in a series may be related one to another (Brazil 1981:156).

Or a pitch sequence may come to an end within an exchange. This is, for instance, the case in:

| EXCHANGE | MOVE |
|---|---|
| D: well ^h\|TÈLL me Mister Smith \|\| ^m\|how are you feeling ↓NÒW \|\| | Opening |

Here the low termination on *now* indicates that a pitch sequence has come to an end, although the exchange is not yet complete. According to Brazil, closing a pitch sequence on an eliciting move in this fashion "serves often as an invitation to reply at length precisely because the addressee is free to begin as he likes" (Brazil 1981:157).

A pitch sequence may likewise come to an end on a response move; in this case, since the speaker does not indicate that he expects an acknowledgement, his response "carries evident overtones of brusqueness or sullenness":

| EXCHANGE | MOVE | |
|---|---|---|
| D: ^h\|how ÒFten \|\| do you ^m\|GÈT these pains \|\| | Opening | |
| P: ^m\|every few ↓DÀYS \|\| | Answering | (Brazil 1981:157) |

## 3.3 Intonation in conversation analysis

Brazil's model of discourse intonation is a tightly constrained system which presents important insights into the nature and organization of asymmetrical discourse. However, if it is applied to more symmetrical interaction (as, for instance, panel discussions such as those on the accompanying cassette), it appears overly rigid and indeed occasionally breaks down. Consider, for instance, the following excerpt:

| EXCHANGE | MOVE |
|----------|------|
| DJ: $^h$\|BĔRnard DeNĪN \|\| | Initiation |
| BD: I $^m$\|think what ↑Alex ↑Woodall ↑↑MEÀNT \|\| ... | Response  (A1/BD$_1$) |

Here although the (re-)initiating move has high key/termination, the response move begins with mid key.[14] [Notice that the textual function of different onset beginnings as hypothesized in §2.1.2 accounts quite nicely for the presence of mid onset here, since what the speaker says represents a continuation of the discourse topic introduced earlier.]

Or consider:

| EXCHANGE | MOVE |
|----------|------|
| DJ: $^h$\|CŌNor \|\| have you got anything to | Initiation |
| $^m$\|ĀDD to that \|\| | |
| CCB: well I $^h$\|think one should ↑CÒNcentrate | Response |
| on the question of... (E1/CCB$_2$) | |

In this instance, although the initiating move has mid termination, the response move begins extra high. Notice, however, that CCB does not interpret DJ's question as an elicitating move requiring a reply; instead it is merely a nomination, granting permission to contribute to the discourse. CCB begins his response high because it represents a new 'topic', or in this case a new comment on the theme under discussion (§2.1.2). We can only conclude that constraints of the sort Brazil et al have postulated for asymmetrical discourse do not necessarily apply to more symmetrical types of discourse such as panel discussions. Here the chairman has the role of coordinating replies to an initial elicitation (i.e. question from the audience). Although the chairman formally opens exchanges by nominating discourse participants, his initiating moves do not set up the same kind of expectation as do those of, say, doctors or teachers. Rather, the key choices with which team members begin their responses appear to reflect only the textual/topical relation of their contributions to preceding discourse.

On the other hand, we do find evidence in our data of a technique involving pitch concord, or matching pitch levels, which is used by discourse participants to influence the process of turn-taking in conversation. Consider, for instance:

---

[14] Initial high and mid key are judged here with respect to the speaker's individual norm.

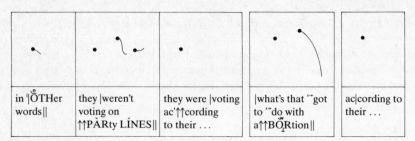

| in ‖ŎTHer words‖ | they |weren't voting on ↑↑PÅRty LÍNES‖ | they were |voting ac'↑↑cording to their … | |what's that ⁻got to ⁻do with a↑↑BŎRtion‖ | ac|cording to their … |
|---|---|---|---|---|

Notice that EP's question has a higher key (with respect to her norm) than BD's speech with respect to his norm. However, BD's key shifts upward in the immediate continuation of his turn.

In conversation analysis,[15] this would constitute an example of an *interruption* – brought about when one conversational participant comes in during another's turn[16] – which is *turn-competitive*: it indicates on the part of the speaker that s/he wishes to have the floor immediately. As French/Local (1982) have shown, turn-competitive interruptions tend to be both louder and (relatively speaking) higher-pitched than ongoing speech.[17] The raised pitch level of BD's attempted continuation would be termed a *return of competition*. That is, the current speaker refuses to give up the turn and comes back in higher (relatively speaking) than before.

This competitive matching of pitch levels is perhaps most apparent during interruptions. However, it is also present during regular turn-taking. For instance:

Fig. XI/12                              $(A1/BD_1 - EP_2 - BD_2)$

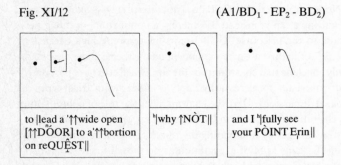

| to |lead a '↑↑wide open [↑↑DŎOR] to a'↑↑bortion on reQUĘST‖ | ʰ|why ↑NÒT‖ | and I ʰ|fully see your PÓINT Erin‖ |
|---|---|---|

Here BD raises his key as if in response to the high key of EP's question, although strictly speaking he is not giving an answer.

---

[15] Conversation analysis represents a less rigidly structured approach to discourse which has arisen from the sociologically oriented, ethnomethodological study of human behaviour (Sacks/Schegloff/Jefferson 1974).

[16] Strictly speaking, interruptions occur only at points during a speaker's turn where there is no indication (syntactic or prosodic) that the current speaker might be finished what s/he is saying.

[17] And/or than the interrupter's norm for loudness and pitch.

Moreover, the matching need not always be upwards:

Fig. XI/13

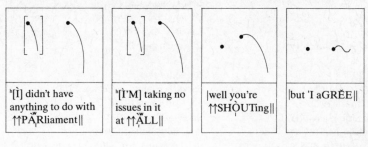

(A1/EP - BD$_2$ - EP - BD$_2$)

Here EP suddenly shifts down to mid key and BD follows suit. [Note too BD's reduplication of EP's rhythm and intonation.] The effect is that of a *pas-de-deux* between two participants who are basically at odds.

A final example will demonstrate that matching pitch levels may even be used for ironic effect:

Fig. XI/14

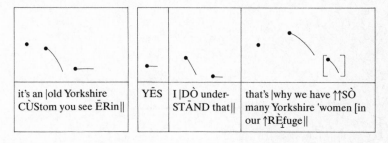

(A1/BD$_2$ - EP)

Here EP's sudden switch to low in response to BD's (condescendingly) low-pitched *Erin* has a distinctly mocking note to it, which heightens the humour of her rebuttal.

In conclusion, both discourse analysis and conversation analysis establish models to describe the organization of linguistic interaction and then attempt to determine how intonation 'fits in' to the pre-established model. But from a prosodic point of view, it would undoubtedly be wiser to establish first of all the basic macro- and micro-units of intonational organization beyond the tone-unit and then to investigate their function in text and discourse or conversation. This is the challenge which intonation specialists will hopefully take up in the future. Indeed it is largely uncharted terrain.

## References

Beattie/Cutler/Pearson 1982
Brazil 1975
Brazil 1978
*Brazil 1981
*Brazil/Coulthard/Johns 1980
Bruce 1982
Coulthard 1977
Coulthard/Brazil/Johns 1979
Coulthard/Brazil 1982
Coulthard/Montgomery 1981
Couper-Kuhlen 1983
Enkvist/Nordström 1978
Fox 1973
French/Local 1982
de Groot ²1968
Gumperz 1982
Halliday/Hasan 1976

Hinds 1979
Leech/Short 1981
*Lehiste 1975
Levelt/Cutler 1983
Liberman/Sag 1974
Pilch 1977b
Rees/Urquhart 1976
Sacks/Schegloff/Jefferson 1974
Sag/Liberman 1975
Schegloff/Sacks 1973
Sinclair/Coulthard 1975
Sinclair/Forsyth/Coulthard/Ashby 1972
Trim 1959
van Dijk 1980
Widdowson 1977
Wunderli 1979
*Yule 1980b

# Epilogue

The preceding five chapters have attempted to give a more realistic appraisal of the function of intonation than heretofore available, in the 'meaning' domains of information, grammar, illocution, attitude and text/discourse. To the extent that research has progressed (and in some areas there is still a regrettable lag), the results are rather modest indeed: the role of intonation seems a good deal less central than many linguists have claimed it to be. In no domain has a strong version of the functional claim been substantiated. At the most only co-occurrence relations have emerged – and these for only a limited range of 'meaning' and select intonational features. With one or two exceptions, 'proper' intonational marking of a given grammatical structure, illocutionary force, attitude, etc. may actually be lacking, with no significant consequence for the type of 'meaning' in question. All this makes it seem that intonation is very dispensable indeed, as linguists such as Hultzén have claimed: "... the sentence does go on and can be put together, if at some small cost in effort, without intonational signals, as the line of print indicates" (1964:89).

However, one important fact is overlooked in conclusions of this sort: intonation CAN be essential, even if it is not always so. In instances when a given type of 'meaning' is not conveyed by other linguistic means, intonation is left carrying the load – and here its function in shaping speaker meaning is undeniable. For instance, as we have seen, (a) a speaker may say something 'new' by accenting formally given information (Ch. VII), (b) a speaker may elicit a *yes–no* response by uttering a grammatically declarative sentence with the appropriate rise (Chs. VIII, IX), (c) a speaker may express disrespect by, say, not observing the convention of pitch concord when it is called for (Chs. X, XI), (d) a speaker may re-structure objectively given text relations by choice of onset level (Ch. XI), etc.

The fact that speakers have the option of giving their utterances informational, illocutionary, attitudinal and textual 'meaning' with intonational means alone constitutes strong evidence for the function of intonation in language. This function is not fully 'distinctive' in the classical sense, but it is potentially of such far-reaching import that students of language can hardly afford to ignore it. It seems hard to escape the conclusion that what is needed is a new approach to linguistic function – but this is a matter for future linguistic debate.

# Recordings

## Side 1

A) *Any Questions?* BBC Radio 4, July 13, 1979

00:37  1) On Parliament restricting legal abortion
mins.      A. Woodall$_1$ – E. Pittsy$_1$ – B. Denin$_1$ – (E. Pittsy$_2$ – B. Denin$_2$)* – D. Jacobs$_1$ –
           B. Denin$_3$ – D. Jacobs$_2$ – A. Woodall$_2$ – T. Taylor – E. Pittsy$_3$ – B. Denin$_4$

07:40  2) On a BBC television interview with members of the IRA
           D. Jacobs – B. Denin – E. Pittsy

10:46  3) On planning one's career
           D. Jacobs – T. Taylor – E. Pittsy – A. Woodall – B. Denin

14:35  4) On lifting sanctions against Rhodesia
           B. Denin – E. Pittsy

17:02  B) *BBC Radio News*, July 14, 1979
           Oxfam – Prior – Benn

19:53  C) *A Word in Edgeways*, BBC Radio 4, July 14, 1979
           B. Redhead$_1$ – G. Bennett$_1$ – B. Redhead$_2$ – G. Bennett$_2$ – B. Redhead$_3$ –
           A. Coffmann – B. Redhead$_4$ – A. Jarwitt

## Side 2

00:00  D) *Let's Get This Settled*, BBC Radio 4, July 18, 1979

       E) *Any Questions?*, BBC Radio 4, July 20, 1979

02:04  1) On buying shares in British Airways
           D. Jacobs – C.C. O'Brien$_1$ – S. Williams$_1$ – H. Wheldon$_1$ – E. Powell$_1$ –
           H. Wheldon$_2$ – (E. Powell$_2$ – H. Wheldon$_3$)* – S. Williams$_2$ – H. Wheldon$_4$ –
           E. Powell$_3$ – S. Williams$_3$ – C.C. O'Brien$_2$ – H. Wheldon$_5$ – C.C. O'Brien$_3$

07:41  2) Parliament on the capital punishment issue
           D. Jacobs – E. Powell – S. Williams – C.C. O'Brien – H. Wheldon

12:26  3) On private medical treatment for members of the TGWU
           D. Jacobs$_1$ – S. Williams$_1$ – E. Powell$_1$ – S. Williams$_2$ – D. Jacobs$_2$ –
           Mrs Baker – H. Wheldon$_1$ – C.C. O'Brien$_1$ – (D. Jacobs$_3$ – C.C. O'Brien$_2$)* –
           E. Powell$_2$ – C.C. O'Brien$_3$ – (D. Jacobs$_4$ – C.C. O'Brien$_4$)*

19:46  F) *News of the Week*, BBC Television, October 19, 1977

[Subscripts index the successive turns by a given speaker within one excerpt; asterisked parentheses ( )* signal a recursive exchange of short remarks between two speakers (internal numbering
suspended).]

# Bibliography

Abdul-Ghani, Christina (1978) Accent in Discourse: An analysis of function. PhD diss., University of Southern California.

Abe, Isamu (1962) Call-contours. In: Proceedings of the 4th International Congress of Phonetic Sciences, Mouton, The Hague, 519–523.

— (1980) How vocal pitch works. In: The Melody of Language, L. Waugh/C.H. van Schooneveld, eds., University Park Press, Baltimore, 1–24.

Abercrombie, David (1964a) A phonetician's view of verse structure. Linguistics 6, 5–13. Also in: Phonetics in Linguistics, W.E. Jones/J. Laver, eds., Longman, London, 6–13.

— (1964b) Syllable quantity and enclitics in English. In: In Honour of Daniel Jones, D. Abercrombie et al, eds., Longmans, London, 216–222.

— (1965) Steele, Monboddo and Garrick (1951). In: Studies in Phonetics and Linguistics, D. Abercrombie, ed., Oxford University Press, London, 35–44.

— (1967) Elements of General Phonetics. Edinburgh University Press, Edinburgh.

— (1971) Some functions of silent stress. In: Edinburgh Studies in English and Scots, A.J. Aitken/Angus McIntosh/Hermann Pálsson, eds., Longman, London, 147–156.

— (1976) "Stress" and some other terms. Work in Progress 9, Edinburgh University, Department of Linguistics, 51–53.

Abramson, A.S. (1961) Identification and discrimination of phonemic tones (Abstract). Journal of the Acoustical Society of America 33, 842.

Adams, Corinne (1979) English Speech Rhythm and the Foreign Learner. Mouton, The Hague.

Adams, C./Munro, R.P. (1978) In search of the acoustic correlates of stress: Fundamental frequency, amplitude and duration in the connected utterance of some native and non-native speakers of English. Phonetica 35, 125–156.

Alkon, Paul K. (1959) Joshua Steele and the melody of speech. Language and Speech 2, 154–174.

Allen, George D. (1972a) The location of rhythmic stress beats in English: An experimental study I. Language and Speech 15, 72–100.

— (1972b) The location of rhythmic stress beats in English: An experimental study II. Language and Speech 15, 179–195.

— (1975) Speech rhythm: its relation to performance universals and articulatory timing. Journal of Phonetics 3, 75–86.

Allen, W. Sidney (1968) Vox graeca. A guide to the pronunciation of Classical Greek. Cambridge University Press, Cambridge.

— (1973) Accent and Rhythm. Prosodic features of Latin and Greek: A study in theory and reconstruction. Cambridge Studies in Linguistics 12, Cambridge University Press, Cambridge.

Allerton, D.J. (1978) The notion of 'givenness' and its relations to presupposition and to theme. Lingua 44, 133–168.

Allerton, D.J./Cruttenden, A. (1974) English sentence adverbials: their syntax and their intonation in British English. Lingua 34, 1–29.

— (1976) The intonation of medial and final sentence adverbials in British English. Archivum linguisticum 7, 29–59.

— (1978) Syntactic, illocutionary, thematic and attitudinal factors in the intonation of adverbials. Journal of Pragmatics 2, 155–188.

— (1979) Three reasons for accenting a definite subject. Journal of Linguistics 15, 49–53.

Anderson, Keith O. (1978) On the contrastive phonetics of English and German intonation. In: Festschrift für Otto von Essen anläßlich seines 80. Geburtstags, Hamburger Phonetische Beiträge 25, Buske, Hamburg, 25–35.

Anderson, John (1969) Syllabic or non-syllabic phonology? Journal of Linguistics 5, 136–144.

Anderson, Stephen R. (1978) Tone features. In: Tone. A linguistic survey, Victoria A. Fromkin, ed., Academic Press, New York, 133–175.

Andrew, Christine M. (1980) On theories of focus. In: Experimental Linguistics, G.D. Prideaux/ B.L. Derwing/W.J. Baker, eds., E. Story-Scientia, Ghent, 55–63.

Antonsen, Elmer H. (1966) Suprasegmentals in German. Language 42, 587–601.

Armstrong, Lilias E./Ward, Ida C. ($^2$1931) A Handbook of English Intonation. W. Heffer & Sons, Cambridge.

Arnold, G.F. (1957) Stress in English words. Lingua 6, 221–267. Repr. North-Holland Publishing Co., Amsterdam, 1957.

Arnold, Roland/Hansen, Klaus (1975) Englische Phonetik. Max Hueber, München (VEB Verlag 1974).

Artemov, V.A. (1978) Intonation und Prosodie. Phonetica 35, 301–339.

Ashby, Michael G. (1978) A study of two English nuclear tones. Language and Speech 21, 326–336.

Atkinson, James Edward (1973) Aspects of intonation in speech: Implications from an experimental study of fundamental frequency. PhD Thesis, Univ. of Connecticut.

Austin, J.L. (1962) How to Do Things with Words. Clarendon Press, Oxford.


Bailey, Charles-James N. (1978) Gradience in English syllabication and a revised concept of unmarked syllabization. Indiana University Linguistics Club, Bloomington [cit. in Bell/ Hooper 1978].

— (1979) Phrasierung und Intonation im Englischen. Arbeitspapiere zur Linguistik/Working Papers in Linguistics 5, Technische Universität Berlin.

— (1980) Evidence for variable syllable boundaries in English. In: The Melody of Language, L.R. Waugh/C.H. van Schooneveld, eds., University Park Press, Baltimore, Md., 25–39.

Baker, Sheridan (1960) English meter *is* quantitative. College English 21, 309–315.

Bald, Wolf-Dietrich (1975) Englische Intonation in Forschung und Lehre: Ein Überblick. In: Contributions to Applied Linguistics I, Christoph Gutknecht, ed., Lang, Frankfurt, 139–163.

— (1976) Contrastive studies in English and German intonation: A survey. In: Papers and Studies in Contrastive Linguistics 4, Jacek Fisiak, ed., Poznán.

— (1979/80) English intonation and politeness. Studia Anglica Posnaniensia 11, 93–101.

— (1980) English tag-questions and intonation. In: Anglistentag 1979, Kuno Schuhmann, ed., TUB-Dokumentation, Berlin, 263–291.

Bar-Hillel, Yehoshua/Carnap, Rudolf (1964) An outline of a theory of semantic information. In: Language and Information. Selected essays on their theory and application, Yehoshua Bar-Hillel, ed., Addison-Wesley, Reading, Mass., 221–274.

Barry, William J. (1981a) Prosodic functions revisited again! Phonetica 38, 320–340.

— (1981b) Grammatik, Intonation and Situation in den englischen 'tag questions': Theoretische und didaktische Überlegungen. In: Angewandte Sprachwissenschaft. Grundfragen-Bereiche-Methoden, Günter Peuser/Stefan Winter, Hrsg., Bouvier, Bonn, 334–350.

Beattie, Geoffrey W./Cutler, Anne/Pearson, Mark (1982) Why is Mrs Thatcher interrupted so often? Nature 300, 744–747.

Bell, Alan/Hooper, Joan Bybee, eds. (1978) Syllables and Segments. North-Holland, Amsterdam.

Bell, Alan/Hooper, Joan Bybee (1978a) Issues and evidence in syllabic phonology. In: Syllables and Segments, A. Bell/J.B. Hooper, eds., North-Holland, Amsterdam, 3–22.

Berman, Arlene/Szamosi, Michael (1972) Observations on sentential stress. Language 48, 304–325.

Bierwisch, Manfred (1966) Regeln für die Intonation deutscher Sätze. Studia grammatica 7, 99–201.

— (1968) Two critical problems in accent rules. Journal of Linguistics 4, 173–178.

Bing, Janet Mueller (1980) Aspects of English Prosody. Indiana University Linguistics Club, Bloomington.

— (1983) Contrastive stress, contrastive intonation and contrastive meaning. Journal of Semantics 2, 141–156.

Bloomfield, Leonard (1933; 1935) Language. Holt, New York; Allen & Unwin, London.

Bolinger, Dwight L. (1947) Comments on Pike's American English Intonation. Studies in Linguistics 5, 69–78.

— (1951) Intonation: Levels vs. configurations. Word 7, 199–210.

— (1957) On certain functions of accents A and B. Litera IV, 80–89.

— (1958a) Stress and information. American Speech 33, 5–20.

— (1958b) A theory of pitch accent in English. Word 14, 109–149.

— (1958c) Intonation and grammar. Language Learning 8, 31–37.

— (1958d) Interrogative structures of American English: The direct question. Publications of the American Dialect Society 28, Univ. of Alabama Press, 97–102.

— (1961a) Contrastive accent and contrastive stress. Language 37, 83–96.

— (1961b) Generality, Gradience, and the All-or-none. Mouton, The Hague.

— (1964) Intonation as a universal. Proceedings of the Ninth International Congress of Linguists, 833–848.

— (1965) Pitch accent and sentence rhythm. In: Forms of English: Accent, Morpheme, Order. Harvard University Press, Cambridge, 163ff.

— (1970) Relative height. In: Prosodic Feature Analysis, P.R. Léon/G. Faure/A. Rigault, eds., Didier, 109–125. Also in: Intonation. Selected readings, D. Bolinger, ed., Penguin, 1972, 137–153.

— (1972a) Intonation. Selected Readings. Penguin, Harmondsworth, Middlesex.

— (1972b) Accent is predictable (if you're a mind-reader). Language 48, 633–644.

— (1978) Intonation across languages. In: Universals of Human Language, Vol. 2 Phonology, J.P. Greenberg/C.A. Ferguson/E.A. Moravcsik, eds., Stanford University Press, Stanford, 471–524.

— (1983) Where does intonation belong? Journal of Semantics 2, 101–120.

Bolton, T.L. (1894) Rhythm. American Journal of Psychology 6, 145–238.

Boomer, Donald S. (1965) Hesitation and grammatical encoding. Language and Speech 8, 148–158.

— (1978) The phonemic clause: Speech unit in human communication. In: Non-verbal Behavior and Communication, A.W. Siegman/S. Feldstein, eds., Lawrence Erlbaum Ass., Hillsdale, N.J., 245–265.

Brand, Ruth M. (1975) Studies in tone and intonation. [Summer Institute of Linguistics] Karger, Basel.

Brazil, David (1975) Discourse Intonation. Discourse Analysis Monographs 1, English Language Research, University of Birmingham.

— (1978) Discourse Intonation II. Discourse Analysis Monographs 2, English Language Research, University of Birmingham.

— (1981) The place of intonation in a discourse model. In: Studies in Discourse Analysis, Malcolm Coulthard/Martin Montgomery, eds., Routledge & Kegan Paul, London.

Brazil, David/Coulthard, Malcolm/Johns, Catherine (1980) Discourse Intonation and Language Teaching. Longman, London.

Breckenridge, Janet (1977) The declination effect. Journal of the Acoustical Society of America 61, 90.

Brend, R. (1972) Male–female intonation patterns in American English. Proceedings of the 7th International Congress of Phonetic Sciences, Mouton, 866–869.

Bresnan, Joan (1971) Sentence stress and syntactic transformations. Language 47, 257–281.

— (1972) Stress and syntax: A reply. Language 48, 326–342.

Brown, Gillian (1977) Listening to Spoken English. Longman, London.

— (1983) Prosodic structure and the given/new distinction. In: Prosody: Models and measurements, A. Cutler/D.R. Ladd, eds., Springer-Verlag, Berlin, 67–77.

Brown, Gillian/Currie, Karen L./Kenworthy, Joanne (1980) Questions of Intonation. Croom Helm, London.

Brown, Warner (1911) Temporal and accentual rhythm. Studies from the Psychological Laboratory of the University of California, Psychological Review 18, 336–346.

Bruce, Gösta (1977) Swedish Word Accents in Sentence Perspective. Travaux de l'Institut de Linguistique de Lund 12. Gleerup, Lund.

— (1982) Textual aspects of prosody in Swedish. Phonetica 39, 274–287.

Bruce, Gösta/Gårding, Eva (1978) A prosodic typology for Swedish dialects. In: Nordic Prosody, E. Gårding/G. Bruce/R. Bannert, eds., Gleerup, Lund, 219–228.

Bublitz, Wolfram (1979) Tag questions, transformational grammar and pragmatics. Papers and Studies in Contrastive Linguistics 9, 5–22.

Burgess, O.N. (1973) Intonation patterns in Australian English. Language and Speech 16, 314–326.

Butler, Charles (1634) The English Grammar. London. [Re-edited A. Eichler, 1910.]

Butterworth, B., ed. (1980) Language Production. Vol. 1 Speech and Talk. Academic Press, London & New York.


Cairns, H.S./Cairns, C.C. (1976) Psycholinguistics. Holt Rinehart Winston, New York. [Esp. pp. 120–144.]

Catford, J.C. (1977) Fundamental Problems in Phonetics. Edinburgh University Press, Edinburgh.

Chafe, Wallace L. (1974) Language and consciousness. Language 50, 111–133.

— (1976) Givenness, contrastiveness, definiteness, subjects, topics, and point of view. In: Subject and Topic, Charles N. Li, ed., Academic Press, New York, 25–55.

Chiţoran, Dimitru (1981) Contrastive remarks on English and Romanian intonation from the point of view of pragmatics. In: Kontrastive Linguistik und Übersetzungswissenschaft. Akten des Internationalen Kolloquiums, Trier/Saarbrücken, W. Kühlwein/G. Thome/W. Wilss, eds., Fink, Munich, 18–24.

Chomsky, Noam (1971) Deep structure, surface structure, and semantic interpretation. In: Semantics, D.D. Steinberg/L.A. Jakobovits, eds., Cambridge University Press, 183–216.

— (1972) Some empirical issues in the theory of transformational grammar. In: Goals of Linguistic Theory, Stanley Peters, ed., Prentice-Hall, Englewood Cliffs, N.J., 63–130.

Chomsky, Noam/Halle, Morris (1968) The Sound Pattern of English. Harper & Row, New York.

Chomsky, Noam/Halle, Morris/Lukoff, F. (1956) On accent and juncture in English. In: For Roman Jakobson, M. Halle/H. Lunt/H. McLean, eds., Mouton, The Hague, 65–80.

Clark, Herbert H./Clark, Eve V. (1977) Psychology and Language. An Introduction to Psycholinguistics. Harcourt Brace Jovanovich, New York.

Classe, A. (1939) The Rhythm of English Prose. Basil Blackwell, Oxford.

Cohen, A./'t Hart, J. (1967) On the anatomy of intonation. Lingua 19, 177–192.

Cohen, A./Collier, R./'t Hart, John (1982) Declination: Construct or intrinsic feature of speech pitch? Phonetica 39, 254–273.

Coleman, H.O. (1914) Intonation and emphasis. Miscellanea phonetica [cit. in Bolinger 1961].

Collier, René (1974) Intonation from a structural linguistic viewpoint: A criticism. Linguistics 129, 5–28.

Collier, R./'t Hart, J. (1975) The role of intonation in speech perception. In: Structure and Process in Speech Perception, Antoine Cohen/S.G. Nooteboom, eds., Springer Verlag, Berlin, 107–121.

Cooper, Franklin S. (1972) How is language conveyed by speech? In: Language by Ear and by Eye, J.F. Kavanaugh/I.G. Mattingly, eds., MIT Press, Cambridge, 25–45.

Cooper, W.E. (1980) Syntactic-to-phonetic coding. In: Language Production, Vol. 1, B. Butterworth, ed., Academic Press, London, 297–333.

Costanzo, F.S./Markel, N.N./Costanzo, P.R. (1969) Voice quality profile and perceived emotion. Journal of Counseling Psychology 16, 267–270.

Coulthard, Malcolm (1977) An Introduction to Discourse Analysis. Longman, London.

Coulthard, Malcolm/Brazil, David/Johns, Tim (1979) Reading intonation. In: Trends in English Text Linguistics, Gottfried Graustein/Albrecht Neubert, eds., Berlin, 29–42.

Coulthard, Malcolm/Brazil, David (1982) The place of intonation in the description of interaction. In: Analyzing Discourse: Text and Talk, Georgetown University Round Table on Languages and Linguistics 1981, Deborah Tannen, ed., Georgetown University Press, Washington, D.C., 94–112.

Coulthard, Malcolm/Montgomery, Martin, eds. (1981) Studies in Discourse Analysis. Routledge & Kegen Paul, London.

Couper-Kuhlen, Elizabeth (1983) Intonatorische Kohäsion: Eine makroprosodische Untersuchung. In: Intonation, Wolfgang Klein, ed., Zeitschrift für Literaturwissenschaft und Linguistik, LILI 49, 74–100.

— (1984) A new look at contrastive intonation. In: Modes of Interpretation. Essays presented to Ernst Leisi on the occasion of his 65th birthday, Richard J. Watts/Urs Weidmann, eds., Gunter Narr, Tübingen, 137–158.

di Cristo, A. (1975) Soixante et dix ans de recherches en prosodie (Bibliographie alphabétique, thématique et chronologique), Etudes phonétiques I. Aix-en-Provence.

Crompton, Andrew S. (1978) Intonational subordination in English. Pragmatics Microfiche 3/2, Jan. A2.

— (1980) Intonation: Tonetic stress marks versus levels versus configurations. Word 31, 151–198.

Cruttenden, A. (1970) On the so-called grammatical function of intonation. Phonetica 21, 182–192.

— (1981) Falls and rises: meanings and universals. Journal of Linguistics 17, 77–91.

Crystal, David (1969) Prosodic Systems and Intonation in English. Cambridge University Press, London.

— (1969a) Review of M.A.K. Halliday, Intonation and Grammar in British English. Language 45, 378–394.

— (1973) Intonation and linguistic theory. In: The Nordic Languages and Modern Linguistics, K.-H. Dahlstedt, ed., Almqvist & Wiksell, Stockholm, 267–303.

— (1975a) Prosodic features and linguistic theory. In: The English Tone of Voice. Essays in intonation, prosody and paralanguage, Edward Arnold, London, 1–46.

— (1975b) Relative and absolute in intonation analysis. In: The English Tone of Voice. Essays in intonation, prosody and paralanguage, Edward Arnold, London, 74–83.

— (1975c) Prosodic and paralinguistic correlates of social categories. In: The English Tone of Voice. Essays in intonation, prosody and paralanguage, Edward Arnold, London, 84–95.

— (1975d) Intonation and metrical theory. In: The English Tone of Voice, Edward Arnold, London, 105–124.

— (1980) The analysis of nuclear tones. In: The Melody of Language, L. Waugh/C.H. van Schooneveld, eds., University Park Press, Baltimore, Md., 55–70.

Crystal, David/Davy, D. (1969) Investigating English Style. Longman, London.

Crystal, David/Quirk, Randolph (1964) Systems of prosodic and paralinguistic features in English. Mouton, The Hague.

Currie, Karen L. (1979) Contour systems of one variety of Scottish English. Language and Speech 22, 1–20.

— (1980) An initial "search for tonics". Language and Speech 23, 329–350.

— (1981) Further experiments in the 'search for tonics'. Language and Speech 24, 1–28.

Cutler, Anne (1977) The context-dependence of "intonational meanings". Papers from the 13th Regional Meeting, Chicago Linguistic Society, 104–115.

— (1980) Errors of stress and intonation. In: Errors in Linguistic Performance. Slips of the tongue, ear, pen and hand, Victoria A. Fromkin, ed., Academic Press, New York, 67–80.

Cutler, A./Foss, D.J. (1977) On the role of sentence stress in sentence processing. Language and Speech 20, 1–10.

Cutler, A./Isard, S.D. (1980) The production of prosody. In: Language Production, Vol. 1 Speech and Talk, B. Butterworth, ed., Academic Press, London, 245–269.

Cutler, A./Ladd, D.R., eds. (1983) Prosody: Models and measurements. Springer Verlag, Berlin.


Daneš, František (1960) Sentence intonation from a functional point of view. Word 16, 34–54.

— (1967) Order of elements and sentence intonation. In: To Honour Roman Jakobson: Essays on the occasion of his 70th birthday, Mouton, The Hague, 499–512. Also in: Intonation, Dwight L. Bolinger, ed., Penguin, Harmondsworth, 1972, 216–232.

Danielsson, Bror (1963) John Hart's Works on English Orthography and Pronunciation (1551, 1569, 1570). Part II Phonology. Stockholm Studies in English XI, Almqvist & Wiksell, Stockholm.

Darwin, Charles (1873) The Expression of the Emotions in Man and Animals. John Murray, London.

Davitz, Joel R. (1964) The Communication of Emotional Meaning. McGraw-Hill, New York.

— (1969) The Language of Emotion. Academic Press, New York.

Delattre, Pierre (1963) Comparing the prosodic features of English, German, Spanish and French. International Review of Applied Linguistics I, 193–210.

— (1964) German phonetics between English and French. Linguistics 8, 43–55.

— (1966) Les dix intonations de base du français. French Review 40, 1–14.

— (1969) L'intonation par les oppositions. Le Français dans le monde 64, 6–13.

Delattre, P./Poenack, E./Olsen, C. (1965) Some characteristics of German intonation for the expression of continuation and finality. Phonetica 13, 134–161.

Denes, P. (1959) A preliminary investigation of certain aspects of intonation. Language and Speech 2, 106–122.

Donovan, Andrew/Darwin, C.J. (1979) The perceived rhythm of speech. Proceedings of the Ninth International Congress of Phonetic Sciences, Copenhagen, Vol. II, 268–274.

Eliason, N.E. (1942) On syllable division in phonemics. Language 18, 144–147.

Engler, Leo F./Hilyer, R.G. (1971) Once again: American and British intonation systems. Acta Linguistica Hafniensia 13, 99–108.

Enkvist, Nils Erik (1979) Marked focus: functions and constraints. In: Studies in English Linguistics for Randolph Quirk, S. Greenbaum/G. Leech/J. Svartvik, eds., Longman, London, 134–152.

Enkvist, Nils Erik/Nordström, Hans (1978) On textual aspects of intonation in Finland – Swedish newscasts. Studia linguistica 32, 63–79.

Erdmann, Peter H. (1973) Patterns of stress-transfer in English and German. International Review of Applied Linguistics XI, 229–241.

Esling, John (1978) The identification of features of voice quality in social groups. Journal of the International Phonetic Association 8/1, 18–23.

von Essen, Otto (1964) Grundzüge der hochdeutschen Satzintonation. Henn, Ratingen.

Esser, Jürgen (1978) Contrastive intonation of German and English. Problems and some results. Phonetica 35, 41–55.

— (1979) Englische Prosodie. Eine Einführung. Gunter Narr, Tübingen.

— (1983) Tone units in functional sentence perspective. Journal of Semantics 2, 121–139.


Fallows, Deborah (1981) Experimental evidence for English syllabification and syllable structure. Journal of Linguistics 17, 309–317.

Fant, Gunnar (1960) Acoustic Theory of Speech Perception. Mouton, The Hague.

— (1960a) Acoustic Theory of Speech Production. With calculations based on X-ray studies of Russian articulations. Mouton, 'S-Gravenhage & The Hague.

— (1967) Auditory patterns of speech. In: Models for the Perception of Speech and Visual Form, Wathen-Dunn, ed., MIT Press.

Faure, G. (1967) La description phonologique des systèmes prosodiques. Proceedings of the 6th International Congress of Phonetic Sciences, Prague, 317–318.

— (1970) Contribution à l'étude du statut phonologique des structures prosodématiques. In: Prosodic Feature Analysis, Analyse des faits prosodiques, P. Léon/G. Faure/A. Rigault, eds., Didier, Ottawa, 93–108.

— (1973) La description phonologique des systèmes prosodiques. In: Interrogation et Intonation, Studia Phonetica 8, A. Grundstrom/P. Léon, eds., Montreal, 1–16.

Faure, G./Hirst, D.J./Chafcouloff, M. (1980) Rhythm in English: Isochronism, pitch, and perceived stress. In: The Melody of Language, L.R. Waugh/C.H. van Schooneveld, eds., University Park Press, Baltimore, 71–79.

Firbas, Jan (1966a) On defining the theme in functional sentence analysis. Travaux linguistiques de Prague 1, Academia, Editions de l'Académie tchéchoslovaque des sciences, Paris, 267–280.

— (1966b) Non-thematic subjects in contemporary English. Travaux linguistiques de Prague 2, Academia, Editions de l'Académie tchéchoslovaque des sciences, Paris, 239–256.

— (1972) On the interplay of prosodic and non-prosodic means of Functional Sentence Perspective (A theoretical note on the teaching of English intonation). In: The Prague School of Linguistics and Language Teaching, V. Fried, ed., Oxford University Press, London, 77–96.

— (1980) Post-intonation-centre prosodic shade in the modern English clause. In: Studies in English Linguistics for Randolph Quirk, Sidney Greenbaum/Geoffrey Leech/Jan Svartvik, eds., Longman, London, 125–133.

Firth, J.R. (1948) Sounds and prosodies. Transactions of the Philological Society, 127–152. And in: Phonetics in Linguistics. A book of readings, W.E. Jones/J. Laver, eds., Longman, London, 1973, 47–65.

Fónagy, Ivan (1971) The functions of vocal style. In: Literary Style: A symposium, Seymour Chatman, ed., Oxford University Press, London, 159–176.

— (1978) A new method of investigating the perception of prosodic features. Language and Speech 21, 34–49.

Fónagy, Ivan/Magdics, Klara (1963) Emotional patterns in intonation and music. Zeitschrift für Phonetik, Sprachwissenschaft und Kommunikationsforschung 16, 293–313. Also in: Intonation. Selected readings, D.L. Bolinger, ed., Penguin, Harmondsworth, 1972, 286–312.

Fónagy, Ivan/Bérard, E. (1972) "Il est huit heures": contribution à l'analyse sémantique de la vive voix. Phonetica 26, 157–192.

Fourquet, J. (1976) Linguistic aspects of expressive language. Journal de Psychologie Normale et Pathologique 73, 261–271.

Fox, Anthony (1973) Tone-sequences in English. Archivum linguisticum IV (New series), 17–26.

— (1981) Fall–rise intonations in German and English. In: Contrastive Aspects of English and German, Charles V.J. Russ, ed., Groos, Heidelberg.

— (1982) Remarks on intonation and 'Ausrahmung' in German. Journal of Linguistics 18, 89–106.

Frank, Diana Crone (1974) The Structure of Intonation: A first approximation. PhD thesis, Cornell University.

French, Peter/Local, John (1983) Turn-competitive incomings. Journal of Pragmatics 7, 17–38.

Fries, Charles C. (1964) On the intonation of 'yes–no' questions in English. In: In Honour of Daniel Jones, D. Abercrombie et al, eds., Longmans, London, 242–254.

Fromkin, Victoria A. (1971) The non-anomalous nature of anomalous utterances. Language 47, 27–52.

— , ed. (1973) Speech Errors as Linguistic Evidence. Mouton, The Hague.

— (1977) Putting the emPHAsis on the wrong syllable. In: Studies in Stress and Accent, L.M. Hyman, ed., University of S. California, Los Angeles.

— , ed. (1978) Tone. A linguistic survey. Academic Press, New York.

Fry, D.B. (1958a) Experiments in the perception of stress. Language and Speech 1, 126–152.

— (1958b) The perception of stress. Proceedings of the 8th International Congress of Linguists, 601–603.

— (1960) Linguistic theory and experimental research. Transactions of the Philological Society, 13–39. Also in: Phonetics in Linguistics, W.E. Jones/J. Laver, eds., Longman, London, 1973, 66–87.

— (1968) Prosodic phenomena. In: Manual of Phonetics, Bertil Malmberg, ed., North-Holland, Amsterdam, 365–410.

— (1974) Phonetics in the twentieth century. In: Current Trends in Linguistics, Vol. 12, Thomas A. Sebeok, ed., Mouton, The Hague, 2201–2239.

— , ed. (1976) Acoustic Phonetics. Cambridge University Press, Cambridge.

Fuchs, Anna (1976) 'Normaler' und 'kontrastiver' Akzent. Lingua 38, 293–312.

— (1980) Accented subjects in 'all-new' utterances. In: Wege zur Universalienforschung, G. Brettschneider/C. Lehmann, eds., Narr, Tübingen, 449–461.

— (1984) 'Deaccenting' and 'default accent'. In: Intonation, Accent and Rhythm. Studies in discourse phonology, Dafydd Gibbon/Helmut Richter, eds., de Gruyter, Berlin, 134–164.

Fudge, E.C. (1969) Syllables. Journal of Linguistics 5, 253–286.

Gandour, Jackson T. (1978) The perception of tone. In: Tone. A linguistic survey, Victoria A. Fromkin, ed., Academic Press, New York, 41–76.

Gårding, Eva (1983) A generative model of intonation. In: Prosody: Models and Measurements, A. Cutler/D.R. Ladd, eds., Springer-Verlag, Berlin, 11–25.

Gårding, Eva/Abramson, A.S. (1965) A study of the perception of some American English intonation contours. Studia linguistica 19, 61–79.

Gay, Thomas (1978) Physiological and acoustic correlates of perceived stress. Language and Speech 21, 347–353.

Gazdar, G. (1980) Pragmatic constraints on linguistic production. In: Language Production, Vol. 1 Speech and Talk, B. Butterworth, ed., Academic Press, London, 49–68. [VII/A Stress and intonation.]

Gibbon, Dafydd (1976a) Perspectives of Intonation Analysis. Forum Linguisticum 9, Peter Lang, Frankfurt.

— (1976b) Performatory categories in contrastive intonation analysis. In: Second International Conference of English Contrastive Projects, D. Chiţoran, ed., Bucarest University Press & Center for Applied Linguistics, Arlington, Va., 145–156.

— (1980) Metalocutions, structural types and functional variation in English and German. Papers and Studies in Contrastive Linguistics 13, 17–39.

— (1981) A new look at intonation syntax and semantics. In: New Linguistic Impulses in Foreign Language Teaching. Narr, Tübingen, 71–98.

Gibbon, Dafydd/Richter, Helmut, eds. (1984) Intonation, Accent and Rhythm: Studies in discourse phonology. de Gruyter, Berlin.

Giegerich, Heinz J. (1978) On the rhythmic stressing of function words: A modest proposal. Work in Progress 11, Department of Linguistics, Edinburgh University, 43–51.

Gimson, A.C. (1956) The linguistic relevance of stress in English. Zeitschrift für Phonetik und allgemeine Sprachwissenschaft 9, 113–149. Also in: Phonetics in Linguistics, W.E. Jones/ J. Laver, eds., Longman, London, 1973, 94–102.

— (1962, ³1980) An Introduction to the Pronunciation of English. Edward Arnold, London.

Glenn, Marilyn (1977) Pragmatic Functions of Intonation. PhD Thesis, University of Michigan, Ann Arbor.

Goes, Alvar Nyqvist (1974) The Stress System of English. Studia Anglistica Upsaliensia 19, Stockholm.

Goody, E.N. (1978) Towards a theory of questions. In: Questions and Politeness, E.N. Goody, ed., Cambridge University Press, Cambridge.

Green, G.M. (1973) How to get people to do things with words. In: New Directions in Linguistics, Roger W. Shuy, ed., Georgetown University Press, Washington, D.C., 51–81. Also in: Speech Acts, Syntax and Semantics 3, Peter Cole/Jerry L. Morgan, eds., Academic Press, New York, 1975, 107–141.

Gregory, O.D. (1966) A comparative description of the intonation of British and American English (for the teaching of English as a foreign language). Diss., Columbia University.

Grice, H.P. (1975) Logic and conversation. In: Speech Acts, Peter Cole/Jerry L. Morgan, eds., Syntax and Semantics 3, Academic Press, New York, 41–58.

de Groot, A.W. (²1968) Phonetics in its relation to aesthetics. In: Manual of Phonetics, Bertil Malmberg, ed., North-Holland, Amsterdam, 533–549.

Grundstrom, Allan W. (1979) Listener reconstruction of the prosodies. In: Problèmes de prosodie, P. Léon/M. Rossi, eds., Didier, Ottawa, 41–47.

Gumperz, John J. (1982) Discourse Strategies. Cambridge University Press, Cambridge.

Gunter, Richard (1966) On the placement of accent in dialog: A feature of context grammar. Journal of Linguistics 2, 159–179. Also in: Sentences in Dialog, Hornbeam Press, Columbia, S.C., 1974, 22–51.

— (1972) Intonation and relevance. In: Intonation. Selected readings, Dwight Bolinger, ed., Penguin, Harmondsworth, 194–215. Reprinted in: Sentences in Dialog, Hornbeam Press, Columbia, S.C., 1974, 52–80.

— (1974) Sentences in Dialog. Hornbeam Press, Columbia, S.C.

Gussenhoven, Carlos (1983a) Focus, mode and the nucleus. Journal of Linguistics 19, 377–417.

— (1983b) Testing the reality of focus domains. Language and Speech 26, 61–80.

— (1983c) A three-dimensional scaling of nine English tones. Journal of Semantics 2, 183–203.

Gutknecht, Christoph (1978a) The function of intonation in the teaching of English. In: Festschrift für Otto von Essen anläßlich seines 80. Geburtstags, Hamburger Phonetische Beiträge 25, Buske, Hamburg, 121–133.

— (1978b) Kontrastive Linguistik: Zielsprache Englisch. Kohlhammer, Stuttgart. [§3.2 Prosodie und Intonation: britische und amerikanische Untersuchungen, 64–86.]

Gutknecht, Christoph/Mackiewicz, Wolfgang (1977) Prosodische, paralinguistische und intonatorische Phänomene im Englischen. In: Grundbegriffe und Hauptströmungen der Linguistik, Christoph Gutknecht, ed., Hoffmann & Campe, Hamburg, 95–132.


Hadding-Koch, Kerstin (1956) Recent work on intonation. Studia linguistica 10, 77–96.

— (1961) Acoustico-phonetic Studies in the Intonation of Southern Swedish. Gleerup, Lund.

Hadding-Koch, Kerstin/Studdert-Kennedy, Michael (1964) An experimental study of some intonation contours. Phonetica 11, 175–85. Also in: Acoustic Phonetics, D.B. Fry, ed., Cambridge University Press, Cambridge, 1976, 431–441. And in: Intonation. Selected Readings, Dwight Bolinger, ed., Penguin, Harmondsworth, 348–358.

Hála, B. (1961) La syllabe, sa nature, son origine et ses transformations. Orbis 10, 69–143.

Halle, Morris/Keyser, Samuel Jay (1966) Chaucer and the study of poetry. College English 28/3, 187–219.

— (1971) English Stress. Its form, its growth, and its role in verse. Harper & Row, New York.

Halle, M./Stevens K.N. (1964) Speech recognition: A model and a program for research. In: The Structure of Language, J.A. Fodor/J.J. Katz, eds., Prentice-Hall, Englewood Cliffs, N.J., 604–612.

Halliday, M.A.K. (1961) Categories of the theory of grammar. Word 17, 241–292. Also in: Halliday: System and Function in Language, Gunther Kress, ed., Oxford University Press, London, 52–72.

— (1963) The tones of English. In: Phonetics in Linguistics, W.E. Jones/J. Laver, eds., Longman, London, 103–126.

— (1967a) Intonation and Grammar in British English. Mouton, The Hague.

— (1967b) Notes on transitivity and theme in English, Part 2. Journal of Linguistics 3, 199–244.

— (1970a) A Course in Spoken English: Intonation. Oxford University Press, London.

— (1970b) Language structure and language function. In: New Horizons in Linguistics, J. Lyons, ed., Penguin, Harmondsworth, 140–165.

— (1976a) Functions and universals of language. In: Halliday: System and Function in Language, G.R. Kress, ed., Oxford University Press, London, 26–31.

— (1976b) Theme and information in the English clause. In: Halliday: System and function in language. Selected papers, G.R. Kress, ed., Oxford University Press, London, 174–188.

Halliday, M.A.K./Hasan, Ruqaiya (1976) Cohesion in English. Longman, London.

Hammarström, Gönar (1966) Linguistische Einheiten im Rahmen der modernen Sprachwissenschaft. Kommunikation und Kybernetik in Einzeldarstellungen 5, Springer-Verlag, Berlin.

— (1976) Linguistic Units and Items. Springer-Verlag, Berlin.

Harris, Katherine S. (1974) Physiological aspects of articulatory behavior. In: Current Trends in Linguistics, Vol. 12, Thomas A. Sebeok, ed., Mouton, The Hague, 2281–2302.

't Hart, J./Cohen, A. (1973) Intonation by rule: A perceptual quest. Journal of Phonetics 1, 309–327.

't Hart, J./Collier, R. (1975) Integrating different levels of intonation analysis. Journal of Phonetics 3, 235–255.

Haugen, Einar (1949) Phoneme or prosodeme? Language 25, 278–282.

— (1956) The syllable in linguistic description. In: For Roman Jakobson, Morris Halle et al, eds., Mouton, The Hague, 213–221.

Haviland, S./Clark, H.H. (1974) What's new? Acquiring new information as a process in comprehension. Journal of Verbal Learning and Verbal Behaviour 13, 512–521.

Heffner, R.-M.S. (1950) General Phonetics. University of Wisconsin Press, Madison.

Heike, Georg (1969) Suprasegmentale Analyse. Elwert Verlag, Marburg.

Hill, Archibald A. (1961) Suprasegmentals, prosodies, prosodemes. Comparison and discussion. Language 37, 457–468.

Hinds, John (1979) Organizational patterns in discourse. In: Discourse and Syntax, T. Givon, ed., Syntax and Semantics 12, Academic Press, New York, 135–157.

Hirst, Daniel (1977) Intonative Features. A syntactic approach to English intonation. Mouton, The Hague.

— (1979) The transcription of English intonation. In: Problèmes de prosodie I, Approches théoriques, P. Léon/M. Rossi, eds., Didier, Ottawa, 29–39.

— (1983a) Interpreting intonation: a modular approach. Journal of Semantics 2, 171–181.

— (1983b) Structures and categories in prosodic representations. In: Prosody: Models and Measurements, A. Cutler/D.R. Ladd, eds., Springer-Verlag, Berlin, 93–109.

Hjelmslev, L. (1938) The syllable as a structural unit. Proceedings of the 3rd International Congress of Phonetic Sciences (Ghent).

Hockett, Charles F. (1955) Manual of Phonology. International Journal of American Linguistics, Memoir 11.

Höffe, W.F. (1960) Über Beziehungen von Sprachmelodie und Lautstärke. Phonetica 5, 129–159.

Hoequist, Charles E., Jr. (1983a) The perceptual center and rhythm categories. Language and Speech 26, 367–376.

— (1983b) Durational correlates of linguistic rhythm categories. Phonetica 40, 19–31.

— (1983c) Syllable duration in stress-, syllable- and mora-timed languages. Phonetica 40, 203–229.

Hooper, Joan B. (1972) The syllable in phonological theory. Language 48, 525–540.

Householder, Fred (1957) Accent, juncture, intonation, and my grandfather's reader. Word 13, 234–245.

Hudson, R.A. (1975) The meaning of questions. Language 51, 1–31.

Hultzén, Lee S. (1956) 'The poet Burns' again. American Speech 31, 195–201.

— (1959) Information points in intonation. Phonetica 4, 107–120.

— (1962) Significant and nonsignificant in intonation. Proceedings of the 4th International Congress of Phonetic Sciences, 1961, Mouton, The Hague, 658–681.

— (1964) Grammatical intonation. In: In Honour of Daniel Jones, D. Abercrombie et al, eds., Longmans, London, 85–95.

Huss, Volker (1978) English word stress in the post-nuclear position. Phonetica 35, 86–105.

Huttar, G.L. (1968a) Two functions of the prosodies in speech. Phonetica 18, 231–241.
— (1968b) Relations between prosodic variables and emotions in normal American-English utterances. Journal of Speech and Hearing Research 11, 481–487.
Hyman, Larry M. (1975) Phonology. Theory and analysis. Holt, Rinehart and Winston, New York.
— (1977) On the nature of linguistic stress. In: Studies in Stress and Accent, Southern California Occasional Papers in Linguistics 4, University of Southern California, Los Angeles, 37–82.

Isačenko, A./Schädlich, H.J. (1970) A Model of Standard German Intonation. Mouton, The Hague.

Jackendoff, Ray S. (1972) Semantic Interpretation in Generative Grammar. MIT Press, Cambridge.
Jakobson, Roman (1960) Closing statement: Linguistics and poetics. In: Style in Language, T.A. Sebeok, ed., MIT Press, Cambridge, Mass., 350–377.
Jakobson, Roman/Halle, Morris (1956, ²1971) Fundamentals of Language. Mouton, The Hague.
James, Allan R. (1976) Dialektaler Transfer in der Prosodie. Auswirkungen des Schwäbischen in der englischen Intonation. Linguistik und Didaktik 7, Heft 28, 261–272.
Jarman, E./Cruttenden, A. (1976) Belfast intonation and the myth of the fall. Journal of the International Phonetic Association 6, 4–12.
Jassem, Wiktor (1952) Intonation of Conversational English (Educated Southern British). Travaux de la société des sciences et des lettres de Wrocław 1/45, Wrocław.
— (1972) The question–phrase fall–rise in British English. In: Papers in Linguistics and Phonetics. To the memory of Pierre Delattre, Albert Valdmann, ed., Mouton, The Hague, 241–251.
— (1978) On the distributional analysis of pitch phenomena. Language and Speech 21, 362–372.
Jassem, Wiktor/Gibbon, Dafydd (1980) Re-defining English accent and stress. Journal of the International Phonetic Association 10, 2–16.
Jassem, Wiktor/Hill, D.R./Witten, I.H. (1984) Isochrony in English Speech: its statistical validity and linguistic relevance. In: Intonation, Accent and Rhythm: Studies in discourse phonology, Dafydd Gibbon/Helmut Richter, eds., de Gruyter, Berlin, 203–225.
Jespersen, Otto (1900) Notes on meter. In: Linguistica. Selected Papers in English, French and German, Copenhagen, 1933. [Repr. McGrath, College Park, Md., 1970, 249–274.]
Jones, Daniel (1909) Intonation Curves. B.G. Teubner, Leipzig & Berlin.
— (1918, ⁹1976) An Outline of English Phonetics. Cambridge University Press, Cambridge.
— (1931) The 'word' as a phonetic entity. Le maître phonétique, 3rd series, No. 36, 60–65. Also in: Phonetics in Linguistics, W.E. Jones/J. Laver, eds., Longman, London, 1973, 154–158.
Jones, W.E./Laver, J., eds. (1973) Phonetics in Linguistics. A book of readings. Longman, London.

Kavanaugh, James F./Cutting, James E. (1975) The Role of Speech in Language. M.I.T. Press, Cambridge.
Kenworthy, Joanne (1978) The intonation of questions in one variety of Scottish English. Lingua 44, 267–282.
Kingdon, Roger (1958a) The Groundwork of English Stress. Longmans, London.
— (1958b) The Groundwork of English Intonation. Longmans, London.

Kiparsky, P. (1966) Über den deutschen Akzent. Studia grammatica VII, 69–98.

— (1973) Elsewhere in phonology. In: A Festschrift for Morris Halle, S.R. Anderson/P. Kiparsky, eds., Holt, Rinehart, Winston, New York.

Klein, Wolfgang (1980) Der Stand der Forschung zur deutschen Satzintonation. Linguistische Berichte 68, 3–33.

Klinghardt, Hermann (1920) Übungen im englischen Tonfall, für Lehrer und Studierende. O. Schulze, Coethen.

Knowles, Gerald (1978) The nature of phonological variables in Scouse. In: Sociolinguistic Patterns in British English, P. Trudgill, ed., Edward Arnold, London, 80–90.

— (1984) Sociolinguistic variables in accent contours. In: Studies in Intonation and Discourse, Catherine Johns-Lewis, ed., Croom Helm, London.

Kohler, K.J. (1966) Is the syllable a phonological universal? Journal of Linguistics 2, 207–208.

— (1973) Phonetische und semantische Aspekte der 'Tag Questions' im Englischen. Linguistische Berichte 24, 35–42.

Kuhlmann, W. (1952) Vergleich deutscher und englischer Tonhöhenbewegung. Zeitschrift für Phonetik, Sprachwissenschaft und Kommunikationsforschung 6, 195–207.


Labov, William/Fanshel, David (1977) Therapeutic Discourse. Psychotherapy as conversation. Academic Press, New York.

Ladd, D. Robert, Jr. (1978) The Structure of Intonational Meaning. Evidence from English. PhD diss., Cornell University. [Pub. Indiana University Press, Bloomington, 1980.]

— (1979) Light and shadow: A study of the syntax and semantics of sentence accent in English. In: Contributions to Grammatical Studies: Syntax and Semantics, Linda Waugh/Frans v. Coltsam, eds., Brill, Leiden, 93–131.

— (1979a) Basic Bibliography on English Intonation. Indiana University Linguistics Club, Bloomington.

— (1981) On intonational universals. In: The Cognitive Representation of Speech, T. Myers/ J. Laver/J. Anderson, eds., North-Holland, 389–397.

— (1983a) Levels vs. configurations, revisited. In: Essays in Honor of Charles F. Hockett, Frederick B. Agard/Gerald Kelley, eds., E.J. Brill, Leiden, 51–59.

— (1983b) Phonological features of intonational peaks. Language 59, 721–759.

— (1983c) Even, focus, and normal stress. Journal of Semantics 2, 157–170.

Ladd, D. Robert/Scherer, K.R./Silverman, Kim (1984) An integrated approach to studying intonation and attitude. In: Studies in Intonation and Discourse, Catherine Johns-Lewis, ed., Croom Helm, London.

Ladefoged, Peter (1962) Elements of Acoustic Phonetics. University of Chicago Press, Chicago.

— (1967) Three Areas of Experimental Phonetics. Oxford University Press, London.

— (1971) Preliminaries to Linguistic Phonetics. University of Chicago Press, Chicago.

— (1975) A Course in Phonetics. Harcourt, Brace, Jovanovich, New York.

Ladefoged, Peter/Draper, M.H./Whitteridge, D. (1958) Syllables and stress. Miscellanea phonetica III, 1–14. Also in: Phonetics in Linguistics, W.E. Jones/J. Laver, eds., Longman, London, 1973, 205–217.

Ladefoged, P./McKinney, N.P. (1963) Loudness, sound pressure, and subglottal pressure in speech. Journal of the Acoustical Society of America 35, 454–460.

Lakoff, George (1971) The role of deduction in grammar. In: Studies in Linguistic Semantics, C. Fillmore/D.T. Langendoen, eds., Holt, Rinehart, Winston, New York.

— (1972) The global nature of the nuclear stress rule. Language 48, 285–303.

Lane, Harlan L. (1965) The motor theory of speech perception: A critical review. Psychological Review 72, 275−309.

Laver, J.D.M. (1968) Voice quality and indexical information. British Journal of Disorders of Communication 3, 43−54.

— (1970) The production of speech. In: New Horizons in Linguistics, John Lyons, ed., Penguin, Harmondsworth, 53−75.

— (1980) The Phonetic Description of Voice Quality. Cambridge University Press, Cambridge.

Lea, Wayne A. (1977) Acoustic correlates of stress and juncture. In: Studies in Stress and Accent, Larry M. Hyman, ed., Southern California Occasional Papers in Linguistics 4, Department of Linguistics, UCLA, 83−119.

Leben, William R. (1976) The tones in English intonation. Linguistic Analysis 2, 69−107.

Lee, William R. (1953) Intonations involving choice and exemplification. Le maître phonétique 99, 2−5 & 100, 35−38.

— (1956a) English intonation: A new approach. Lingua 5, 345−371.

— (1956b) Fall−rise intonations in English. English Studies 37, 62−72; 160−162.

— (1980) A point about rise-endings and fall-endings of yes−no questions. In: The Melody of Language, Linda R. Waugh/C.H. van Schooneveld, eds., University Park Press, Baltimore, 165−168.

Leech, Geoffrey/Svartvik, Jan (1975) A Communicative Grammar of English. Longman, London.

Leech, Geoffrey N./Short, Michael (1981) Style in Fiction: A linguistic introduction to English fictional prose. Longman, London.

Lehiste, Ilse (1970) Suprasegmentals. M.I.T. Press, Cambridge, Mass.

— (1972a) The units of speech perception. In: Speech and Cortical Functioning, John H. Gilbert, ed., Academic Press, New York, Ch. 6.

— (1972b) The role of temporal factors in the establishment of linguistic units and boundaries. In: Phonologica, Wolfgang Dressler/F.V. Mares, eds., Fink, München, 115−122.

— (1972c) The timing of utterances and linguistic boundaries. Journal of the Acoustical Society of America 51, 2018−2024.

— (1973a) Phonetic disambiguation of syntactic ambiguity. Glossa 7, 107−122.

— (1973b) Rhythmic units and syntactic units in production and perception. Journal of the Acoustical Society of America 54, 1228−1234.

— (1975) The phonetic structure of paragraphs. In: Structure and Process in Speech Perception, Antonie Cohen/S.G. Nooteboom, eds., Springer, Berlin, 195−203.

— (1976) Suprasegmental features of speech. In: Contemporary Issues in Experimental Phonetics, Norman J. Lass, ed., Academic Press, New York, 225−239.

— (1977) Isochrony reconsidered. Journal of Phonetics 5, 253−263.

Lehiste, Ilse/Peterson, G.E. (1959) Vowel amplitude and phonemic stress in American English. Journal of the Acoustical Society of America 31, 428−435.

Lehiste, Ilse/Peterson, Gordon (1961) Some basic considerations in the analysis of intonation. Journal of the Acoustical Society of America 33, 419−425. Also in: Acoustic Phonetics, D.B. Fry, ed., Cambridge University Press, Cambridge, 1976, 379−393.

Lehman, Christina (1977) A re-analysis of givenness: Stress in discourse. Papers from the 13th Regional Meeting, Chicago Linguistic Society, 316−324.

Léon, Pierre (1970) Systématique des fonctions expressives de l'intonation. In: Prosodic Feature Analysis, P.R. Léon et al, eds., Didier, Montréal, 57−74.

— (1972) Où en sont les études sur l'intonation. In: Proceedings of the Seventh International Congress of Phonetic Sciences, Montreal 1971, 113−150.

— (1979) BB – ou la voix "charmeuse", "petite fille" et "coquette". In: Problèmes de prosodie, Vol. II. Experimentations, modèles et fonctions, P. Léon/M. Rossi, eds., Didier, Ottawa, 159–171.

Léon, Pierre R./Faure, Georges/Rigault, André (1970) Prosodic Feature Analysis. Analyse des faits prosodiques. Didier, Paris.

Léon, Pierre/Martin, Philippe (1970) Prologomènes à l'étude des structures intonatives. Didier, Paris.

Léon, Pierre/Rossi, Mario (1979) Problèmes de prosodie. Vol. 1 Approches théoriques, Vol. 2 Expérimentations, modèles et fonctions, Didier, Ottawa. ·

Levelt, William J.M./Cutler, Anne (1983) Prosodic marking in speech repair. Journal of Semantics 2, 205–217.

Liberman, A.M. (1957) Some results of research on speech perception. Journal of the Acoustical Society of America 29, 117–123.

Liberman, A.M./Cooper, F.S./Harris, K.S./MacNeilage, P.F. (1963) A motor theory of speech perception. In: Proceedings of the Speech Communications Seminar, C.G.M. Fant, ed., Speech Transmission Laboratory, Royal Institute of Technology, Stockholm. [unpubl. report]

Liberman, A.M./Cooper, F.S./Shankweiler, D.P. et al (1967) Perception of the speech code. Psychological Review 74, 431–461.

Liberman, A.M. et al (1968) On the efficiency of speech sounds. Zeitschrift für Phonetik 21, 21.

Liberman, Mark Yoffe (1975) The Intonational System of English. PhD Diss., MIT. [Publ. Garland Press, 1980.]

Liberman, Mark/Prince, Alan. (1977) On stress and linguistic rhythm. Linguistic Inquiry 8, 249–336.

Liberman, Mark/Sag, Ivan (1974) Prosodic form and discourse function. Papers from the 10th Regional Meeting, Chicago Linguistic Society, 416–427.

Lieb, Hans-Heinrich (1980) Intonation als Mittel verbaler Kommunikation. Linguistische Berichte 68, 34–48.

Lieberman, Philip (1960) Some acoustic correlates of word stress in American English. Journal of the Acoustical Society of America 32, 451–454.

— (1965) On the acoustic basis of perception of intonation by linguists. Word 21, 40–54.

— (1967) Intonation, Perception, and Language. Research Monograph 38, MIT Press, Cambridge.

— (1974) A study of prosodic features. In: Current Trends in Linguistics, Vol. 12. Thomas A. Sebeok, ed., Mouton, The Hague, 2419–2449.

— (1980) The innate, central aspect of intonation. In: The Melody of Language, L. Waugh/ C.H. van Schooneveld, eds., University Park Press, Baltimore, Md., 187–199.

Lieberman, P./Michaels, S.D. (1962) Some aspects of fundamental frequency, envelope amplitude and the emotional content of speech. Journal of the Acoustical Society of America 34, 922–927. Also in: Intonation. Selected readings, Dwight Bolinger, ed., Penguin, 1972, 235–249.

Lieberman, P./Sawashima, Masayuki/Harris, Katherine/Gay, Thomas (1970) The articulatory implementation of the breath-group and prominence: Cricothyroid muscular activity in intonation. Language 46, 312–327.

Lieberman, Philip/Harris, Katherine S./Sawashima, Masayuki (1970) On the physical correlates of some prosodic features. In: Prosodic Feature Analysis, P. Léon et al, eds., Didier, Ottawa, 33–53.

Lindström, Olof (1978) Aspects of English Intonation. Acta universitatis gothoburgensis, Göteberg.

Lipka, Leonhard (1977) Functional sentence perspective, intonation, and the speaker. In: Grundbegriffe und Hauptströmungen der Linguistik, Christoph Gutknecht, ed., Hoffmann und Campe, Hamburg, 133–141.

Loman, Bengt (1975) Prosodic patterns in a Negro American dialect. In: Style and Text. Studies presented to Nils Erik Enkvist, Håkan Ringbom et al, eds., Skriptor, Stockholm, 219–242.

Lyons, John (1962) Phonemic and non-phonemic phonology. International Journal of American Linguistics 28/2, 127–134.

— (1970) Semantics, Vol. 1. Cambridge University Press, Cambridge.

Magdics, K. (1963) Research on intonation during the past ten years. Acta linguistica hafniensia 13, 133–165.

Makkai, Valerie Becker, ed. (1972) Phonological Theory. Evolution and current practice. Holt, Rinehart and Winston, New York.

Malmberg, Bertil (1955) The phonetic basis for syllable division. Studia linguistica IX, 80–87.

— (1963) Structural Linguistics and Human Communication. An introduction into the mechanism of language and the methodology of linguistics. Berlin.

— (1966) Analyse des faits prosodiques – problèmes et méthodes. Cahiers de linguistique théorique et appliquée, Bucarest, 99–107.

— , ed. (1968) Manual of Phonetics. North-Holland, Amsterdam.

Markel, N.N./Bein, M.F./Phillis, J.A. (1973) The relationship between words and tone-of-voice. Language and Speech 16, 15–21.

Martinet, André (1955) Phonology as functional phonetics. Publications of the Philological Society 15, Oxford.

— (1960) Eléments de linguistique générale. Armand Colin, Paris. [Engl. transl.: Elements of General Linguistics, University of Chicago Press, Chicago, 1964.]

— (1962) A functional view of language: being the Waynflete lectures. Clarendon, Oxford.

Mattingly, I.G. (1966) Synthesis by rule of prosodic features. Language and Speech 9, 1–13.

McCawley, James D. (1978) What is a tone language? In: Tone. A linguistic survey, Victoria A. Fromkin, ed., Academic Press, New York, 113–131.

McClure, J. Derrick (1980) Western Scottish intonation. A preliminary study. In: The Melody of Language, L.R. Waugh/van Schooneveld, eds., University Park Press, Baltimore, 201–217.

McNeill, D./Repp, B. (1973) Internal processes in speech perception. Journal of the Acoustical Society of America 53, 1320–1326.

Meyer-Eppler, W. (1957) Realization of prosodic features in whispered speech. Journal of the Acoustical Society of America 29/1, 104–6. Also in: Readings in Acoustic Phonetics, Ilse Lehiste, ed., MIT Press, Cambridge, Mass., 1967, 180–182.

Mol, U./Uhlenbeck, E.M. (1956) The linguistic relevance of intensity in stress. Lingua 5, 205–213.

Morton, John/Jassem, Wiktor (1965) Acoustic correlates of stress. Language and Speech 8/3, 159–181.

Mouchet, Erdmuthe (1978) Der Satzakzent, seine Position und seine Funktion. Untersuchung an 3 Lektionen aus Deutsch 2000, Band 1. Linguistische Berichte 55, 71–89.

Nakatami, L. H./O'Connor, J. D./Aston, C. H. (1981) Prosodic aspects of American English speech rhythm. Phonetica 38, 84–105.

Nash, Rose/Mulac, Anthony (1980) The intonation of verifiability. In: The Melody of Language, Linda R. Waugh/C.H. van Schooneveld, eds., University Park Press, Baltimore, 219–241.

Newman, Stanley S. (1946) On the stress system of English. Word 2, 171–187.

Novak, L. (1978) Die linguistische Auffassung der Silbe. Jazykovedne aktuality 15, 24–25.

O'Connor, J.D. (1955) The intonation of tag questions in English. English Studies 36, 97–105.
— (1965) The perception of time intervals. In: Progress Report 2, Phonetics Laboratory, University College, London, 11–15. [cit. in Gimson 1976]
O'Connor, J.D./Arnold, G.F. ($^2$1973) Intonation of Colloquial English. Longman, London.
O'Connor, J.D./Trim, J.L.M. (1953) Vowel, consonant and syllable – a phonological definition. Word IX/2, 103–122. Also in: Phonetics in Linguistics, W.E. Jones/J. Laver, eds., Longman, London, 1973, 240–261.
Ohala, John J. (1970) Aspects of the control and production of speech. Working Papers in Phonetics 15, University of California, Los Angeles.
— (1977) The physiology of stress. In: Studies in Stress and Accent, Larry M. Hyman, ed., Southern California Occasional Papers in Linguistics 4, 145–168.
— (1978) The production of tone. Report of the Phonology Laboratory No. 2, University of California, Berkeley, 63–116.
Ohala, John J./Hirano, M. (1967) An experimental investigation of pitch change in speech (Abstract). Journal of the Acoustical Society of America 42, 1208–1209.
Osgood, Charles E./Suci, George J./Tannenbaum, Percy H. (1957) The Measurement of Meaning. University of Illinois Press, Urbana, Illinois.

Palmer, Harold E. (1924) English Intonation. With systematic exercises. Heffer & Sons, Cambridge.
Pellowe, John/Jones, Val (1978) On the intonational variability of Tyneside speech. In: Sociolinguistic Patterns in British English, Peter Trudgill, ed., Edward Arnold, London, 101–121.
— (1979) Establishing intonationally variable systems in a multi-dimensional linguistic space. Language and Speech 22, 97–116.
Peterson, G.E./Lehiste, I. (1960) Duration of syllable nuclei in English. Journal of the Acoustical Society of America 32, 693–703.
Pheby, John (1975) Intonation und Grammatik im Deutschen. Akademie Verlag, Berlin.
Pierrehumbert, Janet Breckenridge (1980) The Phonology and Phonetics of English Intonation. PhD diss., MIT.
Pike, Kenneth L. (1945) The Intonation of American English. University of Michigan Publications, Linguistics 1, Ann Arbor, Mich.
Pilch, Herbert (1970) The elementary intonation contour of English. Phonetica 22, 82–111.
— (1977a) Baseldeutsche Phonologie. Auf Grundlage der Intonation. Phonetica 34, 165–190.
— (1977b) Intonation in discourse analysis. With material from Finnish, English, Alemannic German. Phonetica 34, 81–92.
— (1980) English intonation as phonological structure. Word 31, 55–67.
— (1981) Les mots anglais à accent mobile. Motivation pour une théorie de l'accent. In: Problèmes de Prosodie, Vol. 1 Approches théoriques, P. Léon/M. Rossi, eds., Didier, 3–8.
Prince, E.F. (1981) Toward a taxonomy of given/new information. In: Radical Pragmatics, Peter Cole, ed., Academic Press, New York, 223–255.
Pürschel, Heiner (1975) Pause und Kadenz: Interferenzerscheinungen bei der englischen Intonation deutscher Sprecher. Niemeyer, Tübingen.
Pulgram, Ernst (1970) Syllable, Word, Nexus, Cursus. Mouton, The Hague.

Quirk, Randolph (1965) Descriptive statement and serial relationship. Language 41, 205–217.
Quirk, Randolph/Crystal, David (1966) On scales of contrast in connected English speech. In: In Memory of J.R. Firth, C.E. Bazell et al, eds., Longmans, London, 359–369.

Quirk, Randolph/Duckworth, A.P./Svartvik, J. et al (1964) Studies in the correspondence of prosodic to grammatical features in English. Proceedings of the 9th International Congress of Linguists, Mouton, The Hague, 679–692.

Quirk, Randolph/Greenbaum, Sidney/Leech, Geoffrey/Svartvik, Jan (1972) A Grammar of Contemporary English. Longman, London.

Rando, Emily (1980) Intonation in discourse. In: The Melody of Language, L.R. Waugh/ C.H. van Schooneveld, eds., University Park Press, Baltimore, 243–278.

Rees, Martin (1975) The domain of isochrony. In: Work in Progress 8, Department of Linguistics, Edinburgh University, 14–28.

Rees, M./Urquhart, A.H. (1976) Intonation as a guide to readers' structuring of prose texts. Work in Progress 9, Department of Linguistics, Edinburgh University.

Rigault, André (1964) Réflexions sur le statut phonologique de l'intonation. Proceedings of the 9th International Congress of Linguists, Mouton, The Hague, 849–858.

Robins, R.H. (1964, [3]1980) General Linguistics. An introductory survey. Longman, London. [§4.4 Prosodic phonology, 125–134]

— (1972) Aspects of prosodic analysis. In: Phonological Theory. Evolution and current practice, Valerie Becker Makkai, ed. Holt, New York, 264–274.

Rohrer, Fritz (1952) Untersuchungen zur Intonation der Dialekte von Dorset, Gloucester, Westmoreland, Northumberland, Yorkshire, Lincoln und Norfolk. Kessler, Gutenberg, Lachen.

Romportl, Milan (1973) Studies in Phonetics. Janua Linguarum, Mouton, The Hague.

Rosetti, A. (1959, [2]1963) Sur la théorie de la syllabe. Mouton, The Hague.

— (1961) Sur la théorie de la syllabe. Réponse à M.B. Hála. Phonetica 7, 109–113.

Rossi, M. (1971) Le seuil de glissando ou seuil de perception des variations tonales pour la parole. Phonetica 23, 1–33.

— (1978) Interactions of intensity glides and frequency glissandos. Language and Speech 21, 384–396.

Sacks, Harvey/Schegloff, E.A./Jefferson, G. (1974) A simplest systematics for the organization of turn-taking. Language 50, 696–735.

Sadock, J. (1974) Towards a Linguistic Theory of Speech Acts. Academic Press, New York.

Sag, Ivan/Liberman, Mark (1975) The intonational disambiguation of indirect speech acts. Papers from the 11th Regional Meeting, Chicago Linguistic Society, 487–497.

Sanders, Derek A. (1977) Auditory Perception of Speech. An introduction to principles and problems. Prentice-Hall, Englewood Cliffs, N.J. [Ch. 5, Theories of speech perception, 97–133.]

Schane, Sanford A. (1979) The rhythmic nature of English word accentuation. Language 55, 559–602.

Schegloff, Emanuel A. (1978) On some questions and ambiguities in conversation. In: Current Trends in Textlinguistics, W. Dressler, ed., de Gruyter, Berlin, 81–102.

Schegloff, E.A./Sacks, H. (1973) Opening-up closings. Semiotica 8, 289–327.

Scherer, Günther/Wollmann, Alfred ([2]1977) Englische Phonetik und Phonologie. Erich Schmidt, Berlin.

Scherer, Klaus R. (1979) Nonlinguistic vocal indicators of emotion and psychopathology. In: Emotions in Personality and Psychopathology, Carroll E. Izard, ed., Plenum, New York, 495–529.

Scherer, Klaus R./London, H./Wolf, J. (1973) The voice of confidence: Paralinguistic cues and audience evaluation. Journal of Research in Personality 7, 31–44.

Schmerling, Susan F. (1974a) Contrastive stress and semantic relations, Papers from the 10th Regional Meeting, Chicago Linguistic Society, 608–616.
— (1974b) A re-examination of 'normal stress'. Language 50, 66–73.
— (1976) Aspects of English Sentence Stress. University of Texas Press, Austin.
Schubiger, Maria (1935) The Role of Intonation in Spoken English. Cambridge.
— (1953) Notes on the intonation of coordinate sentences and syntactic groups. English Studies 34, 268–273.
— (1956) Again: Fall–rise intonations in English. English Studies 37, 157–160.
— (1958) English Intonation. Its form and function. Niemeyer, Tübingen.
— (1963) Again: The stressing of prepositions. English Studies 44, 275–277.
— (1964) The interplay and co-operation of word-order and intonation in English. In: In Honour of Daniel Jones, D. Abercrombie et al, eds., Longman, London, 255–265.
— (1965) English intonation and German modal particles. Phonetica 12, 65–84. Also in: Intonation. Selected readings, D.L. Bolinger, ed., Penguin, Harmondsworth, 175–193.
— (1967) A note on two notional functions of the low-falling nuclear tone in English. English Studies 48, 53–59.
— (1980) English intonation and German modal particles II: A comparative study. In: The Melody of Language, L.R. Waugh/C.H. van Schooneveld, eds., University Park Press, Baltimore, 279–298.
Scott, N.C. (1939) An experiment on stress perception. Le maître phonétique 44.
Scuffil, Michael (1982) Experiments in Comparative Intonation: A case-study of English and German. Niemeyer, Tübingen.
Searle, John R. (1969) Speech Acts. An essay in the philosophy of language. Cambridge University Press, Cambridge.
— (1971) Austin on locutionary and illocutionary acts. In: Readings in the Philosophy of Language, J. Rosenberg/C. Travis, eds., Prentice Hall, Englewood Cliffs, 262–275.
— (1975a) A taxonomy of illocutionary acts. In: Minnesota Studies in the Philosophy of Science VII, Language, Mind, and Knowledge, Keith Gunderson, ed., University of Minnesota Press, Minneapolis, 344–369. Also in: Language in Society 5, 1976, 1–23.
— (1975b) Indirect speech acts. In: Speech Acts, Syntax and Semantics 3, Peter Cole/Jerry L. Morgan, eds., Academic Press, New York, 59–82.
— (1976) Review of Sadock 1974. Language 52, 966–971.
Searle, John R./Kiefer, Ferenc/Bierwisch, Manfred, eds. (1980) Speech Act Theory and Pragmatics. Reidel, Dordrecht.
Séguinot, Candace (1979) A phonostylistic study of rhythm in English. In: Problèmes de prosodie, P. Léon/M. Rossi, eds., Didier, Ottawa, 149–157.
Selkirk, Elisabeth (1980) The role of prosodic categories in English word stress. Linguistic Inquiry 11, 563–605.
— (1982) The syllable. In: The Structure of Phonological Representation (Part II), H. van der Hulst/N. Smith, eds., Foris Publications, Dordrecht, 337–383.
— (1984) Phonology and Syntax: The relation between sound and structure. MIT Press, Cambridge, Mass.
Sharp, A.E. (1958) Falling–rising intonation patterns in English. Phonetica 2, 127–152.
— (1960) The analysis of stress and juncture in English. Transactions of the Philological Society, 104–135.
Shen, Y./Peterson, G. (1964) Isochronism in English. Occasional Papers 9, Studies in Linguistics, University Press, Buffalo.
Siertsema, B. (1962) Timbre, pitch, and intonation. Lingua 11, 388–398.
Silverman, Kim/Scherer, Klaus R./Ladd, D. Robert (1983) Vocal cues to attitude in non-emotional speech. MS, Dept. of Psychology, University of Giessen.

Sinclair, J. McH./Coulthard, R.M. (1975) Towards an Analysis of Discourse. The English used by teachers and pupils. Oxford University Press, Oxford.

Sinclair, J. McH./Forsyth, I.J./Coulthard, R.M./Ashby, M.C. (1972) The English Used by Teachers and Pupils. Final Report to S.S.R.C., Mimeo, Birmingham University.

Sledd, James (1960) Review of Kingdon, The Groundwork of English Intonation. Language 36, 173–178.

Sonnenschein, E.A. (1925) What is Rhythm? Blackwell, Oxford.

Stankiewicz, E. (1964) Problems of emotive language. In: Approaches to Semiotics, Th.A. Sebeok et al, eds., Mouton, The Hague, 239–264.

Steele, Joshua (1775) An Essay Towards Establishing the Melody and Measure of Speech (to be expressed and perpetrated by peculiar symbols). [Prosodia rationalis 1779] Repr. The Scolar Press, Menston, 1969.

Stetson, R.H. (1945) Bases of Phonology. Oberlin, Ohio.

— (²1951) Motor Phonetics, a Study of Speech Movements in Action. North-Holland, Amsterdam.

Stevens, K.N. (1968) Speech movements and speech perception. Zeitschrift für Phonetik 21, 102.

— (1972) Segments, features and analysis by synthesis. In: Language by Ear and by Eye, J.F. Kavanaugh/I.G. Mattingly, eds., MIT Press, Cambridge, 47–52.

Stevens, K.N./Halle, M. (1967) Remarks on analysis-by-synthesis and distinctive features. In: Models for the Perception of Speech and Visual Form, W. Wathen-Dunn, ed., MIT Press, Cambridge.

Stevens, S.S./Volkman, J./Newman, E.B. (1937) A scale for the measurement of psychological magnitude of pitch. Journal of the Acoustical Society of America 8, 185–190.

Stevens, S.S./Volkman, J. (1940) The relation of pitch to frequency: A revised scale. American Journal of Psychology 53/3, 329–353.

Stock, E./Zacharias, Ch. (1972) Deutsche Satzintonation. VEB Verlag, Leipzig.

Stockwell, Robert (1960) The place of intonation in a generative grammar of English. Language 36, 360–367.

— (1962) On the analysis of English intonation. Proceedings of the 2nd Texas Conference on Problems of Linguistic Analysis in English, A.A. Hill, ed., Univ. of Texas Press, 39–55.

— (1972) The role of intonation: Reconsiderations and other considerations. In: Intonation, D. Bolinger, ed., Penguin, Harmondsworth, 87–109.

Studdert-Kennedy (1974) The perception of speech. In: Current Trends in Linguistics, Vol. 12, T.A. Sebeok, ed., The Hague, Mouton, 2349–2386.

— (1975) From continuous signal to discrete message: Syllable to phoneme. In: The Role of Speech in Language, J.F. Kavanaugh/J.E. Cutting, eds., MIT Press, Cambridge, 113–125.

— (1976) Speech perception. In: Contemporary Issues in Experimental Phonetics, Norman J. Lass, ed., Academic Press, New York, 243–293.

Studdert-Kennedy, M./Liberman, A.M./Harris, K.S./Cooper, F.S. (1970) The motor theory of speech perception: A reply to Lane's critical review. Psychological Review 77, 234–249.

Sumera, Magdalena (1970) The temporal tradition in the study of verse structure. Linguistics 62, 44–65.

— (1980) The handling of three-syllable feet by Dr. William Thomson. A survey and interpretation. In: Work in Progress 13, Department of Linguistics, Edinburgh University, 29–49.

Sweet, Henry (1892, ²1906) A Primer of Phonetics. Clarendon Press, Oxford.

— (³1900) A Primer of Spoken English. Clarendon Press, Oxford.

Taglicht, J. (1982) Intonation and the assessment of information. Journal of Linguistics 18, 213–230.

Tarone, Elaine E. (1973) Aspects of intonation in Black English. American Speech 48, 29–36.

Thorsen, Nina (1978) An acoustical analysis of Danish intonation. Journal of Phonetics 6, 151–175.

— (1980) A study of the perception of sentence intonation: Evidence from Danish. Journal of the Acoustical Society of America 67, 1014–1030.

Tibbitts, E.L. (1966) Barking up the wrong tree?, or Does a rise follow a fall? Some thoughts on the teaching of English intonation. English Language Teaching 21, 24–33.

Tillmann, Hans Günther (1964) Das phonetische Silbenproblem. Eine theoretische Untersuchung. Diss., Bonn.

Tillmann, Hans G./Mansell, Phil (1980) Phonetik. Lautsprachliche Zeichen, Sprachsignale und lautsprachlicher Kommunikationsprozeß. Klett-Cotta, Stuttgart.

Trager, G.L. (1972) The intonation system of American English. In: Intonation. Selected Readings, D. Bolinger, ed., Penguin, Harmondsworth, 82–86.

Trager, George L./Smith, Henry Lee Jr. (1957) An Outline of English Structure. Studies in Linguistics: Occasional Papers 3, American Council of Learned Societies, Washington, D.C. (5th printing).

Trim, J.L.M. (1959) Major and minor tone-groups in English. Le maître phonétique, 3rd series, No. 112, 26–29. Also in: Phonetics in Linguistics. A book of readings, W.E. Jones/J. Laver, eds., Longmans, London, 1973, 320–323.

— (1964) Tonetic stress marks for German. In: In Honour of Daniel Jones, David Abercrombie et al, eds., Longmans, London, 374–383.

— (1970) Some continuously variable features in British English intonation. Proceedings of the 10th International Congress of Linguists IV, Editions de l'Académie de la République Socialiste de Roumanie, Bucharest, 263–268.

Trojan, F. (1957) General semantics. (A comparison between linguistic and sub-linguistic phonic expression). In: Manual of Phonetics, Louise Kaiser, ed., North-Holland, Amsterdam, 437–438.

Trubetzkoy, N.S. (1939) Grundzüge der Phonologie. Travaux du cercle linguistique de Prague 7, Prague. [Repr. Göttingen 1958.]

Uldall, Elizabeth (1960) Attitudinal meanings conveyed by intonation contours. Language and Speech 3, 223–234. Also in: Phonetics in Linguistics, W.E. Jones/J. Laver, eds., Longman, London, 1973, 324–335.

— (1964) Dimensions of meaning in intonation. In: In Honour of Daniel Jones: Papers contributed on the occasion of his 80th birthday, D. Abercrombie et al, eds., Longman, London, 271–279. Also in: Intonation. Selected readings, D. Bolinger, ed., Penguin, Harmondsworth, 1972, 250–259.

— (1971) Isochronous stresses in R.P. In: Form and Substance: Phonetic and linguistic papers presented to Eli Fischer-Jørgensen, L.L. Hammerich et al, eds., Akademisk Forlag, Copenhagen, 205–210.

— (1972) Relative durations of syllables in two-syllable rhythmic feet in R.P. in connected speech. In: Work in Progress 5, Department of Linguistics, Edinburgh University, 110–111.

— (1978) Rhythm in very rapid R.P. Language and Speech 21, 397–402.

Vanderslice, Ralph (1970) Occam's razor and the so-called stress cycle. Language Sciences 13, Indiana University Research Center for the Language Sciences, 9–15.

Vanderslice, Ralph/Ladefoged, Peter (1972) Binary suprasegmental features and transformational word-accentuation rules. Language 48, 819–838.

231

van Dijk, Teun A. (1980) Macrostructures. An interdisciplinary study of global structures in discourse, interaction, and cognition. Lawrence Erlbaum Associates, Hillsdale, New Jersey.

Vanvik, Arne (1961) On Stress in Present-Day English (Received Pronunciation). Norwegian Universities Press, Bergen & Oslo.

— (1978) Some remarks on Norwegian prosody. In: Nordic Prosody, E. Gårding/G. Bruce/ R. Bannert, eds., Travaux de l'Institut de Linguistique de Lund, Lund University, 161–163.

Vennemann, Theo (1972) On the theory of syllabic phonology. Linguistische Berichte 18, 1–18.

Wang, W. S.-Y. (1967) Phonological features of tone. International Journal of American Linguistics 33, 93–105.

Waugh, Linda R./van Schooneveld, C.H., eds. (1980) The Melody of Language. University Park Press, Baltimore.

Weinrich, U. (1956) Notes on the Yiddish rise–fall intonation contour. In: For Roman Jakobson, Morris Halle/H.B. Lunt et al, eds., Mouton, The Hague, 633–643.

Wells, Rulon S. (1945) The pitch phonemes of English. Language 21, 27–39.

Widdowson, H.G. (1977) An applied linguistic approach to discourse analysis. Unpubl. PhD thesis, University of Edinburgh [cit. in Coulthard 1977].

Williams, C./Stevens, K. (1972) Emotions and speech: Some acoustic correlates. Journal of the Acoustical Society of America 52, 1238–1250.

Winkler, Henry J. (1973) A comparison of the intonation patterns of Black English and Standard English. Paper presented to the Annual Meeting of the Acoustical Society of America.

Wittig, Kurt (1954) Amerikanische und englische Intonation. Studium generale 7/10, 579–589.

Witting, Claes (1962) A method of evaluating listeners' transcriptions of intonation on the basis of instrumental data. Language and Speech 5, 138–150.

Wodarz, H.W. (1960) Über vergleichende satzmelodische Untersuchungen. Phonetica 5, 75–98.

— (1962) Über syntaktische und expressive Relevanz der Intonation. Proceedings of the 4th International Congress of Phonetic Sciences, The Hague, 800–804.

Wode, Henning (1966) Englische Satzintonation. Phonetica 15, 129–218.

— (1971) Review of Crystal, Prosodic Systems and Intonation in English. Phonetica 24, 188–192.

Wunderli, Peter (1979) Satz, Paragraph, Text – und die Intonation. In: Text vs. Sentence: Basic questions of text linguistics, Part 1, Janós S. Petöfi, ed., Buske, Hamburg, 319–341.

Wunderli, Peter/Benthin, Karola/Karasch, Angela (1978) Französische Intonationsforschung. Kritische Bilanz und Versuch einer Synthese. Gunter Narr, Tübingen.

Wunderlich, Dieter (1976) Studien zur Sprechakttheorie. Suhrkamp, Frankfurt.

— (1980) Methodological remarks on speech act theory. In: Speech Act Theory and Pragmatics, J.R. Searle/F. Kiefer/M. Bierwisch, eds., Reidel, Dordrecht, 291–312.

Yorio, Carlos Alfredo (1973) The generative process of intonation. Linguistics 97, 111–125.

Yule, George (1980a) Intonation and givenness in spoken discourse. Studies in Language 4, Amsterdam, 271–286.

— (1980b) Speakers' topics and major paratones. Lingua 52, 33–47.

— (1980c) The functions of phonological prominence in one variety of Scottish English. Archivum linguisticum 11, 31–46.

— (1981) New, current and displaced entity reference. Lingua 55, 41–52.

Zillig, Werner (1982) Emotionen als perlokutionäre Effekte. Grazer Linguistische Studien 17/18, 317–349.

Zinkin, N.J. et al (1975) Über die Wahrnehmung der gesprochenen Sprache. Linguistics 148, 45–60.

# Index

Boldface numbers refer to pages where definitions and/or illustrations of technical terms can be found.

physiological basis for the syllable 11f.
physiological sources: of increased intensity 21; of increased $f_0$ 20
physiology: of emphatic stress 21; of stress 21
pitch 3f., 7, 9, 19, 20, 55, 63, 67, 117, 154, 173, 176; as a cue to stress perception 23; in stressed syllables 21; ~ perception 6, 63, 88; ~ prominence 29, 31f., 35
pitch accents 24, **29**, 72, 135
pitch concord 76, **202**f., 205, 209
pitch configurations 66
pitch direction 71, 92, 108, 112, 117
pitch glide 20, 32, 55, 79, 98, 100f.
pitch height 71, 82, 90ff., 104, 106, 108, 128, 134, 137, 198f.
pitch jump 32, 55, 79, 98, 100f.
pitch level 64ff., 72, 181, 186
pitch movement 29, 31, 63, 67f., 79ff., 90, 92, 94, 100
pitch obtrusion **24**, 29f., 31, 35, 79f.
pitch phonemes 27, **64**f.
pitch range 66, 69, 92, 98, 104, 108, 112, 117, 181, 185f., 198f.
pitch sequence 103f., 193, 203f.
pitch width 71, 90ff., 104, 106, 108
pitch-accent language, *see* word-accent language
polite, politeness 177, 184
polysyllabic pitch-range features 101, 104f.
position of nucleus, *see* nucleus, location of
post-tonic 68
pre-contour (Pike) 68
pre-head 68, 70, 76, 78, **86**, 105
pre-ictic vs. post-ictic pitch movement 29
pre-tonic (Halliday) 71, 123
presupposition **41**
primary accent (Crystal) **32**
primary acoustic cues to stress 20
primary information 129, 131
primary stress **27**, 39, 42, 68, 132
primary tones (Halliday) 71
promise **160**
prosodic analysis (Firth) 1
prosodic features, components of speech 4, 32, 55, 71, 91, 93, 119, 180f.
prosodic phonology (Firth) 1
prosodic unit 73
prosody, prosodic level 1, **2**ff., 8, 71

psychoacoustic studies: of pitch perception 63, 82; of stress perception 26
pulmonic muscular activity 20f.
purposiveness of linguistic signs 118, 186
quality, *see* vowel quality
quantity 2
question: illocution 148, 156, 166, 169, **170**ff.; sentence-type 111, 139, 146, 148f., 155, 176f., 179
range of intonational function 115, 209
rate of speech 9, 21, 38, 58, 173, 185
relative clauses 141f., 144
relative height 63, 67f., 106, *see also* pitch height
relative onset level 101ff.
relative probability of phoneme combinations 14f.
relative syllable length 56ff., 59
request 111, 139, 155, 162f., 166ff., 182
rheme (FSP) **124**f.
rhythm 2, 4, 51ff., 173; perception of ~ 52
rhythmic alternation 34f., 37, 60
rhythmic break 99, 106, 108
rhythmic group 58, **59**, 196
rhythmic hierarchy 34, 60f.
rhythmic pattern as a cue to stress perception 22
rhythmic principle of stress distribution 37f.
rhythmic stress beats 4, 33f., 35, 107
rhythmic view of stress 25, 33ff.
rhythmic well-formedness 60f.
rhythmicality **55**, 71
rightmost rules 43, 47
rise, rising contour 66, 67, 69f., 75, 79f., 86, 90, **92**ff., 98, 106, 111, 134, 139, 150, 155f., 172, 182f., 198
rise–fall, rising–falling contour 67, 71, 92, 95, **97**f., 150, 198
rise + fall nucleus, nuclear tone 98, 196
rising heads 84f.
rising–falling heads 84
R.P. 38, 57, 70, 92
salient syllable 33
secondary accent (Crystal) 32
secondary acoustic cues to stress 20
secondary information 129, 131, 148
secondary stress **27**, 66
secondary tones (Halliday) 71
segment, segmental level **2**, 4, 7f.